Paul O'Grady
– not the same without you

Paul O'Grady – not the same without you

The Man. The Magic.
The Friendship.

MALCOLM PRINCE

HarperCollins*Publishers*

HarperCollins*Publishers*
1 London Bridge Street
London SE1 9GF

www.harpercollins.co.uk

HarperCollins*Publishers*
Macken House, 39/40 Mayor Street Upper
Dublin 1, D01 C9W8, Ireland

First published by HarperCollins*Publishers* 2025

1 3 5 7 9 10 8 6 4 2

A catalogue record of this book is
available from the British Library

ISBN 978-0-00-872919-6

Printed and bound in the UK using 100%
renewable electricity at CPI Group (UK) Ltd

For Paul, who never needed a gimmick

Contents

Introduction

'We must enjoy life for as long
as the adventure lasts'
Paul O'Grady

Paul O'Grady often told me that writing a book isn't easy. And he would know: he'd published bestsellers for adults and children, a guide to life in the Kent countryside and another bursting with tips, courtesy of Miss Lily Savage.

And if you've read them, you might think you would know all there is to know about Paul O'Grady. But you'd be wrong.

I worked with Paul for 20 years, usually producing his popular, long-running BBC Radio 2 show. The Paul O'Grady I knew was not only a versatile presenter, broadcaster and entertainer, he was a campaigner, a political advocate and a trailblazer. He was also a son, a father and a grandfather. But most of all he was a friend.

And I'd like to share that person with you.

At his core, Paul was a talented and complicated individual, an incredible and mercurial man, and one who fiercely protected his privacy – in many an interview, he would deftly deflect a personal question with an amusing anecdote. So some might say I'm setting out to do the impossible, especially because his radio programme presented a carefully curated 'version' of the man. But I like a challenge.

That task began 6 months after Paul died, when I received a phone call from his husband André. He had a proposition for me: would I be interested in helping him write a book about his life with Paul? I agreed to a meeting, but it quickly became clear to me that the story of their intimate relationship wasn't mine to tell; fortunately, soon after that book was abandoned.

I wanted to write about the Paul O'Grady who was my work colleague, my sparring partner and my trusty friend.

This is Paul's story, as I discovered it.

In so doing, the important milestones are here, nearly all of which he told me about in detail, from Birkenhead to Battersea. I wouldn't go so far as to say it's warts and all, and while I have been careful not to break his confidence, I have attempted to complete the story of his career and friendships his autobiographies only partly told.

It's also a journey through a life, if you will. In simple terms, Paul travelled from the northwest of England of the 1950s and 1960s, ending up in the southeast 50 or so years later; but there was nothing straightforward about it. It's a convoluted and astonishing tale which took in outrageous and seedy bars and nightclubs, the finest theatres in the land, millions of front rooms and even a royal palace.

The time we spent working together at the BBC was Paul's longest regular gig, but his job as a host of a weekly radio show often took third place behind his TV shows and appearances in panto. And that's fine. But now it's time to reveal the story we shared.

To help me, I have spoken with numerous friends and colleagues, and visited the places that helped create the Paul O'Grady so many of us loved. I've also had the good fortune to talk to Paul's daughter and grandchildren. Their insights have been invaluable and revealing, and provide different facets of the man we knew. As a result, this book, just like him, is heartfelt, candid – and even has a little bit of bite.

Loyal fans will know that Paul wrote four accomplished and successful volumes of autobiography, a process he enjoyed – eventually. Those books are rich in memories, anecdotes and detail about his formative days, and if you haven't read them, I wholeheartedly recommend you seek them out. As ever, no, I'm not on commission and as Paul once said on his radio show: 'Other autobiographies are available – but they're nowhere near as funny or as good.'

For various reasons, however, he decided against writing about his later years, so this book – in part – takes up the mantle, and I have charted some of the many highs and occasional lows which Paul O'Grady experienced after he had retired Lilian Maeve Veronica Savage in the early 2000s. But this is really a story about friendship, drawn from years of work and worries, regular rants and countless hearty doses of laughter.

When he died in March 2023, many of Paul's 'loyal listeners' contacted me to tell me of their heartache. He might have been embarrassed by public displays of affection, but he was aware that people held him in high regard; he also knew that most of them, if not all, considered him as their friend. The affection his listeners held for him, and indeed the connection many believed they had with him, was there thanks to the mediums in which he worked. When he appeared on television, Paul O'Grady was in your living room, while on the radio, you could hear him while you were in the bath, driving a car or, as was often the case on a Sunday evening between 5 p.m. and 7 p.m., doing your ironing. Fundamentally, he had an intimate relationship with his fans.

The last song Paul played on his BBC radio show was by Bette Midler. Released as a single back in 1973, Bette first performed 'Friends' during one of her now legendary 'intimate' shows in front of hundreds of gay men – who would have been wearing nothing but a towel – at the Continental Baths in New York. Paul and I both loved Bette (although I should add neither of us saw her perform in a gay sauna). I chose the track because I had produced two radio specials with the star, while Paul had enjoyed her company on his ITV chat show in 2010, so I hoped something by her was a fitting way to bow out. And 'Friends', or 'You've Got To Have Friends' as some people call it, was the perfect choice. Despite its melancholic undertones, the number is both rousing and heartfelt, and emphasises the importance of human connection; it represented the ethos of Paul's radio show.

The song was originally the first choice as the theme for the American sitcom *The Golden Girls* although, ultimately, that honour went to Andrew Gold's 'Thank You For Being A Friend' – another one we sometimes featured on the radio show. Looking back, I can see that Paul's programme had a lot in common with the Miami-based comedy. *The Golden Girls* changed mainstream television by showing that four independent older women could be interesting, funny and wise. And, most of all, friends. The same was true of Paul's Sunday show. Yes, he and I were pals, and we both certainly knew what made each other tick, but he was also a friend to his listener at home. And it is because of his special relationships – with you and me – that I've written this book.

Friendships were important to Paul, and he worked hard to maintain them. I have discovered, researching this project, there was an inner circle of pals who protected Paul O'Grady, or 'Savage' as they knew him, throughout his life. They continue to do so and I am grateful many of them have supported this project. He loved people and was constantly fascinated – and sometimes rattled – by them. And it says a lot about him that some, like Vera, were there from almost the beginning to the end of Paul's life. Yes, Vera was a real person! But more on her later.

Much has been chronicled about the decade or more during which Paul O'Grady perfected his alter ego's character and act in gay pubs and clubs across the country: his hard work during the 1980s and 1990s ultimately led to Lily Savage becoming part of the entertainment establishment, with her own shows on mainstream prime-time television. She had, to quote one of Paul's idols, Gypsy Rose Lee, 'descended from a long line her mother listened to'. Lily was, as he explained, 'a hard-bitten hooker from Birkenhead, with her roots showing, ripped tights and a big handbag'. For a very long time, Paul was hidden by Lily, a character who allowed him to break down boundaries and, as Sir Elton John commented, go 'places nobody had gone before'. Miss Savage was part of a transformation in Britain – perhaps for a time she led it – and her journey is a good measure of how far LGBTQ+ people have come in the last 50 years or so: from the downtrodden and hidden to the shining stars of popular entertainment.

But as Lily became part of British show business royalty, it was her manager and Paul's life partner Brendan Murphy who helped 'the man behind the lippy' realise the only way he could go to the next level was to be himself. As Paul later explained to me, Lily Savage became a financial means to an end.

The screenwriter and television executive Russell T Davies was 'heartbroken' to hear Paul was retiring Lily: 'I actually couldn't believe it. I cynically rolled my eyes and thought, "Two years, give him two years and Lily will be back." I thought, "How bold is that?"' Comedian and broadcaster Alan Carr was equally shocked by the move: 'I thought it was madness. I was, like, "What?!" and naively thought, "Well, that's the last we'll hear of him!"' But for Paul's close pal, comedian and author Julian Clary, retiring Lily was a 'genius thing to do, extremely brave, it opened a whole new world for him. And as it turned out it was a brilliant thing to do.' Broadcaster and author Graham Norton agrees: 'I totally understood why he wanted to "become Paul". Was I sure he could do it? No, I wasn't. But when you saw him, you realised it was simply Lily without lipstick – there wasn't much method acting when he was her. So, yes, it was a bold thing to do, a big decision, but not irreversible, and there wasn't a bonfire of wigs out back. And if people hadn't warmed to Paul in the same way, it would have been, "Hello! Here's Lily again."'

But Paul's decision to say goodbye to Lily Savage did work – and after spending time in a convent in Brittany, Lily finally relocated to Amsterdam where she was last seen running a home for young ladies.

I never 'knew' Lily Savage as such. I began working with Paul just after he had semi-retired her in the early 2000s, and even though I loved watching Lily on telly, with her forthright 'Bet Lynch brass', I think I was lucky. Bear with me here. You see, I'm not so sure I could have survived working with the demonic Blonde Bombsite (Paul's description, not mine) because her quick wit would have exhausted me; simply put, I wouldn't have been able to keep up with her. Back in the nineties and early noughties, Paul and I were poles apart – I was never a party animal and I'm a life-long teetotaller, and, as I often reminded him, I was much younger.

But as time's gone by since we lost him, I've realised those differences were the very reason we became such good friends years later.

The man I knew and worked with for two decades was fiercely loyal and supportive, constantly witty, and uncompromisingly fascinating – he was never short of a story, an anecdote or a juicy piece of gossip. He was well-read but never lecturing. He was opinionated and a champion of the underdog – both two- and four-legged – moody and unpredictable, and yet so easy to read. And even though he was a highly successful star, he was extremely down-to-earth and always the first to acknowledge his modest background. He was excellent company and, as I write this introduction, I still can't believe I'll never receive another phone call from him: 'Hiya, Malcolm!'

Oh, how I miss him: our conversations and all the drama that always seemed to follow him around. I'd never met anyone quite like Paul O'Grady, and don't think I will again.

Throughout the years I worked with him, Paul remained creatively ambitious while giving the impression that he was always about to give it all up. He was genuinely proud of the programmes he presented, the books he had written and the stage performances he had given, but he seldom boasted of his achievements. And while he appreciated his huge and diverse fan base, Paul loved nothing more than being at home, feeding his pigs, talking to his chickens and walking his ever-growing family of dogs – but he wasn't a saint, as all his friends will tell you.

I have continued to be inundated with funny and outrageous messages and stories about him. It's no surprise really, given the huge audiences who tuned into 'the dog show' on ITV, or who listened to his weekly radio programme. So many people really felt that they knew him. And they did, or at least a part of him. And that was just one of the many remarkable attributes that he had: Paul O'Grady made us *all* feel we were his best friend, whether we knew him intimately, directly or hardly at all.

It's said, 'A man is known by the company he keeps', and in Paul's case, there were millions of us. There were those who knew him on the gay circuit as Lily Savage, and her later incarnation as a TV hostess. Some people knew him as the man who loved dogs, elephants and orangutans; while, for others, he was Miss Hannigan, or the wicked attraction of a spectacular pantomime.

For me, the Paul O'Grady I knew was first and foremost a radio presenter. The *Radio Times* contacted me the day after he died, asking if I'd be willing to talk about him. After checking with Joan Marshrons, Paul's long-serving and long-suffering agent, I agreed and spoke about the years I had spent working with Paul. You never know how such things will turn out, but the article seemed to be well received, and nor was I surprised when the magazine highlighted one quote out of my conversation: 'I was paid to laugh.' It was true, and what a job it was! I know I was very lucky.

Paul's wit, which was his superpower, was an instrument that he had mastered in the pubs and clubs where he held court as Lily Savage. In the radio studio, he would riff stories and I'd despair, thinking, 'This isn't in the script, he's gone rogue. How am I going to get him back on track to play Dollar?'

For 14 years and across 500 or more TeamPOG radio shows, Paul created a safe place, one where, as the *Guardian* wrote, 'He was both acerbically funny – Lily without the wig – and incredibly warm, the kind of warmth you can't fake without sounding oily. And O'Grady never sounded oily … The fact that a lot of people who wrote in [to the show] seemed to be of advanced years … said a great deal about the breadth of his appeal. Pensioners seemed to adore him.' And they did. And so did young mums and their children, animal-loving middle-aged couples, and those of all ages with a lonely heart. We were all friends together, and no matter who you were, or where you were, it was his 'loyal listener' who was at the heart of every programme.

Around the time of our 300th show, and without help from BBC Marketing or an audience focus group, we adopted a motto, a mission statement if you will, and I featured it in all our posts on social media, and later on air. It was intended to make the listener aware that we knew the programme was not only *for* them, but that it also wouldn't be a show *without* them. One guest presenter – a professional funny man brought in to hold the fort while Paul was on a short break – took offence at the strapline, which he felt was a criticism directed at him, telling his agent to complain to Radio 2 management. Fearing they might lose the support of said comedian, I was told to stop using the strapline while Paul was away. Annoyed, I complied.

I can laugh about it now, however, because that line has given me the title of this book, and those few short words remain as pertinent as ever, even though today they have an added and more poignant meaning.

Paul, it truly *is* … not the same without you.

1.

Are You Sitting Comfortably?

> 'I have a high pain threshold,
> no need for anaesthetic'
> Paul O'Grady

It was Broadcasting House in London where I first encountered Paul O'Grady. I can remember that meeting as if it were yesterday, even though it was decades ago now.

'BH', as it's often referred to, is the main headquarters of the BBC. It's located in Portland Place, just north of Oxford Circus in London's West End and has been home to the Corporation in one guise or another since the early 1930s. BBC Radio's stations 1 and 2 launched in 1967. They were part of a major change for the Corporation as it responded to the emergence of pirate radio and a demand for programmes from a younger, 'pop-loving' audience. Radio 2 focused initially on 'light' entertainment and music, much like its rather frumpy predecessor, the Light Programme. During the next 20 years or so, it became home to such broadcasting legends as Jimmy Young, Pete Murray, Ray Moore and John Dunn.

11

Everything changed in the mid 1990s with the arrival of new management in the guise of a former head of light entertainment at the BBC, James Moir, and his managing editor, Lesley Douglas. Jim's tenure saw significant modernisation as he repositioned the network. And within 5 years his plans had succeeded, as BBC Radio 2 replaced BBC Radio 1 as the most listened-to station in the UK.

It was in BH that Paul and I first began making programmes for Radio 2. Paul was no stranger to the medium as he'd been a regular guest on many shows ever since the early days of Lily Savage. In 1996 he had hosted an edition of the network's clip-show *Talking Comedy* in which he explained what made him laugh, while also admitting that he wasn't a fan of comics and comedians, 'in fact, I hate comedy' he disclosed. And a few months before I first began working with him in 2003, Paul had sat in for Jonathan Ross on his Saturday morning radio show, where he was joined by Lily Savage's 'daughter' Bunty, aka the singer Sonia. But Paul O'Grady's appearance on the station some months later, purely as the presenter of a music documentary, was perhaps a more unexpected one and it was all because of Cilla Black.

I began producing programmes for the station in 1998 and had made numerous documentaries for them about singers and songwriters. Five years later, Cilla Black was celebrating her fortieth anniversary in show business. She had signed with The Beatles' manager Brian Epstein in September 1963, going on to enjoy huge success in the music industry with her UK number ones, 'Anyone Who Had A Heart' and 'You're My World'. To commemorate her ruby anniversary in the business, and her sixtieth birthday, Radio 2 commissioned me to produce a two-part documentary which would boast a new 3-hour interview with Cilla – conducted by me at her holiday home in Estepona, Spain. It also featured guest contributions from her friends and peers, including Cliff Richard, Burt Bacharach, Lulu, Michael Winner, Terry Wogan and Tim Rice.

As with all of Radio 2's documentaries back then, the network wanted an equally starry name as presenter. Cilla suggested her pal, Paul O'Grady. Since the death of her husband Bobby in 1999, the two stars had become firm friends. A call was made to Paul's manager, and the response was an immediate 'yes'.

I was thrilled *and* worried. To be honest, I was wary of Paul O'Grady. I had never met him before, and all I had to go on was the Paul I'd seen on television and the Lily Savage I'd witnessed in gay clubs. Let's not beat around the bush here: Paul O'Grady had a bit of a reputation back then. 'The stories when he was Lily Savage were that he was an absolute night-mare', says theatre impresario, Michael Harrison. 'Wigs being thrown in the dressing room, bottles of champagne being chucked out the window, so his reputation back in those days was that he was tough to work with.'

Dressed in a smart suit, he arrived at studio 1H to record the script for the Cilla documentary a little worse for wear: he had just had significant dental surgery, and I remember think-ing, 'How on earth will he be able to speak properly?' As though reading my mind, Paul had said: 'Don't worry, Malcolm', going on to explain the dental treatment had been completed without any anaesthetic. I began to feel queasy at the thought of it. Realising I was a bit squeamish, or 'nesh' as he called it, Paul proceeded to go into great detail about the invasive procedure he had just endured, laughing as I began to turn pale. Unpacking his WH Smith's carrier bag, he produced his copy of the script, and a bottle of Lucozade, and settled into the familiar surroundings. He relished working in such iconic studios, with their aged mixing desks, dusty furniture and Bakelite fixtures.

The job of a radio producer depends on the programme you're working on – and the station you're working for too, come to think of it. In the main, though, it's about organisation, preparation and, in the case of a documentary, storytelling. The challenge when making these radio documentaries is that often the producer doesn't get the chance to meet their presenter before recording their links or 'narration'. If you're lucky, you might have a quick phone call, but all I'd had was an email from Paul's manager confirming the date and location of the recording session. I had no idea what Paul would be like to work with – *to produce* – and I had no inkling what he even thought about my work.

Much to my relief, Paul told me he was happy with the script and was impressed with the list of contributors and my choice of Cilla's music. But, most of all, he was interested to know what she'd said during our intimate interview. While it was obvious that Paul O'Grady was a huge fan of Cilla, it should be noted that, as Lily Savage, he had said some derogatory things about her while he'd been working the nation's pubs and clubs, and often sent her up, especially when it came to the wannabe-star deserting the north to find success down south.

Thankfully, by 2003, Cilla had forgiven Lily.

One of the contributors I had interviewed was the broadcaster, writer and musicologist Russell Davies (not to be confused with the television writer Russell T Davies). When Paul discovered I also produced Russell's weekly Radio 2 show, he went off on a rant in which he delivered a scathing review of the series, the presenter and the choice of music. Paul's condemnation surprised me, but it was hilarious nonetheless, especially as it happened so spontaneously. This impromptu tirade – the first of many I would witness in the years that we worked together – was four-and-a-half minutes of pure, unfiltered O'Grady, and all of it totally unsuitable for broadcast. I now realise he was also testing me.

Words on paper need some magic to make them into a compelling listen on radio, and Paul O'Grady was undoubtedly a magician. He not only brought the script to life, but he also improved it by adding small but subtle ad libs here and there. For example, introducing a rare Cilla performance, while sharing the date and location of the appearance, he gently sent up his friend's age: 'Buried in the bowels of the BBC's archives for nearly forty years,' he began, 'here's Cilla's interpretation of "The In-Crowd", originally broadcast from Blackpool's Jubilee Theatre in August 1966 … I was five!' Typical Paul, always one to exaggerate to make an anecdote work – he would actually have been 11.

Another link detailed some of the products Cilla advertised or promoted in the 1970s, which included chocolate, fresh cream cakes, tea bags and baked beans. 'I bet her pantry was full!' he quipped.

As a producer, there's nothing more frustrating or alarming than to discover the presenter doesn't know how to interpret the written word or isn't engaged with the subject in hand. Thankfully, with Paul O'Grady there was no need to worry. His personal and intimate knowledge of the places I'd written about, and his huge affection for its central subject, gave the two programmes added gravitas.

An hour or so later, and with everything I needed safely recorded onto quarter-inch tape – it was 2003 and the BBC hadn't fully embraced the digital age – Paul thanked me and left the studio. I hurried back to my office over the road in Western House to begin mixing the programmes. I was thrilled: Paul's words combined with Cilla's story and music made for a compelling listen.

The next day, Paul phoned me. 'Hiya, Malcolm … remember that ad lib I did about fleas? Could you cut it out, please? If Cilla hears it, she'll have my guts for garters.' During the recording session, in a reference to growing up in Vauxhall, Liverpool, Paul had joked, 'By the time Cilla was twenty-five, the girl from Scottie Road, with great legs, a load of flea bites and dyed red hair, was a millionaire.' I had thought at the time: 'I hope she's OK with that,' but Paul had obviously been mulling it over ever since he had left the studio. I'd assumed recording the script for my documentary was just another job to him, and that he would quickly be on to the next, but I was wrong. He cared about the programme *and* his pal, and he wanted it to be right. The reference to fleas never made it to the final broadcast, and Cilla was none the wiser.

Sadly, the studio in BH where Paul and I recorded his links is long gone, as it was demolished along with the whole extension to Broadcasting House soon after we worked there (the two events were unrelated, before you ask). The space it occupied is now part of what is known as New Broadcasting House, home to the BBC's news operation. BBC Radio 2 relocated across the road to Western House – later renamed in honour of Sir Terry Wogan – until early 2024. But Paul often spoke of the old studios in BH – he joked about the state of them: the random pianos and ill-matching chairs, the haunting smell of nicotine from a time when smoking was allowed at the BBC, gram players and record racks, and ill-fitting headphones with cables that Paul always managed to tangle up into a knot. His comments about those old studios were made with great affection. He loved 'Auntie Beeb' or 'Auntie', as the broadcaster was commonly referred to by those of Paul's generation. The familial nickname was most likely inspired by the likes of Uncle Arthur, Auntie Violet and Uncle Caractacus who read stories on *Children's Hour*. And like millions of others, Paul had fond childhood memories of sitting on his mum's knee while tuning in to *Listen With Mother* on the BBC's Light Programme, and decades later admitted he would very happily host the record request show *Housewives' Choice* – if it was ever resurrected. Yes, Paul O'Grady was very proud to be associated with the British Broadcasting Corporation.

I didn't know it at the time, but interviewing Miss Black on the Costa del Sol for that radio documentary would change my life. I would go on to work with her again on other radio shows, and we would often bump into each other at the opening of a West End musical or similar production. And it was because of her that I met the man who is the subject of this book.

Recorded in late November 2003, and first broadcast a few weeks later, *Cilla – What's It All About?* was a documentary Paul and I were both proud of. The *Radio Times* agreed, selecting the programme as a 'Radio Choice', adding that Miss Black was 'in fine form' and that Paul was an 'impeccable host'. That project was also the start of our radio partnership, which would last until the day he died. Those years were filled with lots of laughs, countless rants and an abundance of drama.

The same could be said for all of Paul O'Grady's life.

2.

A Quaint Little Fishing Village

'23, Holly Grove … I loved that little house
… It's in my blood'
Paul O'Grady

For the years I knew him, Paul O'Grady lived 'down south' in Kent, but his story began not far from the west bank of the River Mersey, near the Woodside Ferry Terminal in Birkenhead.

If you make the pilgrimage there, you'll find an impressive piece of spray-paint art by the Wallasey-based artist Adam Brezaux. Commissioned in 2023, the mural is one of a series that reflects the area's history, culture and notable figures along the historic waterfront. Using a heightened realism that is both striking and sympathetic, the piece of art captures an avuncular man in his later years, opposite his former larger-than-life alter ego. Paul would have probably been both embarrassed and delighted by the artistic tribute, but its striking likeness to its subject is just part of the work's appeal. Equally important is its location: Birkenhead on the Wirral, where Paul was born in 1955.

In the many tributes and articles written about him, some refer to Paul as a Liverpudlian, but they are mistaken; he came from the other side of the Mersey, and he was proud of that and wouldn't hold back in correcting anyone who got it wrong.

He was born in the suburb of Higher Tranmere and grew up in a modest, rented house on a small road called Holly Grove. Paul compared the property to being 'like a doll's house inside' and 'always cold … No, not cold – freezing. You could've hung meat in the bedrooms during the winter months.' Situated in an elevated position, the family home offered views to the front over the river and Liverpool city skyline. 'It was the view I got to see every morning taking the "ferry cross the Mersey" on my way to work in the Cunard Shipping Office. The train over from Birkenhead to Liverpool was much quicker but I loved taking the ferry,' he once noted. Paul later described his first home: 'It was just an ordinary two-up, two-down house.' Today, there's no blue plaque and, without wishing to offend its current inhabitants, for anyone making a trip there the property is somewhat underwhelming given the person who spent his formative years inside. But it's a significant location in the story of Paul O'Grady.

Two of his four volumes of autobiography chronicled, in blistering detail, the time he spent growing up in the north-west. When his mother died in 1988, Paul considered buying his family home in Holly Grove because 'to let it go,' he later wrote, would be 'akin to an act of betrayal … [that house] meant so much to me.' Ultimately, however, he returned the keys to the landlord, taking as much of the contents of his childhood bedroom that he could carry back with him to London.

In essence, he had enjoyed a very happy upbringing, one that was full of affection. Like many in the area, Paul's parents were of Irish descent. His father, Paddy Grady (the 'O' was added in error to a form when he later joined the RAF), hailed from Galway and Ballincurry, County Roscommon; while Paul's mother, Mary 'Molly' Savage, had links to County Louth, where her parents grew up. Paul would often speak about his fondness of the Emerald Isle: 'I loved it as a kid … we'd go for the summer holidays,' and told RTÉ radio in 2015: 'I remember me dad when we were kids, he used to say, "We're related to Irish royalty!" We all just used to laugh at him. I quite fancy being Irish royalty. [But] I know with my luck I'll be in the kitchens, scrubbing the floors.'

Paul had a brother, Brendan, who was 14 years older than he was, and a sister, Sheila, who was 11 years older than Paul. The brothers weren't that close, but Sheila was another matter. Many years later, when Paul had become a household name, he would ring her most Sunday evenings for a catch-up. 'I was born late – what my mother called the last kick of a dying horse,' he explained in his 2009 autobiography *At My Mother's Knee … And Other Low Joints*. It's no accident his mother received top billing; he chose her maiden name for Lily after all.

'I was an indulged child and completely protected from anything bad,' he wrote. Even so, Paul recalled his mother was always threatening to put him in an orphanage if he didn't behave, something that filled him with dread: 'I didn't want to eat bread and dripping and be beaten with a belt by nuns so I'd be on my best behaviour for a while, making my mother instantly suspicious.' The sassy women of his youth, including his aunties Chrissie and Annie, and the neighbours who lived nearby, were all an influence on him. During one of the rare occasions we ventured out onto London's gay scene many years later, he told me: 'Lily owed a lot to the women I encountered in my childhood.'

His Aunty Chrissie had been a 'clippie' (a bus conductor) on the local 79 bus route. She was also a single parent and was, he said 'as hard as nails and very glamourous, she was the captain of the darts team in the pub and she liked a drink and she smoked, and she swore like a trooper. This woman to me was like a goddess,' adding, 'There was a whiff of Marlene Dietrich about her, and she couldn't resist the odd smart one-liner … but some of her stories were full of it, full of rubbish.' A typical example: 'When I was little, she told me, "Some fella shoved something down my bra today and said 'Have a drink on me.' I asked her what it was, and she replied, "A teabag."'

Characteristics that were observed, embellished and ulti- mately employed by Lily.

His Aunty Annie told the young Paul to, 'Think of the past, but don't dwell on it' – advice he observed. Nevertheless, he later admitted: 'For me, everything seems rosier in retrospect.'

Growing up in the 1960s, the women in the north were a completely different breed to those anywhere else in the world, according to Paul. 'My Aunty Chrissie [later] got a job as a manageress of an off-licence. Two fellas came in: "This is a stick-up." She said, "I'll just open the safe for you, love," went out the back, got a brush and battered them. This is who they were … [These women] were all very resilient.'

And none more so than his mother, Molly. Paul described her as 'very cynical and very dry,' she was, he explained, 'a mistress of the one liner'. He told me, 'I knew she wasn't what you'd call normal. She'd love to kick off.' Apparently, Molly was the sort of woman who would pop into a shop and ask if the ham on sale was fresh, just to get a reaction from the shopkeeper. 'That was the woman she was, Malcolm. You can see where I got it from,' adding, 'Your funny bone is forged in childhood.' He would say the same to many a journalist – as Paul told the *Big Issue* in 2022: 'A lot of the stuff I used to say as Lily stemmed from those days. [Those women] were all funny. I didn't realise at the time.'

But one thing he didn't tell his mum was the fact he was gay. He skirted around the issue, and she turned a blind eye. 'Taboos were swept under the carpet.'

As writer and playwright Jonathan Harvey explains, 'Telling his mother he was working in catering up and down the country rather than as a drag queen still tickles me, but they were such different days. She was worried he was a drifter who wouldn't settle down.' Indeed, Paul was the first to admit that, as a young man, he sought excitement and would go out of his way to find it: 'I just wanted to get on with my life.' There's often a kernel of truth in a joke, and Paul said his mother wouldn't have cared if he was running a brothel in Amsterdam – as long as he had a pension.

He failed his eleven-plus exam but eventually left school with four 'O' levels and a handful of CSEs to his name.

Speaking to the *Big Issue* in 2022, Paul reminisced about his teenage years. 'I had no ambition, I floated from job to job to job. As a young kid, I had a paper round and used to go around the hospital selling newspapers and ciggies, would you believe – on maternity as well. I was always quite self-sufficient. I worked in every single shipping office in Liverpool … you name it, I did it. I'd do any old job, me, as long as it paid enough money for me to go out, [and] buy new clothes.'

Aged 17, he found work at Liverpool Magistrates' Court where he met Diane Jansen, who was working in the same office. He was 9 years her junior and was, according to her, 'A catch, very handsome.' He described her as 'a bit of a party animal'. In fact, the two became such a pairing that their mutual employers had to keep them apart because Paul and Diane used to laugh and talk too much in the workplace. And, for a short while, the couple became a bit of an item. Some 50 years later, in 2024, Diane spoke to me at her home in Liverpool. She says she always knew that Paul liked both men and women: 'We didn't think of it as being gay or straight back then.' Paul was always acting out films and musicals, and he loved to dress up. 'You could see the talent was there,' remembers Diane. 'It wasn't organised and ordered … but I knew he was very clever and intelligent … It was just a part of him, dressing up, drag, it's what he did. I never suggested he did it professionally, though. He was just flamboyant. I got annoyed with him once, as I was sick of going to gay bars, so we went to a straight bar and I made him dance. He hated dancing, but he did it because I wanted him to … We did have a laugh. He'd say and do wicked things, but it was all for effect. We had a good time together.'

Those good times came to a shattering halt when his father died, at which point the 17-year-old Paul also discovered he was to become a dad himself.

I'm sure I wasn't the only one to be surprised when I heard Paul had a child, and I asked him about it many years later. He simply explained, with a wink, 'I put it about a bit, Malcolm.'

Contrary to the stories that appeared in the *Sun* in August 1995, Paul, who was then a rising star, didn't try to hide the fact he had a daughter, Sharyn. The front-page headline announced, 'Dad Lily meets his long-lost lovechild' and, inside, a further two pages were devoted to the 'revelations' that the two had met up recently in London. They had only agreed to appear in the paper because another tabloid was threatening to run their own version of Paul's private life, and he wanted to scupper their plans with his 'official', approved account.

Years later, with more time to reflect on the events of his youth, Paul wrote about discovering he was going to be a father, describing the news as, 'Life over. The end of my world as I knew it.'

As far as Diane was concerned, that response was character-istically over-dramatic because it was going to be she, and not he, who would be bringing up their child. She remembers that Paul 'did say he would stand by me' – something she took with a pinch of salt. 'He also said he would marry me, but I knew it was just words. He didn't mean it.'

Paul was never, as he later suggested, a single father. 'I knew what he was like,' Diane recalls. 'But it was quite hard for me.

I remember my grandma saying there was an article in the *Woman's Own* if you wanted to get rid [of the baby], but that never entered my head.' The same was true for Paul.

Sharyn was born in May 1974, when Paul was 18 years old. Diane stopped working at the courts to bring their daughter up; her own parents, though nearby, couldn't support her financially. Money was tight, and sometimes Diane would try to visit her mum and dad at teatime just so she and Sharyn would have something to eat.

Soon after the birth of his daughter, Paul left his hometown, with £100 in cash given to him by Diane. 'I wasn't surprised he left Birkenhead as soon as he could.' He headed for London and for many years continued to drift in and out of their lives, staying in touch by phone and through letters and cards – many of which featured his talented doodles and drawings. From time to time, he returned to Birkenhead, often staying with his mum, and would visit Sharyn and Diane, both of whom remember him as being a constant in their lives in those years, just not a physical one. 'He was there,' recalls Sharyn, 'maybe not daily, or weekly, but he was around. My mum would dress me, and sometimes he wouldn't turn up. But there are photographs of my birthday parties and he was there. And there were loads of phone calls, loads of letters, he would write to me all the time, and I would write to him at Holly Grove.'

Later on, Paul's mother would occasionally stop by the stall in Birkenhead Market where Diane was working with £1 for Sharyn – possibly offered out of Catholic guilt – but there was very little other contact between Grandmother O'Grady and grandchild. 'She was just a woman in a head scarf, I didn't know who she was, and she didn't want to be in my life,' notes Sharyn. Her early recollections of her father were more memorable: 'He took me to the cinema to see Disney films, and we saw *Snow White*. And he later bought me a Lady Di doll from the toy shop near the market. He also gave me a little Pluto toy when I went to see him at Holly Grove. And he would always send cards and presents at Christmas. He was like an uncle. I called him Paul, and when I was a teenager, I occasionally used to visit him in London. I'd go to Vauxhall, but I wasn't living with him.'

In *Open the Cage, Murphy*, the final volume of his autobiography, Paul explained that he looked forward to Sharyn's detailed and 'charming' letters – written on *Hello Kitty* notepaper – in which she expressed no sign of anger towards her 'excuse for a father'.

Diane never hid the fact from Sharyn that her dad was the hard-bitten hooker character, Lily Savage, though because of her young age Sharyn didn't witness Paul perform for many years. Even so, she grew up with drag. 'It wasn't a secret,' Sharyn told me. 'It was just something he had done, it was ordinary. I thought nothing of it. I was just proud of him.' There was one memorable occasion when the teenage Sharyn, accompanied by her mother, went to see 'the dragon' (as Diane called Lily) at the Empire Theatre in Liverpool. As they exited the building after the performance, Diane recalls Sharyn telling a departing audience member, 'That's my dad,' as she pointed to a poster outside the theatre.

The live performance would also prove a significant one because two worlds of Paul O'Grady's life collided that night.

'We went backstage to see him,' recounts Sharyn. 'We walked into his dressing room and Sheila, Paul's sister, was there with her husband. I didn't know who she was and asked her. She had no idea who we were, either. Paul just said, "Oh my god" and went into the bathroom.' Not for the first time, Paul O'Grady had tried to keep two sides of his personal life apart. 'Paul liked to keep everything separate then, it must have been exhausting for him.' Following the 1995 article in the *Sun*, Sheila and Sharyn connected properly and have remained in contact ever since.

Sharyn tried to maintain a meaningful relationship with her father. In 2001, she took her partner Phil Mousley to see Paul at his home in Kent; it was Phil's first meeting with his future father-in-law. 'He told us to get a cab from Ashford and we were dropped off at the gate to the house,' recalls Phil. 'We were walking down the long path in the dark as the lights were broken, and I was expecting the house to be imposing, flamboyant, with marble floors and chandeliers everywhere … but when we walked inside, it wasn't like that; it was like a single man's flat: there were open jam jars and butter trays in the kitchen, it was unkempt but homely. And Paul came down the stairs in a pair of chinos, a jumper with what looked like jam or egg on it, he didn't look like he'd had a shave in a couple of days, and he was belching and laughing. And I just thought, "He's not what I was expecting." He was making spaghetti Bolognese, and he asked me, "Where do you want it, at the table?" and I said, "No, in our laps, in front of the TV," and he replied, "You'll do me." We hit it off straight away.' Sharyn recalls after dinner that night: 'Paul played the piano in the living room and Phil was impressed, not knowing it was an automated piano and the music played itself.'

When Paul was the castaway on *Desert Island Discs* in 2003, he told presenter Sue Lawley: 'I love the bones of (Sharyn). It's a really happy-ending story. We got used to each other, and it's true that what's in the dog comes out in the pup because I'll have a go at her and she'll have a go back at me and I can't answer her back, I can't top her … and I'm really proud to say now that I love her dearly.' Father and daughter may have bonded, but Diane decided against maintaining a relationship with Sharyn's dad. 'Paul did invite me and a load of others down to Kent, but I thought, "No, I have my own life."' Paul was equally happy not to persevere.

In July 2005, he was given an honorary fellowship to Liverpool John Moores University, for services to television and entertainment. During the oration, he was described as 'a magnificent Merseysider'. Eight days later, Paul gave his daughter away in a lavish ceremony at the city's town hall.

Sharyn remembers when he arrived at Diane's flat, where they were all getting ready: 'And then Paul O'Grady walks in, larger than life; that's when sometimes you'd think, "Oh god, don't be so loud." But later, he was quieter, he wasn't performing.' In the car on the way to the ceremony, Paul turned to Sharyn and jokingly told her, 'I've got a plane on standby to Shanghai if you don't want to go through with it. If you want to get out of the marriage, come now.'

Sharyn wasn't impressed. 'Fancy saying that!'

At the wedding breakfast, seated on the top table with the groom's parents, and Diane, Paul tapped his champagne glass, got up and gave a speech – with no notes. Phil recalls, 'He just rattled it off, yappin', and everyone was just crying and screaming-laughing. Then I had to get up and give mine! I was dreading it, but I got through it.'

As far as Sharyn is concerned: 'My dad loved Phil. And Phil could see him for who he was, a complete nightmare half the time, which people didn't really witness, but Phil had seen my dad behind closed doors. They would text each other a lot, and they had great banter, often joking about my mother. My dad loved that.'

Phil adds, 'He didn't give me advice at the wedding, though he did say, "I know she's in safe hands." Sharyn didn't pull any punches, she would speak back to him and tell him off; she almost acted as if she was his mother. And he was in awe of his daughter. But later, Paul did give me good life advice about my family: he taught me not to worry about what people think and get on with my own life, to "look after your own". He did worry about things like we all do, but he had a good way of dealing with it. I do miss being able to ring him with a question because he'd always say, "If there's anything you ever need, lad, give me a ring."'

Sharyn agrees. 'Dad was always thinking about us. If you got something through the post, you knew his writing – he had very distinctive handwriting – and you realised that he'd gone to the shop and got a box; he had packed it and then gone to the post office himself. And he would always be messaging us. The last text I had from him was asking what Halo's [his granddaughter] shoe size was. We were always in his thoughts.'

During one of Paul's radio shows, we chatted about his plans for Easter that year. He explained with great excitement he had 'that lot coming down'. I hadn't really seen that side of Paul before: 'Little Halo is a stunner, Malcolm, and Abel's got his mam's brains.' He was undeniably proud of them. And then he joked, 'The family's visits always give me pleasure – if not the arrival, the departure.'

In November 2023, Paul's life was celebrated in his home-town, Birkenhead, where he was posthumously awarded the Honorary Freedom of the Borough, the highest award the local council can bestow as it's only granted to someone who has made an exceptional contribution to the area. The mayor of Wirral spoke at the ceremony, explaining: 'Paul O'Grady exemplified the best that our borough has to offer. Birkenhead-born, he dazzled his way to the national stage … but never forgot his roots.' The mayor went on to present Paul's assembled family with a scroll that depicted illustrations of the star's early life, including St Catherine's hospital where he was born, his family home at Holly Grove, the number 11 bus he used to take and Birkenhead library, where he was a frequent visitor.

A decade earlier, the city across the water had also celebrated Lily Savage when the Walker Art Gallery and Museum of Liverpool became the first venues to host *Savage Style*, an exhibition featuring 11 of her most famous outfits, all of which the fashion icon had worn in her dazzling career. The opening day was a significant event for Paul's then six-year-old grandson, Abel. In 2024 he told me, 'It was when I first realised he was famous, and that other people loved him too.

It was strange. Generally, we weren't included in the big, grand events like that with him, so I hadn't seen the suited and booted side to GanGan [the name Sharyn's family called Paul]. We were more used to seeing him in an apron at home, wearing his Vans [shoes] with a broken-down heel, and his hair in a mess. He often gave me a lot of advice, but simply being with him was just a lesson, I looked up to him so much. To me he was just GanGan.'

Names were significant in the story of Paul O'Grady, as they helped him compartmentalise different aspects and areas of his life. To the inner circle of his friends, no matter where they were, he was 'Savage', or 'Lil'; across the Mersey and beyond, he was Lily Savage, the 'deadly white flower of the Wirral'; while in Birkenhead, he was simply Paul O'Grady, son to Paddy and Molly, and brother to Sheila and Brendan.

And to those who worked with him, he was the title of his favourite Elvis Presley song: 'Trouble'.

3.

From The Black Cap to Blackpool

'I questioned this accidental career path
and wondered if the life of a drag queen
was really for me'
Paul O'Grady

While it goes without question that Birkenhead and Liverpool
both played a significant role in the formative years of Paul
O'Grady, it would be the pubs and clubs of London, the
northwest and beyond where he – and Lily – would find the
kind of success he had only dreamt of in his youth.

It would be convenient if Paul O'Grady's first foray into
the drag scene of the capital had resulted in instant, overnight
fame, but that's not how it happened. As I have discovered,
Paul's life was anything but straightforward.

Unlikely as it might seem, the diminutive star Jimmy
Krankie and the town of Blackpool were instrumental in
Paul's success. I'll come back to 'Wee Jimmy' shortly, but Paul's
association with the Lancastrian resort was an important one,

and it was far from fleeting. In fact, it would be Blackpool where Lily cemented her commercial star status.

Back when Lily Savage started her career in the late 1970s, she was, like so many drag artistes then, a mime act. In those days, it was all about lip-syncing and performing to recorded music. And if you'd had the chance to ask the rising star about her professional debut, she would have told you it had taken place at the Blue Balloon Club in Huddersfield where she had performed a 'very artistic and tasteful strip' under the stage name Lily La Douce, which she thought, 'sounded French and exotic'. But the reality was somewhat different.

The Black Cap in Camden, London, had been a pub for over 250 years and later became an important LGBTQ+ venue, even before homosexuality began to be decriminalised in 1967. And it was famous for drag cabaret. During the 1996 radio programme *Talking Comedy*, Paul explained the venue 'had lots and lots of acts on, most of them rubbish ... but there were a few good ones including Marc Fleming, whose act was called Auntie Flo, who was a vicious old queen, absolutely vitriolic. And there was Mrs Shufflewick.' Comedian Rex Jameson's character was a 'gin-soaked old tart who was broadminded to the point of obscenity'. Shuff, as Paul called him, had been a big star on the stage and radio in the 1950s until his addiction to alcohol got in the way. Paul described his early encounter with the comedian with great affection: 'When I began working there, he asked me to be his dresser, which I did ... and even though he was often blind drunk, he did the act ... with his off the wall mad monologues ... and was very, very funny.' Mrs Shufflewick's rambling spiels would eventually influence those of Miss Savage.

Lily made her debut at the pub in October 1978, miming to the song 'Nobody Makes a Pass at Me'. And somebody who saw that performance was Black Cap barman, and Paul's longtime friend, Vera, whose real name is Alan Ralph.

'Lily had to learn the ropes, and gain confidence,' explains Vera, who first encountered Paul on Liverpool's gay scene in the early 1970s. Vera would go on to witness first-hand the emergence of Miss Savage, first as part of The Glamazons, which saw Lily working alongside Joyce (aka Paul Banks), then paired up with Hush (aka David Hunter) as The Playgirls, and a trio called LSD – Lily, Sandra and Doris – comprising Paul, Hush and the drag artist David Dale. As ever, the acts mimed to recorded music.

For a decade or so, Lily Savage and her pals would continue to work London's gay venues and eventually those further afield, from The New Penny in Leeds to Madame Arthur's in Copenhagen. These were usually establishments of varying degrees of suitability and often saw Miss Savage competing with 'bum-grinding' strippers. The money wasn't great, but Paul enjoyed what he later described as 'this new lifestyle and … the peripatetic existence'.

Following a triumphant Christmas gig at Liverpool's Masquerade Club in 1983, The Playgirls, now featuring a refreshed line-up of Lily and Vera, went on to play at the original Flamingo Club – Blackpool's first gay nightclub – on Talbot Road, not far from the North Pier. The venue special-ised in drag acts and the duo went down well, though Vera now admits, 'Lily bullied me into it, really – I was terrified!' Ultimately, a life on the stage wasn't for Vera.

Julian Clary was one of many who enjoyed Lily's early performances with The Playgirls, The Glamazons and LSD. 'Lily was always notable, she was a complete character which worked on all dimensions, and you forgot it was drag. I suppose she was a hybrid, because what you were waiting for was for Lily to attack.'

Paul persevered and it wasn't until 1984 that Lily truly became Savage. Taking over from Hush as compère at a *Stars of the Future* evening at the Elly – the Elephant & Castle pub in Vauxhall – Paul had to use the microphone to introduce acts, and thus Lily finally found her voice. And a new star began to rise. As Alan Carr puts it, 'When that happened, Lily went up a gear, not with her costumes, not with hair and make-up, but with her wit. You can look fantastic, you can mime perfectly – most drag queens come alive when the music starts. But when it ends, you're on your own. But Lily was different as she came alive when the tape stopped. She was as sharp as a whip, she thought on her feet, she was in her element.' When Lily first arrived in Blackpool in the 1980s, her act was quickly identified as being 'a dame comedian with a difference'. And that distinction was a voice like barbed wire.

As Lily's early act evolved, the gigs she landed were by and large in Blackpool's gay venues, and those around the UK: she was still very much targeted at a gay clientele. For example, in 1988, although she was now being promoted as 'The Queen of Comedy', she was topping the bill of shows like *Royal Burlesk*, a daring revue at the Wimbledon Theatre, which saw her accompanied by a company of top male strippers. The production, according to its promotional flyer, was 'the most outrageous show in Britain – the show that Brighton tried to ban!'

I remember seeing Lily in a rare appearance at Madame Jojo's in Soho in 1988 or thereabouts. The cabaret club was usually home to Ruby Venezuela, the hairiest drag queen I had ever seen, but on this night it was Lily, and she was picking on anybody and everybody. I recall she did something with a whip, and I hid behind a bride-to-be who was there on her hen-do. When I shared this story with Paul years later, he laughed and said, 'She must have been the size of a fucking house!' Charming, as always.

Lily's leap to mainstream popularity seemed elusive until she received a Perrier Award nomination in Edinburgh in 1991. From then onwards, it wasn't only a gay clientele that embraced Birkenhead's favourite daughter. After years working intimate clubs around the country, including a long residency at the legendary Royal Vauxhall Tavern in London, the acid-tongued star in a towering blonde wig had climbed her way up the ladder into larger and more prestigious venues. Now her fans were an eclectic mix of leather clones, drag queens and 'respectable-looking people' dressed up for a night at the theatre.

And as the audience changed, so did Paul's creation: Lily was still daring and dangerous, intelligent and inclusive, and as blisteringly sharp as always; but now her artistry and left-leaning political beliefs were matched by her ability to appeal to a broad audience of scale.

In 1995, Lily was back in Blackpool when one of the town's social clubs was chosen as the location for a television series called *Live from the Lilydrome*. The variety show was filmed at a Blackpool live music venue, the Layton Institute, which had previously enjoyed performances by the likes of The Nolans, Joe Longthorne and Matt Munro. Lily's TV offering used a format that owed much to another series, *The Wheeltappers and Shunters Social Club*, which ran on Saturday nights on ITV from 1974 to 1977.

This new, six-part incarnation saw Lily 'The Queen of the Cabaret Scene' as compère, with guests including Boy George, Ian McKellen as a priest and *Coronation Street* star Liz Dawn. In one episode, Lily was joined by Australian comedian Mark Trevorrow, whom Paul had met at the Edinburgh Fringe Festival in 1991. Mark was known for his flamboyant alter ego, the Prince of Polyester with dazzling teeth, Bob Downe, who gave a memorable interpretation of Peggy Lee's 'Fever' with Lily on bongo drums.

The series also featured Jayne Tunnicliffe, as the ukulele-strumming, leopard-print-coat-wearing northern strumpet, Mary Unfaithful. Jayne recalls, 'It was set in a real social club in Blackpool, with real regulars who didn't hold back if they didn't like you. A couple of more "alternative" acts suffered at their hands! Paul was on stage constantly as Lily. Between takes he was his own warm-up act and floor manager. The show I appeared on had George Melly and John Chiltern's Feetwarmers, and Odyssey. I had a ball. Lily … had to go on and apologise for my ribald act afterwards. To quote her: "The Union of Catholic Mothers had a face like a smacked arse."'

The late-night series was a little rough around the edges, and while he enjoyed making it, Paul later admitted he was disappointed with the version that made it on screen and told his closest friends how embarrassed he was of *Live from the Lilydrome*, because it hadn't looked as polished as he had hoped.

It wasn't Paul O'Grady who was becoming famous in the 1990s, it was Lily Savage. And before his own name was widely recognised, Paul paid a visit to one of Blackpool's famous fortune-tellers.

Gypsy Petulengro had provided readings for visiting stars like The Beatles, Tom Jones and Tony Bennett, so Paul was in good company. On this occasion, once the fortune-teller had settled her customer into the booth on the North Pier, she revealed – with what we now know was alarming accuracy – his future: 'You'll work hard and achieve great success, but look after your heart.'

Gypsy Petulengro wasn't wrong, and Blackpool soon witnessed a record-breaking engagement by Lily Savage with her now legendary residence at the theatre on the same pier.

In 1996, two acts separately headlined at that venerable seaside venue. Both starred men who appeared on stage as women, both stars were of Irish descent, and both had an adoring – but very different – following. For all their apparent similarities, the two artists couldn't have been more different, however, and neither could have their shows: one offered tried and tested genteel nostalgia; the other a variety extravaganza hosted by the edgiest drag act in the country.

Back then, Danny La Rue was a 69-year-old mainstream entertainer who, at his peak in the 1970s, had been earning the equivalent of £2 million a year, had four homes, a Rolls-Royce and an entourage of 60. In the 1960s, La Rue had taken female impersonation out of the clubs and pubs and into the nation's most popular theatres. And while Danny was definitely dazzling, he was conservative too: 'I'm vulgar, yes, but never crude.' La Rue cultivated his respectable image as a 'comic in a frock' for decades, almost until the day he died. As the *Guardian* wrote, 'In his heyday, he could fill West End theatres and ... was an old-fashioned music-hall performer with an outsize personality and a big heart.' American comedian Bob Hope even described him as 'the most glamorous woman in the world'. Danny La Rue kicked off the summer season in June 1996 on Blackpool's North Pier in a production of *The Good Old Days*, inspired by the long-running BBC series. It was a dependable format, both the stage and screen versions celebrating the Victorian-Edwardian music hall. But by this point, Danny La Rue's fame had peaked, his act was regarded as 'of its time' and, although respected, younger audiences were seeking something more daring, less traditional.

Paul O'Grady's Lily Savage – who used to carry his oversized wigs around in a black bin liner and not a Rolls-Royce – was that alternative, and she was the antithesis of La Rue's polished drag act. Lily told the *Lancashire Telegraph* in August 1996: 'When they first offered me the show [on the North Pier], I wasn't keen ... I didn't come to Blackpool until I was about 28 because my mother thought it was tacky and downmarket ... But now I love Blackpool – I think it's got a certain feel to it you don't get anywhere else ... I love sitting at bus stops and tram stops and talking to all the old ladies and a lot of the time they don't realise I'm a man, so they tell me everything.' As he reminded me years later: 'If it was good enough for Marlene Dietrich' – who had caused a sensation when she performed two concerts at the Blackpool Opera House in July 1955 – 'then it was good enough for Mary "Hellcat" Savage's daughter.'

Lily and Blackpool were made for each other: 'People are very snobby about it, but I think it's wonderful … Pier shows have got a bad name. Down in London everyone was saying, "What? You're going to *Blackpool*?" like it was some terrible thing, but I feel honoured to be headlining.'

For Paul's longtime friend Moira Stewart (not the broadcaster), Lily was perfect for the seaside resort, and vice versa. 'I think he enjoyed hiding behind her character, he could say all sorts of stuff and get away with it, and what he liked most of all was when he had a load of pensioners in, he could harangue them for their incontinence and they used to howl with laughter … Blackpool shows were his favourite – he'd tell me, "Give me a roomful of pensioners any day!"'

The town's residents and holidaymakers had plenty of traditional entertainment options on offer in the summer of 1996: at The Grand Theatre, Cannon and Ball headlined a bill which included the Three Degrees' lead singer Sheila Ferguson. The theatre on the South Pier was home to the comedian Duncan 'Chase me!' Norvelle, while at the Opera House, Darren Day and Faith Brown were starring in a stage production inspired by the 1963 Cliff Richard film *Summer Holiday*. Lily Savage over on Blackpool's North Pier was, therefore, a bit of a contrast.

To publicise her variety show, Lily popped down to London to be a guest on Channel 4's *The Big Breakfast*, where she also managed to solve viewers' problems with *Lily's Agony Line* and provide a commentary on the day's news with Keith Chegwin and Zoë Ball. The public was interested in Lily and the publicity worked: her fifteen-week seaside run in *The Lily Savage Show* broke all records.

Talking to Des O'Connor on his ITV chat show, Lily said of Blackpool: 'It's my spiritual home, I love it [even though] the North Pier Theatre is a Nissen hut on a pole in the middle of the Irish sea … And there's a tram that takes you down the pier. Now, all the time I was there, when I was in the theatre, the tram was at the other end, and when I was at the other end, the tram was always down there [at the theatre]. And yet I never saw it move. Honest, I swear to God, if you want to commit suicide, throw yourself on the tram lines of the North Pier because you'll have three hours to think it over before anything comes! But it's a fab place.' Paul would later refer to his 15-week stint as his 'National Service'.

Lily's end-of-the-pier spectacular featured guests such as juggler Pete Matthews, an upcoming vocalist called Russ (Russell) Watson, The Kim Gavin Dancers with the Dave Bintley Sound, and the singer Sonia, who performed a couple of cover versions plus her Stock, Aitken and Waterman hits. 'I was overjoyed when Paul asked me to join him for that long, long summer season run. We had such a laugh.'

By the end of the engagement the November weather was 'just horrendous' and Sonia and Lily would sometimes struggle to get to the theatre at the end of the long pier without being blown into the sea. 'When there were gales, the theatre itself would shake, and Paul was worried about it collapsing into the sea,' she recalls. Sonia used to hang out in his dressing room, 'gassing'. Paul's dog Buster was there too, often tucking into a portion of Harry Ramsden's finest. 'They were precious times. I would spend hours with Lily and Buster trying to tidy up his dressing room and sticking his false nails back on as they used to fall off all over the stage. One memory that sticks in my mind is when Paul decided to have a massive party on the roof of the North Pier – for Bonfire Night. Oh my gosh, there were huge fireworks everywhere, sparklers and everything, and loads of people complained but Paul wasn't having any of it. "It's Bonfire Night!" he said. I loved him to bits, and I treasure every single moment with him.'

Lily Savage was now a bona fide star, the souvenir programme explaining that she was 'undoubtedly one of the hottest entertainers in show business today, having graced (and, indeed, disgraced) many a famous television sofa – from Richard and Judy's to Des O'Connor's'.

By 1996, Lily was as much a part of Blackpool as its famous tower, illuminations and rock. Rounding off the year, she moved across town for a festive show at Blackpool's 3-thousand seater Opera House. *Lily's Christmas Cracker* ran from 20 December until New Year's Eve and featured *EastEnders* actor Sean Maguire, and Lily's regular sidekick, the 'former Page Three stunner' Gayle Tuesday, aka Brenda Gilhooly.

Being in a busy Christmas show suited Paul. 'I hate Christmas,' he told the *Bolton News* in 1996, 'so it's great to be working during the festive season.' Brenda Gilhooly remembers, 'Paul really loved the idea that he had the freedom and budget to do a big production number in the show. He was brought up on Hollywood and showbiz, so he loved bringing it all to life. We did big dance numbers, we paid homage to *The Wizard of Oz*, and it was like Paul was in a candy shop, he wanted to do stuff with scale and now that he was a star, he was able to deliver it.' The programme for the show has Lily in fake snapshots with Elizabeth Taylor, the pope and President Reagan. Paul was, however, reluctant to describe Lily's *Christmas Cracker* as a family show: 'I would hate to come out and find wall-to-wall kids facing me,' he said. '[I'd] turn into Dana.'

While Paul was performing in the 1996 festive show, Paul's manager and partner, Brendan Murphy, had been undergoing treatment for liver cancer. Brenda remembers that time well: 'Brendan was such a stoical character, even though he was very ill, he never complained, and you wouldn't have known it. Paul was the same, the show had to go on.' It did, although privately, Paul wanted to focus on Murphy's health. Brendan and Paul were, according to close friends, inseparable in the early days, even though Paul wasn't Brendan's typical type, and their personal relationship was, at times, volatile. He told the *Guardian*, 'Murphy and I used to fight, proper punch-ups. We'd fight in the green room of the BBC. And that was love.' When it came to business, work came first. The former actor and now Labour peer, Michael Cashman, explains, 'Brendan focused Paul. He made him think about what he could get away with and, more importantly, what he couldn't. Paul never accepted the boundaries; they were for other people. Brendan honed the act, and without him, Paul's career wouldn't have developed as it did.'

As Paul's career began to take off in the late 1980s, Brendan accompanied him the length and breadth of the country, often driving Paul's bright red Citroën BX, complete with electric windows, because Paul couldn't drive. Paul described Brendan as 'a man of few words' and 'one stubborn bastard,' while admitting he was 'devastatingly handsome'. He likened their relationship to that of the middle-aged couple Martha and George in Edward Albee's play *Who's Afraid of Virginia Woolf?*

Murphy had also been booking the acts for the Royal Vauxhall Tavern, and by 1988 a complicated and complex partnership started to take shape as he took on the unenviable position as Paul's manager. 'I knew Murphy didn't pull his punches when it came to negotiating fees,' he later explained. But it wasn't just about money: Brendan began to orchestrate Paul's career, while simultaneously being his adviser, publicist, confidante, counsellor, partner and non-exclusive lover.

For tourists, Blackpool was all about excitement and big thrills, but for Paul O'Grady it was more about bloody hard work, combined with equally full-on partying – usually involving sessions at Yates's Wine Lodge where they sold champagne on tap, excursions to the Pleasure Beach and more refined visits to the Tower Ballroom. Joan Marshrons confirms, 'He had great affection for the town. Had things turned out differently, he would have returned there for another project of some sort. He never forgot how important it had been to him in the early days.' The feeling was mutual. In 2009, Blackpool Zoo named the latest addition to its herd of giraffes 'O'Grady' after Paul, who was so pleased he announced the arrival of his namesake to the nation on his Channel 4 teatime telly show. In 2023, when Blackpool's Showtown Museum opened its doors, artefacts from Lily's association with the resort were included as part of its permanent collection.

But perhaps the best illustration of the significance the town had on Paul's career can be found at the National Portrait Gallery in London. Image reference NPG x135364 is one of five pictures of Lily Savage/Paul O'Grady in its collection, and was included in the 2009 *Gay Icons* exhibition. It's a chromogenic print taken by Paul Massey, simply titled *Paul O'Grady as Lily Savage*. Measuring just 13 inches by 13 inches, it sees Lily, fag in mouth, sitting on the North Pier's famous wrought-iron green and white benches, her handbag resting on her lap. Lily is wearing leopard-print tights, white shoes and a gold tasselled cowboy jacket. And in the background, there's Blackpool's famous tower. The striking image is a powerful one, and it captures Paul at peak Savage.

When Danny La Rue's death was announced in May 2009, I suggested to Paul that we mark it in some way on the radio show, thinking he must have been a fan. I was wrong. Although Paul admired Danny's career, he didn't see himself as a disciple – far from it. According to Vera, La Rue initially called Lily Savage 'a filthy pub act,' but, despite that short-sighted description, Paul did respect him and understood how the elder statesman of drag might have been threatened by 'an up-and-coming pretender to his throne' (Paul's words, not mine). They were hardly rivals. Unlike Lily Savage, Danny La Rue never let his audience forget that he was really a man, and they were always in on the secret. He didn't become a gay icon because his act played to a core audience of blue-rinsed ladies of a certain age who sent gushing letters congratulating him on his awards, hair and clothes, and not his opinions or political views; while behind the scenes, according to Paul, Danny La Rue was 'an old dragon'.

Now, let's return to that important brief encounter with Jimmy Krankie. It happened during 1982, when the Scottish husband and wife comedy duo The Krankies were topping the bill on one of Blackpool's three famous piers. The story goes that Paul was a big fan and, seeing Wee Jimmy (Janette Tough), told her he admired her work and hoped one day he would match their success with his drag act, explaining he had ambitions to play bigger venues than the clubs he was used to. Janette invited him for a cup of tea in a café. As Paul later remembered, 'Janette told me to just keep doing what I was doing and eventually I'd get there, as they'd had a long slog too. I was a total stranger to her, but that's the sort of friendly place Blackpool is.' He never forgot Janette's kindness and in 2005, when his own success had eclipsed theirs, he invited The Krankies onto his TV show. That appearance, according to Janette's husband Ian, was the reason their *Best of British Variety* tour became a sell-out success.

During his life, Paul's affection for Blackpool was never far beneath the surface. We once discussed taking Paul's radio show to the seaside town for an outside broadcast. I wanted to reunite him with Gypsy Petulengro on the North Pier; in return, he suggested he would buy me a ticket to ride the Big One, referring to the resort's famous roller-coaster. Sadly, the Covid pandemic got in the way. Speaking on his teatime Channel 4 show to Blackpool-born actress Jodie Prenger in 2009, Paul described the town as his 'second home'. It was true.

4.

Firemen, the Fringe and a First Flush of Fame

'[I] loved working in Edinburgh. I lived on
fish suppers; I came back with hardened
arteries and teenage acne'
Paul O'Grady

Paul O'Grady was appreciative of so many of his early
stomping grounds, and he remembered them fondly, be it the
Nightingale in Birmingham, Heroes in Manchester or the
Fleece in Bradford. But there was one old haunt in another
favourite city which deserves a special mention, because it
changed Paul O'Grady's life entirely.

Of all the places that helped him forge a career, Edinburgh
is perhaps one of the most significant, because it was where
the critics discovered Lily, and later applauded and celebrated
the man behind her lipstick and leopard-print mini skirt.

The Edinburgh Fringe is the world's largest performance
arts festival. Established in 1947, it is now a leading celebration of arts and culture. Comedy didn't feature as such until
1981 when the big Perrier Award winner was the Cambridge

Footlights team, which included Emma Thompson, Stephen Fry and Hugh Laurie. As Paul's good friend the comic and presenter Jo Brand explains, 'At that time, the Fringe was like a display case or a shop window for new talent, and if you won, or were nominated, it was a real stepping stone for someone's visibility. All the important executives from telly decamped to the city for the month, there was no one left in London pretty much, and the Perrier Award really meant something – it had a massive cachet about it.' Within a few short years, the Fringe became widely regarded as the 'spiritual home' of Britain's funny folk.

Paul O'Grady's affection for Edinburgh began in the mid 1980s when Lily and Hush appeared at the city's legendary gay club, Fire Island, on Princes Street. 'We loved working [there … they had] a very appreciative audience,' he wrote in *Still Standing – The Savage Years*. Paul later explained it had been Brendan's idea to go to the Fringe and that appearing there had opened doors which would have otherwise been closed. It also exposed him to a much wider audience than he had been accustomed to. In many ways, the Scottish capital was the place where Paul O'Grady's star began to shine, albeit it as shoplifting, mouthy housewife Lily Savage.

Back in 1991, the Wildman Room on George Street was one of four key locations for the city-wide arts festival. For the first time as a Fringe headliner, Lily was starring in the graveyard midnight slot, wearing her soon-to-be signature platinum wig, knee-high boots, mini skirt and fur coat. *Lily Savage: The Live Experience* promised 'a glittering extravaganza from the radical Marxist sex kitten,' accompanied by Dave

Lynn and Katrina and the Boy. Legend has it the first performance that year – to a half-full venue – did not go according to
plan. During the fire-eating segment of Lily's act, she set off
all the alarms and the place had to be evacuated. And it wasn't
just Lily's show which had to up sticks: it was 'every act, every
room, all the audiences out into the street. I wanted to crawl
under a rock. I was mortified,' Paul later explained. He apparently hadn't counted on the low ceiling of the Wildman
Room and the sensitivity of its smoke detectors. The unexpected publicity stunt was the best thing that could have
happened, however. 'People were roaring laughing,' he
recalled, as theatre-goers were evacuated to the middle of
George Street. 'There I was in full drag, and someone asked
me to pose with the firemen.' Taking pride of place,
surrounded by good-natured fire fighters, the photographs
ended up on the front page of all the papers and the run
became a sell-out.

By the end of the Festival, Lily had made the shortlist for
the Perrier Award in the category of 'Best Comedy Show'.
She was in good company, as fellow nominees included Jack
Dee, Eddie Izzard and the ultimate winner, Frank Skinner.

'For a long time, the people who did well at Edinburgh
weren't working class,' argues Jo Brand. 'They were Oxbridge
types, who had all gone through the Cambridge Footlights.
Lily was a complete breath of fresh air on that comedy circuit;
she harked back to the generation of comics before, from
working men's clubs and pubs … a fusion of the old and the
new. Lily didn't do jokes as such, but almost everything she
said was funny and it was because of the character itself. It was

quite unusual. Before Lily came along, drag queens hadn't really centred on comedy, it was about their look and how they mimed. It wasn't to do with what they said. Lily was so quick, so bright, so political, she was a real mix, so many people could identify with her. Basically, Lily was revolutionary.'

Vera agrees: 'Paul was a raconteur; the whole thing with Lily was a complete character, with a sister and kids; she was a different type of drag artist.' Brenda Gilhooly remembers, 'Paul would make me roar with laughter; he was the most naturally funny person I had ever met. He chose drag at that point in his career as the prop for his comedy. He couldn't fail but be funny, and, once you got to know Paul, you realised that Paul and Lily were interchangeable – if Paul was in a bad mood, then Lily would be in a bad mood on stage. And even if he was in a bad mood, he would still be hilariously funny. It was in his bones, and I didn't really see him as a drag artist, he was just funny.'

Paul later described the atmosphere at the Edinburgh Festival as 'intoxicating as it is infectious'. He told me appearing there had been 'an exhilarating time, but not for my liver'. He also admitted not winning initially meant he went from 'being everyone's darling' to becoming Mr Cellophane, i.e. a bit of a nobody. But that was short-lived, and he was back the following year in *Savage II: The Return*. Once again he was at the Assembly Rooms, but this time Lily was performing in the considerably larger Ballroom.

For Graham Norton, who later also enjoyed success at the Fringe with his act as a tea-towel-clad Mother Teresa of Calcutta, Paul 'had the ambition and imagination to get out of performing in gay bars. And all the other drag queens at the time thought, "What? How did you do that?" And when he announced he was going to the Festival, I remember thinking, "How does a gay bar act do an hour at the Edinburgh Fringe?" But that was stupid of me because he killed it. So, it was his intelligence, both professional and emotional, to know he could upgrade outside that particular world.'

Lily Savage's act and material may have been sharp, unapologetic and fearless, but she wasn't the first to display the hallmarks of what was becoming known as 'alternative comedy' – a form that broke away from the predictability and prejudice found on the working men's club circuit. The Edinburgh Fringe had witnessed the likes of Tony Allen and Alexi Sayle with their *Late Night Alternative* cabaret as early as 1980, but there was an added depth to Miss Savage. Jo Brand explains: 'People saw in her what they wanted to see, she was likeable and hilarious, but never really threatening. And Lily really stood out. Your average drag queen – if there was such a thing then – was two-dimensional, and they wouldn't be that interested in politics, and would far less express political views, and far less express *left-wing* views, but Lily did, and people accepted her.'

Lily's forthright stance emerged against the backdrop of the AIDS epidemic, and the discriminatory legislation known as Section 28, which prohibited the 'promotion of homosexuality' by local authorities. For the author Matt Cain, Paul O'Grady's 'greatest talent was as a storyteller, a communicator. And he provided a crucial link for the gay community to our history.' Drag acts and openly gay performers were frequently marginalised and disrespected as an art form, and 'underground entertainment' seldom cut through to the mainstream. When they did, female impersonators like Danny La Rue, Hinge and Bracket, and Stanley Baxter were, often, seen as novelty acts.

There were exceptions, however, probably most notably one of Barry Humphries' longstanding alter egos, Dame Edna Everage, who, along with Paul's creation, would pave the way for a wider social acceptance and the precursor of today's drag boom. Significantly, as Michael Cashman points out, 'Barry wasn't gay, but Paul O'Grady was, and he was unapologetic about it.'

I wonder how many of Edinburgh's paying audience back in 1991 realised that Paul as Lily would drag the art form into the mainstream? And yet, in later years, Paul O'Grady pointed out that he was only labelled a 'drag artist' because he was openly gay. Paul said, 'Barry Humphries was never called a "drag act" because he's a heterosexual male,' and he suggested in his own case the use of the moniker was, 'homophobic and wrong … I dressed up as a woman for financial purposes'.

It was in Edinburgh that Lily really started earning her keep. As Graham Norton suggests, 'Going to Edinburgh was a game-changer for Lily and it changed Paul's life and career. Now, for my money, as someone who grew up watching Lily at the Royal Vauxhall Tavern, "mainstream Lily" was never as funny as she was there [because] as rude as she was, there was always a slight brake on compared to who she was in the Tavern. That was Paul at the height of his powers, firing on all cylinders. But he was very smart, and he knew if he wanted to cross over, the act couldn't stay exactly the same.'

Paul O'Grady never forgot Miss Savage owed much of her success to Auld Reekie, and Vera remembers spending many a happy evening – and early morning – with Paul on return visits: 'They were great times – Lil really loved Edinburgh.' Years later, Paul was always happy to recall his frequent outings in the city, away from the Festival, on his radio show. He told me of the wild times he enjoyed playing the Laughing Duck in Howe Street, and CC Blooms right next to the Playhouse Theatre on Greenside Place. '[They] had fabulous lock-ins. I'd go in at night with sunglasses on because I knew I'd be staggering out in daylight.' And so it was no surprise that the city was chosen as the location to record a home video of one of 'mainstream Lily's' live theatre shows, released in 1998. The venue was the city's Festival Theatre, and the evening's performance included a duet of 'You Don't Bring Me Flowers' with Fringe regular Mark Trevorrow as Bob Downe, and a cameo from Sonia as Lily's daughter, Bunty, who was seen trying to flog merchandise. Miss Savage admitted to having two children: Bunty was her eldest and a carbon-copy of her mother, only shorter; while Lily's youngest, Jason, was 'in a private boys' school – for the next twenty-five years'.

For theatrical impresario Michael Harrison, by this point, 'It was a bit like Ken Dodd and the Diddymen: with Lily, Paul had created a world you could believe in, with her sister Vera and her daughter Bunty, and even though we didn't live in it, we all wanted to. Her house might not have been all that nice, but we wanted to be with her.'

To open her Edinburgh show, Lily performed a version of a song first featured in the 1976 Goldie Hawn film,

The Duchess and the Dirtwater Fox. The number 'Please Don't Touch Me Plums' owed much to the traditions of old time British music hall and vaudeville, something Paul admired greatly. (He would later support the preservation and legacy of the genre when he succeeded Roy Hudd as President of the British Music Hall Society in 2020.)

As the on-screen credits rolled 70 minutes later at the end of the triumphant Edinburgh performance, three other significant names could be seen: the future producer of his ITV and Channel 4 teatime chat shows, Robert 'Bert' Gray; the woman who would work alongside Paul O'Grady until the day he died, Joan Marshrons; and Paul's partner and then manager, Brendan Murphy.

The 1998 Edinburgh show was a far cry from Lily's first home video, which was a rather bumpy live performance of Lily Savage that had been recorded 5 years earlier at the Hackney Empire Theatre in London. In that time, Miss Savage had matured into an accomplished artiste, though the humour which had helped make her name was still as blunt as ever: 'Doctors are obsessed with stools, aren't they? They said would you bring a stool sample in? What! Sitting on the bus with a turd in your handbag! Disgusting!' She went on to explain that her Edinburgh show was sponsored by the soft drink, Oasis. She had recently been providing the voice-overs for their television adverts, and she admitted, 'I quite like doing the advertising, it's a few bob, isn't it, easy money. Ten grand in your pocket beats standing at a bus stop giving somebody a hand shank for fifteen quid.'

Thirty or so years later, it is interesting to see what was included in that Edinburgh performance, for which Paul O'Grady received sole writing credit. Within the scurrilous, filthy and fast-flowing material were subjects that foretold much of his future career: gags about his beloved *Coronation Street* and the trials and tribulations of Deirdre Rachid (née Barlow); he talked about the hidden depths of fairy tales; learning how to drive; and the appeal of the TV docu-series *Animal Hospital*. There was a reference to the prospect of appearing at *The Royal Variety Performance*, and a story about a South African safari where Vera had been attacked by a rogue elephant. All these subjects would go on to feature in Paul's subsequent life away from Miss Savage.

By the end of the 1990s, Lily, the Queen of the Provident Cheque and former Miss Pears 1957, was one of the biggest names in British show business. Not only that, she was main-stream, hosting family TV game shows, appearing on chat shows and starring in her own series. It was hardly the first time the Fringe had served as a launch pad for new perform ers on television, but Lily's journey is one of those rarer occasions where a character or concept travelled from the Festival to the small screen intact. And that transformation was significant because he was an openly gay man representing others at a time when their queerness was still demonised.

More and more, people were taking notice of Miss Savage.

5.

Ranting and Raving

'You need people to go out and say, "No, no, no,
we're not putting up with this – we're not
second-class citizens"'
Paul O'Grady

Throughout his life, unlike so many of his peers, Paul O'Grady had been no stranger to speaking his mind in public. He cleverly used his celebrity platform to stand up for what he believed in. It was brave, given the potential was always there to damage his career, and sometimes controversy was just a breath away.

Writing this book, I have wondered what his legacy is. The answer lies in his work.

Shortly after his death in 2023, the *Metro* explained that Paul had 'made fun of the stuck-up, stuck up for what he believed in, and he would stick up for you in a fight – provided you weren't a total bastard.' That same week, the then Labour deputy leader Angela Rayner described him, unsurprisingly, as a 'national treasure' – a term he loathed because he felt it implied he was part of the establishment – while a lazy deputy prime minister, Dominic Raab, standing in for Rishi Sunak, got Paul's name wrong and said, 'Paul Grayson was an incredible comic'. Heckled by members of the House, Raab corrected himself and continued, suggesting Paul was a man who 'broke boundaries'.

You can imagine how Savage would have described him!

Arguably nearer the mark, the *Evening Standard* described Paul as, 'Grassroots, working-class gay culture personified. Funniest man in the pub. Sharpest tongue on the block. In the gradients of razor-sharp regional gay humour, Scousers frequently win the comic lottery. O'Grady was a gold medallist across all disciplines.'

His tongue was certainly cutting. I'll always remember one wet Wednesday evening when Paul took me on a night out. Leaving Broadcasting House, we couldn't find a taxi. As we stood in the rain, Paul finally managed to hail one, only for a young woman to jump into it before we could. As the cab drove off, the language he used to describe her actions was so shocking I wanted the proverbial ground to swallow me up. It was the first time I'd been witness to Paul being so loud and outrageous in public. Thankfully, nobody caught his tirade on a mobile.

Paul was proud to have been born to a working-class Irish migrant family in the 1950s. That being said, he didn't embrace the idea of a typical 9-to-5 existence, and it was while he was working at a gay bar called the Bear's Paw 'hidden down' a small alley in Liverpool that Paul was first introduced to the city's gay scene of the 1970s.

At first he was 'a shy young man' but he soon acclimatised, and he started to attend meetings at the Campaign for Homosexual Equality, where he told me he had 'turned a few heads – and stomachs'.

By the time he relocated from Birkenhead to London at the end of the decade, and was employed by Camden Council in social care, he was witnessing and experiencing a seismic change in political power. It was a period of protest, something Paul O'Grady wasn't afraid to embrace. (Neither was Lily, who once confided, 'You need two things in a riot – flat shoes and a pram.') The capital city offered Paul employment and personal freedom, something he was perhaps less confident to fully embrace and explore back at home while living with his Catholic mum.

In 1977, Paul participated in, as he called it, 'a marriage of convenience' to Portuguese model and barmaid Teresa Fernandes. They had met while the two were working at a bar in Westbourne Grove, London. 'No, we didn't consummate it, Malcolm', he shared, when I questioned his motives years later. 'Teresa was under threat of being deported.' The couple drifted apart in the early 1980s, as Paul's career was starting to take off, and were officially divorced in 2005.

Paul's easy-going existence didn't last long, however. The political watershed of the late 1970s and 1980s, which saw a swing from a Labour to a Conservative government, coincided with a threat to his recently adopted liberated lifestyle. 'He ascended out of a terribly dark period in British social history,' recounts Michael Cashman, 'where we had AIDS and HIV, which was used by the media to pummel gay and bisexual men in particular, when they tried to drive us underground, where they brought in a new law banning the so-called promotion of homosexuality, which was all about banning acceptance. And out of that came Paul O'Grady – and Lily Savage – who challenged the establishment and what broadcasters thought audiences would accept. He didn't break the mould; he crushed and destroyed it.'

In the 1980s, at the height of the crisis – which some papers referred to as a 'gay plague' – drag queens became the natural leaders during the epidemic. None more so than Lily Savage who was being gloriously unapologetic as she ruled the roost at the Royal Vauxhall Tavern in south London. In their obituaries of Paul in 2023, the press delighted in reminding readers about the infamous Saturday night in January 1987, when the Metropolitan Police raided the venue in another attempt to intimidate the gay community. On seeing the rubber-gloved officers, Lily reassured her alarmed audience: 'Looks like we've got help with the washing up.' If only the papers had shown such empathy back then.

Paul's creation wasn't the first working-class drag act to use their voice – there was the radical performance troupe Bloolips, founded by Bette Bourne in 1977, renowned for its 'glamour-on-a-budget' with costumes made from plastic laundry baskets, broken lampshades and mops as wigs. There was also Blackpool-born anti-capitalist performance artist David Hoyle, who recognised that drag could be a medium for political disruption – but, for Jonathan Harvey: 'Both Lily, and Paul, were pretty fearless. At the Vauxhall Tavern in the Clause 28 and AIDS years he was never afraid to hold people to account in his act. People flocked to that bar like it was the village hall and they'd be looked after and listened to, while outside the world was burning and hating on us. And that attitude lived on in his later years when he wasn't afraid to slag off the government on his TV shows, if something was annoying him. He certainly wasn't a "yes man", and knew his own mind.'

Paul would return to the 'village hall' many times in the years that followed the infamous 1987 police raid. There was a party in 2012 at the Grade II-listed venue to celebrate the publication of *Still Standing*, the third volume of his autobiography, and various interviews with the press and media. It was all a far cry from his days of being called 'a lascivious act'.

When the political and cultural news magazine the *New Statesman* summed up Paul's life, he was described as 'one of us'. The 'everyman' moniker is a simple yet appropriate accolade and one that was echoed in countless other similar tributes. As Michael Cashman explains, 'Savage knew poverty, he knew what it was like to be shunned, and he knew what it was like to be in a room and not be noticed, he knew what it was like to be shouted at, and he never forgot where he came from. Lily Savage could never have been a success if she didn't speak about her roots, and Paul's roots and Savage's roots were exactly the same. Comedy only works if it's true, and he spoke truth. Lily gave him the excuse to say exactly what he thought, she was his alter ego. So often, we, as LGBT people, grab a persona we can use to navigate our world and the world of others, which is sometimes welcoming [or] hostile and challenging.' And the 1980s were certainly that.

Fuelled in part by the publication in 1983 of a book called *Jenny Lives with Eric and Martin*, which aimed to give children information about different types of family relationships, Margaret Thatcher's government introduced the infamous Section 28 legislation, which outlawed any mention of homo-sexuality in schools. Like many, Paul was furious. In April 1988, he took part in a thirty-thousand-strong march against the law – now known as Clause 28 – which had been drafted by Dame Jill Knight; or, as Paul later called her, 'the Delores Umbridge of politics'.

As a social worker, Paul had seen first-hand how regressive government policies impacted the individual. He believed you needed to bring up others with you. Years later, after Lily Savage had made him a mainstream star, Paul insisted vacant positions on *The Paul O'Grady Show* were advertised in the local Job Centre because he wanted everyone to be able to apply so they could get a break. And for one generation of children, seeing Lily Savage on the box was the first time they had probably seen queerness on screen.

I recall watching one of Lily's early TV appearances on a Channel 4 series called *Out On Tuesday*, a gay magazine-style programme broadcast in 1990 which also included Julian Clary. Watching them didn't change my life, but it was encouraging in a 'safety in numbers' kind of way. And who would have thought that, a few years later, a Scouse, working-class drag queen making veiled jokes about being a hooker would end up on mainstream TV shows like *This Morning* and *Des O'Connor Tonight*?

The actor and writer Ian Hallard recalls, 'Like most people, I was first introduced to Paul via Lily Savage. I was instantly drawn to her dry wit, and I do remember getting a video of her stand-up for Christmas. Only in later years, after I had come out, would I discover Paul's pioneering work as an activist at the Royal Vauxhall Tavern, and his ballsy and unapologetic campaigning for the LGBT+ community.'

As a thank you, Ian invited Paul to record the voice of the 'Radio DJ' in his 2023 stage play, *The Way Old Friends Do*.

Visibility was as important to Paul as self-promotion. In the autumn of 1993, the London Palladium was the venue for Stonewall's *Equality Show*. The gay variety event had been staged to raise money for the organisation's first national campaign for an equal age of consent, beginning 10 years of major law reform for lesbians and gay men. As one of the movement's most glamorous warriors, Lily Savage topped the bill. For Jo Brand, 'He was an everyman, with strong views on politics, and how things should be. Today, most people in the public eye are absolutely terrified to say anything mildly political for fear of the avalanche of shit you get from social media, not to mention a vociferous right-wing press.'

But not Lily.

Unquestionably, Miss Savage had a filthy mouth and a caustic wit, and with her as the klaxon, Paul O'Grady was able to bring left-wing, political, working-class representation to the mainstream. As the writer Mic Wright says: 'Paul and Lily were not comfy characters; they were fighters.'

In early interviews, Paul regularly said that he couldn't do stand-up comedy as himself because he'd be too embarrassed to say what he really thought, but he was happy and comfortable for Lily to say it. Years later, however, when Paul had retired Lily to a convent in France, it was the opinions of Paul O'Grady and not Lily Savage which were finally out in the open: 'I hated that I could never say exactly what I thought. It always had to be warped through Lily,' he told the *Guardian*.

He was more than happy to share his loathing for the Conservative Party, irrespective of their leader, be it Margaret Thatcher ('She was a tyrant'), David Cameron ('I loathe him') or Boris Johnson ('He is a complete and utter disgrace').

In 2010, on his live 9 p.m. ITV show, Paul delivered a witty yet devastating takedown of right-wing politicians and their austerity policies, calling the coalition government 'bastards' for its policy of cuts, and suggesting that the Tories probably would have laughed when Bambi's mother got shot. Shouting over horns blaring the French national anthem, he declared, 'We should take to the streets! We should be vocal in our fight against oppression!' He was so full of passion that he inadvertently smacked his hand against a glass of water on his desk, which flew across the stage. 'Oh, shit!' he remarked, raising his hands in shock. The audience screamed with laughter as O'Grady rose from his seat. 'Vive la Birkenhead! Vive la revolution!'

It wasn't the first time he'd been so vocal on the small screen. Years before, while presenting *The Lily Savage Show* on the BBC, he had given a similar rant which never made it to air as the show was pre-recorded. The outtake is available on YouTube.

Paul simply didn't care what the establishment thought of him, and, just like Lily before him, he remained indomitable and unfiltered.

And it wasn't only politicians he targeted. In September 2010, Paul spoke out against Pope Benedict XVI's visit to London. 'Christian Brothers? I was taught by Christian Brothers. They didn't sexually abuse me but physically they did. They were a group of sadist losers.' The former altar boy added, 'Gay Catholics! How can you be? It's almost like Anne Frank joining the Gestapo.' His disappointment extended to wider social injustice. He later told the *Guardian*: 'Carers are the neglected souls. We leave them alone … It should've got better, but it's got worse, much worse … we don't respect the elderly, and we don't look after the disabled. We pretend to.'

In 2013, Paul was given the perfect platform to air his views when he presented a BBC television documentary called *Paul O'Grady's Working Britain*. Originally, it was intended to be called *Paul O'Grady's Working Class*, but according to reports at the time, the then controller of BBC One got nervous and changed it. The programmes were made with the Open University, using the expertise of its academics to develop what promised to be a lively account of working-class history, values and identities grounded in balanced factual context.

On screen, Paul explained, 'There's a solid bedrock of working-class people in this country … The younger generation don't [believe that]. They consider themselves classless. But watch as they get older, they'll soon find themselves a slot that they fall into … It's a badge of pride … it's a set of values.'

The series certainly had the best of intentions but, for me at least, it became a somewhat misguided venture. As he did with most of his non-radio projects, each week Paul would come into the studio with an update on the documentary's progress and it was clear from his stories it wasn't going well. Sure enough, by the time it made it on air, the three-part series had become just two, and the resulting episodes were an unstructured muddle of sentimentality and cliché. As the *Observer* put it: 'In the documentary, [O'Grady] spoke of his childhood in Birkenhead at a time and place where elders and the police were respected and everyone looked out for each other. That's a generous statement for a gay man. For while Merseyside may have been many things in the 1960s and 1970s, it could not be described as the frontline of gay liberation or pride.' It continued, 'O'Grady had little original or pertinent to say. [His] heart might be in the right place, but his mind was lost in a treacle of misplaced sentimentality.' The academic Lynsey Hanley was someone who had advised the programme-makers on an unaired segment about council housing: 'You can't fault the choice of presenter', she later wrote in the *Guardian*, 'but what has transpired is something so different [from the original concept] that [we] have asked for [our] names to be removed from the credits.'

On this occasion, Paul's voice wasn't enough. But he continued to speak his mind.

In February 2014, despite a transport strike and appalling wintry weather, he joined hundreds of protestors in Whitehall, where he denounced Russia's anti-gay laws and criticised the escalating homophobic violence that was being widely reported. His pal Vera remembers, 'Although Paul was, by this time, "in" with the establishment, he wasn't afraid to fight. He had just done the teatime telly show, and he dragged me down to the demo, just like he'd done during the 1981 Toxteth riots.

He got up and gave a speech, encouraging everyone to go down to the Russian embassy to protest, declaring, "I'll pay for all the taxis, come on!" Paul also suggested that a photograph of Vladimir Putin, which was being widely shared on social media and in the press, showing the political leader riding bare-chested on horseback, was homoerotic and asked if he might be in the closet, which went down a storm with the assembled demonstrators.

As Julian Clary reminded me, 'Paul once had business cards printed that said, "Lily Savage. Riot Consultant – Brixton/Toxteth/Los Angeles".'

When it came to his own BBC radio show, where Paul's voice was perhaps most powerful, there were no such demonstrations of his political beliefs. Instead, he was much more subtle. Each week, he was keen for us to recognise carers, teachers, NHS doctors and nurses in the 'Thank You' slot, where listeners nominated their everyday heroes. It was perhaps his way to circumvent the Corporation's impartiality guidelines, which irritated him – trust me, they *really* got on his nerves – but Paul never abused his position as a BBC broadcaster to the nation. Instead, he used press interviews to share his views – often when he was promoting the launch of a new TV series or book, or when he was attending a media event.

When Paul was interviewed he was usually refreshingly candid, and generally there wasn't a backlash to his political views. He was probably more 'Old' as opposed to 'New' Labour, and in the 2015 General Election announced to attendees of a rally that he would leave the UK if the Tories won – a promise he repeated on various red carpets, and one which came back to bite him the following year. After the result of the referendum in which a slight majority voted in favour of Brexit, his radio show email inbox was inundated with hundreds of messages asking why, as he had been so fervently opposed to the withdrawal of the United Kingdom from the European Union, he hadn't left the country as he'd promised to. The radio show probably lost a fair few listeners as a result.

Two years after the referendum, Paul told the *Daily Mirror* he feared leaving the EU would cause economic ruin and would wreck the NHS. 'With Brexit, we won't have as many overseas members of staff – good doctors, good nurses, chiropodists, speech therapists, everything. We're not going to have them.' He also predicted, 'Going abroad won't be as easy as it is now, our farmers will really suffer without grants, food prices will go sky-high, and all the businesses are leaving.' And then, just to ensure his thoughts were widely reported in the same articles which were supposed to be promoting his latest ITV series, he added, 'It's all about immigration and Farage and Johnson. I cannot stand either of them.' He went on to explain what he'd do to the former if he bumped into him in a lift. Job done, the press duly focused on Paul's political comments, with headlines declaring, 'Paul O'Grady wants to rip Nigel Farage to shreds.'

In another interview in 2018, this time with the *Guardian*, Paul stated that he was still 'ashamed' of the state of the country under the Tories, particularly when it came to the continued underfunding of the National Health Service. He went on to suggest the austerity measures implemented by the Conservative government had caused unnecessary hardship for many people.

While some criticised Paul for his political activism, many of his fans applauded him for using his platform to speak out on issues which he was passionate about and had been all his adult life. He couldn't care less if he lost a few hundred followers on Instagram, or if Joan Marshrons and I had some emails and letters of complaint to deal with; he knew what he was doing: he was – and had been since the early days of Lily – a master manipulator of the media and press.

Unlike many of his show business peers, Paul O'Grady's views were in plain sight.

It wasn't just the politics of Westminster which angered Paul. AIDS had decimated his circle of friends and acquaintances 'like a tsunami' in the 1980s. In his 2015 autobiography *Open the Cage, Murphy* he wrote, 'Watching your friends slowly dying around you was all too commonplace, part of the daily routine, like cleaning your teeth or making tea.' He later shared, 'People my age will never get over the horrors.' In character as Lily, he would visit AIDS wards, sneaking in alcohol and cigarettes for patients. 'I was either at a hospital looking after people, or at cemeteries. I got to a stage where I could identify the Co-op funeral cars. And you try and find humour in all this misery because that's what it was – terrible.' Because the illness was such a taboo, Paul would occasionally have to pretend to some of his friends' families that they were dying of cancer as he nursed them, rather than from AIDS-related complications.

He also witnessed the role The Salvation Army played in helping those afflicted. 'They'd counsel, they'd tell parents who had no idea their child was even gay, let alone doing a drag act and was dying, they'd pay for funerals for people who had no money, they'd go in and sort their houses out … And I realised why they're called an army, because that's how they perform: they're as efficient as an army.' Thirty years later, in 2016, when he presented *Paul O'Grady: The Sally Army and Me*, a BBC TV series about the church and international charitable organisations, he attempted to tackle its policy which stated people from the LGBTQ community couldn't become soldiers. Broadcast to mark its one hundred and fiftieth anniversary, in the concluding episode, he spoke with Commissioner Clive Adams and said, 'It's always bothered me … [It's] upsetting, really, because I know so many men and women who are gay and lesbian, and they'd be the most wonderful officers.' After Paul's death, Salvation Army Captain Jo Moir, who mentored him when he trained as a volunteer for the documentary, said: 'We worked together for six months … Paul's compassion, sensitivity and genuine enthusiasm enabled him to connect with people from all backgrounds, whatever their circumstances and challenges … We are thankful and grateful for the many years of support Paul has given both publicly and privately to The Salvation Army's work with the most vulnerable in society.' Today, the organisation's website explains, 'Like many other Christian churches, we have much to learn from LGBT+ people and are encouraging conversations and dialogue.'

It was in the battle for LGBTQ rights and the AIDS epidemic where Lily Savage had proved she was much more than 'just a drag act'. In later years, Paul continued to be angry that, even after the partial decriminalisation of homosexuality in 1967, thousands of gay and bisexual men had been arrested for consenting, victimless behaviour. Shortly before he died, he was set to be part of a new campaign demanding the police apologise for their decades-long harassment of the queer community. The human rights campaigner Peter Tatchell said on ITV's *Good Morning Britain*: 'It was shocking, and he was very angry. Paul wanted that apology not just for himself, but for everybody.' Just three months after Paul died, the Metropolitan Police Commissioner, Sir Mark Rowley, finally apologised for the force's homophobic failings. In what Peter Tatchell described as a 'ground-breaking step forward,' Sir Mark's letter said he was 'sorry to all of the communities we have let down'. Over the course of the following year, the campaign attracted apologies from the heads of eleven other UK police forces. Paul would have been pleased, but he would have likely remained annoyed it had taken them so long to say sorry.

He also had strong views on the T in LGBT+. In March 2022, he told Times Radio, 'I've known so many trans people. It's no big deal … I'm so familiar with it. Fair play to them … There's a lot of fuss about toilets and changing rooms. And what I always say about trans people is … if you're serious about it you go through the most appalling operation … Trans people are extremely brave because once they've made that transition, they've then got to slot into what you would call "normal society". But I'm afraid society isn't very normal; it never has been and it never will be. I think it's about time we accepted people.'

One area where Paul O'Grady was heard loud and clear was animal rights and, through his television and radio programmes, he was able to remind his audience he believed it was our duty to treat animals with respect. As one animal rights charity put it, Paul O'Grady had a 'lifelong determination to make the world a kinder place for animals'. As well as being the nation's foremost advocate for helping dogs and cats find permanent homes, he also supported a ban on the use of fur. His objections to sheep being herded across London Bridge in a recently revived medieval tradition were ignored by the Lord Mayor of London in 2014, but Paul did succeed in drawing attention to the treatment of orcas in marine parks, and he also joined a call to ban foie gras.

There are many examples of his concern for animals, but one back in 2011 is worth closer examination. When he heard that South Derbyshire District Council was considering a planning application by Midland Pig Producers to build one of the UK's largest factory pig farms in Foston, he wrote to register his thoughts. The plan would have seen a new facility housing 25-thousand pigs at any one time, with 1 thousand being transported to slaughter each week. His letter to the planning committee is revealing. In it, Paul explained, 'Most people haven't spent much time around pigs. I was the same until I welcomed Blanche and her sister, Jane, into my home. They showed me that pigs are fun, loyal, inquisitive and naughty – very much like dogs. In fact, studies have shown that they are actually smarter than dogs and have a level of intelligence similar to that of a 3-year-old human child. Not that I think their worth or treatment should be based simply on how intelligent they are. No, like the overwhelming majority of the British public, I believe that in the twenty-first century, it is our duty to treat animals with respect … Perhaps you should challenge the owners of Midland Pig Producers, and see if they would be up for living like the pigs they would like to lock away! I bet they wouldn't like it.' The application for the factory pig farm was withdrawn.

Paul's voice didn't always change things, though. The same year, he attempted to save a hand-reared sheep called Marcus which had been kept by children at Lydd Primary School near Paul's home in Kent. He was unsuccessful, and the animal was slaughtered.

Paul O'Grady usually won the battles he fought. Collecting the Trailblazer prize at the British LGBT Awards in 2017, he told the assembled audience: 'If someone's being bullied, Christ, I'm in there. Whether it's kids or adults, or whatever, I won't have it.'

He was fiercely protective of his friends too. I had been asked to produce a seasonal show for Radio 2 presented by Alan Carr. I hadn't worked with him before; this was 2007 and the programme would have been his first solo show on the network. My mobile went and it was Alan's agent asking which A-list stars I had managed to book.

To put this conversation into context, the *Guardian* had once described this man as 'the Darth Vader of the fringe comedy scene'. The agent gave me not only a grilling but threatened that, if I didn't book huge Hollywood names, he would personally see to it that I never worked in radio again. His actual turn of phrase was peppered with numerous menacing expletives.

When Paul heard about it, he told me that he had worked with Alan's manager during one of Lily's tours in 1995, and the man had a bit of a reputation for being hot-headed and vocally aggressive. Paul then asked, in all seriousness, if I would like him to pop round and thump said manager. I declined but was grateful that Paul understood my position. Bear in mind, Paul O'Grady was no stranger to a good rant himself, but, on this occasion, he understood that there was no room for such bullying behaviour in the workplace. He had my back.

Paul later explained in another example of a press interview where he *should* have been promoting his latest TV project, that when it came to bullying, homophobia and misogyny, 'I've got no time for it at all, I never have. I was brought up that way, so I'm quite gobby, which has been my downfall on many occasions.' During a rare lunch we had together after Covid restrictions were lifted in 2021, he reminded me of the battles he and his friends had fought, and he warned me, as a gay man, 'The fight isn't over, Malcolm. We should not and cannot become complacent. Our equal rights were hard fought, but they can be easily lost.'

Goodness knows what he'd make of how quickly things have changed in the few years since his death. He once wrote, 'We're not second-class citizens, we shouldn't be in the bloody shadows. What we've been through with AIDS and everything, seeing our friends dying, our loved ones, it's hard, but we're strong people.' And Paul O'Grady really was.

Cliff Joannou, *Attitude* magazine's editor in chief, wrote on Instagram the day Paul's death was reported: 'O'Grady used his platform to do so much good, for the queer community and others … He showed me that you could be the most fabulous freak, and also have the greatest humanity.'

To some, he might have been a treasured entertainer, but he was much more than simply that. He was a campaigner, a champion and, it must be said, a highly rewarded one. As one of the most popular entertainers in the country, by the time he died, Paul's personal fortune ran into the millions. His fans could be forgiven for thinking his wealth was at odds with his political beliefs and that he had sold out in some way, but Paul O'Grady never sacrificed his opinions, his politics or his gayness in return for becoming a household name. His unapologetic ascent to public prominence was, instead, a class act.

6.

Prison Cells, Cottages and Boudoirs

'Nothing, and no one,
is safe, so stick with me, kid'
Paul O'Grady

In 1992, Paul went Down Under. Touring with the Australian comedian and personality Mark Trevorrow meant that Lily Savage and Bob Downe spent three months playing comedy festivals in Sydney, Adelaide and Melbourne.

Paul was initially apprehensive about going so far from home but soon found himself experiencing for the first time gay Mardi Gras, tom yum goong soup and the drug ecstasy. When I spoke to him about his Aussie adventure, Paul's memories seemed to be more about the quality of their dressing rooms – shabby on the whole – than their shows, though he did remember sharing the stage with Dillie Keane of Fascinating Aïda, Bea Arthur from *The Golden Girls* and the American singer Tiny Tim.

Australia quickly became a career highlight for Paul, who later wrote: 'I'd gone from aching-to-go-home to couldn't-give-a-monkey's if I never went back.'

Possibly part of that transformation was due to a visit to Network Ten (as it was then) in Melbourne, home to *The Bert Newton Show* where Lily and Bob promoted their tour and performed the song *Somethin' Stupid*. It was a notable appearance for Paul because the show was filmed in the studios where the drama series *Prisoner: Cell Block H* was made. Paul explained: 'I instantly recognised the red-brick corridors that were used as a location for the prison. This had the effect of releasing my inner crazed fan.'

Prisoner was an Australian television serial which ran for eight seasons and 692 episodes. Shown at varying times on ITV during the 1980s, it became very popular in the UK and was one of Australia's most successful media exports, and was later reimagined as the 2013 TV series *Wentworth*. Paul loved both.

Looking back, Paul seemed to be a fan of any programme that featured women in confinement – step forward *Tenko* and *Within These Walls*. I've often wondered why he was fixated with this particular small-screen genre, and I think part of the attraction was because, much like *Coronation Street* and *Crossroads*, which he also enjoyed, they gave prominence to female protagonists. He could recognise these strong women as his formative years had been filled with them: his mum Molly, Aunty Chrissie and his big sister Sheila to name just three. As Michael Cashman puts it, 'Paul O'Grady grew up around women, he knew how to listen to women, and women don't often find that many men who can listen so well. It's where his comedy came from.'

The prison setting of the Australian drama made it ideal source material for a stage production, and a play toured the

UK in 1989, which was followed by another attempt in 1990. But it wasn't until 1995 that Lily Savage (not Paul) became an inmate at the detention centre in the fictional suburb of Wentworth in Melbourne, Victoria.

This time, the soap had been turned into a stage musical. When it opened at the Queen's Theatre (now The Sondheim) in London's West End, the *Independent* reported that the first night audience included such luminaries as Andrew Lloyd Webber and Terence Conran.

The concept, music and lyrics were originally devised by Australian-based writers Don Battye and his partner Peter Pinne but, during rehearsals, it became apparent that the original script was somewhat lacking, resulting in a complete rewrite which included Lily Savage receiving writing credits for the lyrics of two songs: 'Life on the Inside' and 'I'm Innocent'.

The plot saw Lily going to Oz, having won a competition, but clashing with Aussie authorities and being slammed up for the double crime of stealing a fondue set – and murdering her sister. The promotional posters showed Lily in a bright yellow shirt, a blue waistcoat and short blue skirt, with a series of questions: 'Can a fragile English flower survive the harsh climate of Australia's Cell Block H? Can Lily clear her name? Can she assume the role of Top Dog? Can she work the laundry press? Can she ever!?!' It was hardly Ibsen, but for the many fans of the soap that didn't matter.

To further please devotees, the stage musical's cast included Maggie Kirkpatrick, who had appeared in the original TV show, as Jean 'The Freak' Ferguson, who later wrote: 'Night after night we romped our way through that silly show, often ad-libbing, veering from the script and sending each other up unmercifully. For me it was a master class in comedy timing. Paul and I worked hard ... and [we] loved every minute of it. We also partied hard ... sometimes a tad too much, but oh boy, it was fun.' Liz Smith also joined the cast in the Lizzie Birdsworth role, Penny Morrell played the governor and Alison Jiear was Meg Morris.

Prisoner Cell Block H: The Musical opened in London on 30 October 1995. The *Observer* called it 'a huge hit,' while the *Daily Telegraph* described the production as 'a cross between *The Rocky Horror Show* and Victoria Wood's *Acorn Antiques*.' The musical played everything for laughs: punches failed to connect, lines overlapped, and the sets occasionally wobbled as much as the plot, but the reviewer in the *Independent* nailed it: 'That it worked was largely down to the personality of Lily Savage, the drag queen who has the makings of becoming the biggest blonde star this side of Marilyn Monroe.'

Prisoner completed its twelve-week West End engagement before undertaking a national tour. By the time the show had left London, featuring some new songs, and with Linda Nolan now as the governor, Paul O'Grady was sharing the directing credit. It ran for two UK-wide tours in 1996 and 1997, and audiences delighted in witnessing Lily Savage and Bella Emberg (as Lizzie) getting stuck in a tunnel they'd dug to escape from the prison. The tours sold well and, 25 years after the original production, Paul remembered *Prisoner* with great affection: '[It was] a bit of insanity. But we had a blast ... It felt good to be in a hit.'

It was while Lily Savage was doing her best to survive the torrid conditions of Wentworth that she also somehow managed to take up residence in one of the most recognisable houses on British television. The property at Old Ford Lock, on Dace Road in East London, was nestled in a secluded oasis on the banks of the River Lee. In 1992, a determined work-force had completely transformed the dilapidated buildings into a bespoke television studio for a new Channel 4 series called *The Big Breakfast*.

Not only was the setting in Bow different, so was the programme. The innovative early morning show injected a cheeky, irreverent flavour into an otherwise stuffy mix of current affairs and lifestyle features. Unlike the rolling news format of the BBC's *Breakfast News*, and ITV's more comfort-able *GMTV*, both of which featured presenters behind formal news desks or on studio-bound sofas, this newcomer broad-cast from a houseful of anarchic locations: a bright and airy living room, a large outdoor garden, a busy kitchen, and a bathroom inhabited by puppets Zig and Zag. As the opening titles rolled, and the theme music began, the anaemic and beige landscape of Britain's breakfast TV became firmly multi-coloured.

The new approach and laidback manner trounced its competitors in the ratings. Produced by Bob Geldof's produc-tion company, Planet 24, *The Big Breakfast* employed a radio 'zoo' format which encouraged its presenters, Chris Evans and Gaby Roslin, and their many contributors, to chat infor-mally among themselves. In a review of its launch, the *Guardian* wrote: 'Not everyone is ready for fried eggs on the wall at 7 a.m. The colour is like catching your head between a couple of cymbals. Anyone under 25 will love it.' The reviewer wasn't wrong. Unlike the offerings of the BBC and ITV, the new programme spoke directly to a younger audience with its mix of cheeky chaos, randy vicars, schoolboy humour and friendly banter. And no item on the show better encapsulated the refreshing approach to breakfast telly than the innuendo-packed *On the Bed* interviews.

For the first 3 years, Bob Geldof's wife Paula Yates had held court in the *Big Breakfast* bedroom interviewing actors and rock stars, and her flirtatious encounters were often the highlight of the programme as she casually asked 'killer' questions. In 1995, however, Paula resigned. Needing a replacement, Planet 24 gave Lily Savage an initial four-week trial called *Lie-in with Lily*. She had previously been a guest on Paula's bed, plugging her tours; but a permanent gig was an unlikely move as Paul was a nightbird. Lily Savage explained, 'I'm not what you would describe as a morning person. To be blunt I feel like shit, and I look like shit ... I'll admit I'm foul-tempered and unreasonable in the crucial early hours.'

It was down to Brendan Murphy to manage the process of ensuring Lily arrived on time at the studio for the early morning broadcasts. Brendan had negotiated an impressive fee, which included an additional allowance for new clothes for the star – something she readily took advantage of with the aid of designer Martin Owen-Taylor. Paul had discovered the talents of Martin during his days at The Black Cap, and for Lily's new day job he conjured up an impressive wardrobe of bright and garish clothes to complement the show's character. For the first time, the nation's early risers were introduced to Miss Savage over bowls of cornflakes and slices of toast. It was a bold move for both the producers and the performer, and it worked a treat.

On many occasions Paul simply stayed up all night, as he was still appearing as Lily in the West End, for *Prisoner*. He loved to tell me about the punishing schedule he endured with both the musical and *The Big Breakfast*, and I was staggered by his workload. 'I was younger then!' he'd remind me, adding, 'It was all a blur, I don't know how I managed it, getting up at 4 a.m. five days a week. But the money helped.'

There had been drag queens on TV before but never one quite like Lily Savage. And this early morning version of the former 'lady of the night' was markedly different to the one who'd held court at the Royal Vauxhall Tavern in the 1980s. For Graham Norton, 'No one should really see a drag queen before lunch! *The Big Breakfast* must have been a hellish gig for him, but it got Paul onto mainstream television. That show got him out there and people became familiar with the character of Lily, so it was a good idea.'

Not for the first time, Paul managed to blur the line between queer culture and mainstream entertainment. As Lily Savage on *The Big Breakfast*, he brought queer voices out of the shadows. For Jonathan Harvey: 'It was incredible, really. I'm guessing even the bigots liked Lily as she was so bloody funny. And you can get such a strong message across if you make people laugh … Drag queens on telly before tended to be quite sexless. Lily loved sex. And shoplifting. There was nothing middle-of-the road or fuddy-duddy about her. And that was ground-breaking.'

Lily's pioneering boudoir residence says something about television and opinion today, according to Russell T Davies. 'Now there are so many objections to the way drag is being dragged into the culture wars and sexualised, and criticised and banned – did you think you would live in an age when drag acts were banned? I like to think I can see what's coming next but that's a new one on me – and *The Big Breakfast* came out of an age of experimentation and strange, beautiful innocence, absolute innocence. And the stars getting in on it, everyone was laughing and loving it.'

As Paul's friend, the actor and director Amanda Mealing, told me, '*The Big Breakfast* was an enormous gamble for him and Channel 4. But he was intelligent, articulate and well read, and he was also good at his craft. He made it look easy.'

Even though Paul knew his act inside out, Lily brought an air of chaos and excitement with her to the proceedings. Asked what it was like to step into the shoes of fellow blonde bombshell, Paula Yates, Lily replied: 'Well, she never wore any knickers, you know … I wear a good double gusset, 100 per cent cotton, Marks & Spencer's drawers. And I'm not flirting with the customers.' She then corrected herself, 'Not *customers* – I'm confusing them – no flirting with the interviewees! Paula was all over them, I'm having none of that nonsense!'

In her book, *A Sort of A–Z Thing*, Lily Savage claimed that a bedroom should be like a tomb, i.e. pitch dark, and she confided that she hadn't opened the curtains in hers since she had put them up 10 years before. In contrast, her *Big Breakfast* boudoir was bright and welcoming. 'The thing is about *The Big Breakfast*, they're all so nice … and I'm sat in the corner like *The Exorcist*,' explained Lily in the same book. Despite this, she was a daily fixture on the show for over a year.

One *Big Breakfast*-related story Paul loved to tell was when the Channel 4 programme sent Lily Savage to Los Angeles to cover the Academy Awards. Paul was happy for his alter ego to embrace all that Tinseltown had to offer. At one Oscars' party, screen legend Charlton Heston met Lily and, according to Paul, mistook his drag queen persona for a woman. Paul recalled, 'He began flirting up a storm with Lily at the buffet table … I'm chatting back and "Blah blah blah" and he was very, *very* friendly. When Charlton Heston walked off, the actor Robin Williams came over and said, "He's got a shine on you … he thinks you're a woman." Every time Charlton saw me, I got a wink and a nod, and I gave him a wink and a nod back and I thought, "I'm in here, I hope he's got his chariot outside." … Picked up at a buffet by Chuck Heston, *and* I had a sausage roll in my hand at the time!' When Paul's recollection of the unlikely Hollywood pairing was aired on his radio show, it made the newspapers the next day.

There's little doubt that Lily's breakfast job at Old Ford Lock in Bow was extremely important in securing Lily Savage's place as a permanent fixture in British television entertainment. Performing on early morning telly and nightly in the West End was hard graft, but also a rewarding time for Paul O'Grady: it was during this pivotal period that he restrained the savage, and his fan base grew as a result. As fellow *Big Breakfast* alumna Zoë Ball noted: 'The thing about

Paul, whenever people bumped into him in the street, you always felt you could share anything with him … He just felt like such a friend to everyone, [and] he looked after me through some crazy times in that cottage in East London.'

But it wouldn't just be on Channel 4's madcap breakfast show where Lily cemented her place in the television schedule, as there was another surprising and playful BBC family game to come. And while she didn't receive a blank cheque for hosting it, she was welcomed by an even greater adoring public.

7.

Channel Hopping

'I dress up as a middle-aged prostitute
and do a game show'
Paul O'Grady

You could be forgiven for thinking Paul O'Grady's rise to national fame followed a carefully charted course. There was a plan, yes, albeit it an ad hoc one, but he was also ready to embrace unexpected opportunities, such as the case of his appearance on the popular game show *Blankety Blank*.

Based on an American series called *Match Game*, the BBC One incarnation began in 1978, first hosted by Terry Wogan and later Les Dawson. After a six-year break, the series returned to the Beeb, this time presented by Paul O'Grady's alter-ego on Boxing Day 1997. Paul later wrote, 'The celebrity game show was one I enjoyed watching,' and he admitted that it had taken him three seconds to agree to the job offer, despite recognising that Lily would have 'big shoes to fill'.

Much like Edinburgh's Fringe, the format gave Miss Savage a prime-time shop window to display her comedic wares. 'It was,' Paul recognised, 'designed to be gently mocked.' Sure enough, introducing one episode, Lily claimed, with more than a hint of sarcasm in her voice: 'It's fun, fun, fun. I'm riveted. I'm drooling here …' Lily, it seemed, wanted to be anywhere but standing in front of a collection of B-list celebrities. And viewers lapped it up. She later told chat show host Michael Parkinson that *Blankety Blank* was 'a load of rubbish, really,' but 'good fun … [and] a hoot'.

Unlike Messrs Wogan and Dawson before her, and Bradley Walsh after, Lily's name eventually made it above the title: this was *Lily Savage's Blankety Blank*. And it was notable: a drag queen presenting a family game show on mainstream television. For actress Jodie Prenger, watching at home, 'Nobody questioned it. She was such a complete character, we just wanted to see Lily, and if she was the host of a hit game show, so be it.' Graham Norton notes, 'People loved Lily. But I never felt like TV executives were ahead of the audience, they weren't thinking, "Let's give them something shocking and new." It was very traditional in lots of ways, and I don't think audiences found it jarring. There is such a tradition of drag in mainstream entertainment in Britain, and it ebbs and flows, and when I was growing up there was lots of drag on television – or at least men dressed as women: Dick Emery, the two Ronnies, Les Dawson … for so many acts it was part of their repertoire. There is a cultural vocabulary around drag which British people understand, they get it. So, it wasn't that outrageous to see Lily front a game show. But I think the big difference was that Paul was an out gay man doing it. And that's what made it seem modern: Paul's drag did not seem old-fashioned in any way.'

Speaking of fashion, Lily wore a different, flamboyant and bespoke outfit for every show, designed with aplomb once again by Martin Owen-Taylor.

As they usually recorded two shows back-to-back on the same day, it was an extremely busy time for Lily. And not only was she hosting *Blankety Blank*, but she also had her own BBC series, *The Lily Savage Show*.

For 6 weeks during 1997, this ambitious series saw the eponymous star in a variety of sketches, spoofs and musical numbers. Paul was in his element. Lily's new starring vehicle was a throwback to the golden era of BBC light entertainment, and I remember later suggesting to Paul it owed much to *The Two Ronnies* and *Morecambe and Wise*. He agreed. Notable highlights included a *Doctor Who* spoof in which Lily played the Time Lord in an appearance – which arguably marks the first televisual sight of a female Doctor. She was joined by Gayle Tuesday as companion Gayler, and a robotic dog, K.Y. The production team built Lily her own TARDIS, which Paul later relocated to his home in Kent where it remained for many happy years in his garden.

Who fans have since wondered if Lily's incarnation is 'canon'. 'Yes! I'm officially saying it's canon,' confirmed *Doctor Who* showrunner Russell T Davies in 2024.

Paul would be chuffed to know that.

Another memorable sketch paid homage to his favourite sixties' drama series, *The Avengers*, with a seven-minute affectionate send-up complete with a faithful recreation of the iconic title sequence. This version featured Simon Williams as Steed, Denis Lill as The Colonel, and Lily as Mrs Peel who declared she was, 'too pissed to fight'. (Unlike Lily's TARDIS excursion, this episode isn't considered canon by *Avengers* fans.)

The Lily Savage Show rounded off the series with an equally impressive 'Birkenhead Films' production of *Shanghai Lil*. The lavish eight-minute black-and-white sequence featured Lily's duet with a scene-stealing Michael Ball, supported by a cast of 20 telly and soap stars including Bob Holness, Carol Vorderman and Barry from *EastEnders*. According to Paul's longtime friend Mark Trevorrow, the number was 'one of the greatest musical comedy sketches ever to have been put on screen'.

Even though *The Lily Savage Show* was a sizeable hit, a budget-conscious BBC didn't renew it. But 'the other side' was watching.

In 1999, Carlton Television's controller of entertainment, Mark Wells, received a phone call from Waheed Alli. Having met Paul during *The Big Breakfast* days, the future Lord Alli was now brokering media deals for him. In the call, Waheed explained to Mark that he had just negotiated a new contract to bring Lily to ITV.

The agreement wasn't just for a series starring Miss Savage; it also included new projects that were designed to introduce the nation to the man *behind* Lily. This led to television travelogues about Southeast Asia and America but, closer to home, the lucrative ITV package also resulted in *Lily Live!* which ran for two 9 p.m. Friday night series, starting in September 2000. One of the project's writers and contributors was Jayne Tunnicliffe: '*Lily Live!* was a fantastic experience for me, the pressure of writing topical material for a totally live show was immense, but very good discipline. Paul's opening monologue was the most important bit, but there were sketches, skits and links to write too. My favourite part of the week was when we rehearsed the show in Brixton just before the broadcast. Paul would come in, ranting and raving, spouting a stream of consciousness – totally hilarious. I was trying to write bits down and really wish[ing] I had a Dictaphone to record it all.'

As Mark Wells told Colin Edmonds in his *Behind The Scenes* podcast in 2023, 'The atmosphere in the studio when the show was live was just absolutely electric, and it was the element of danger that helped it as well – you didn't know what he was going to say and sometimes Paul didn't either, and the whole thing was a second away from a catastrophe. But I was never in any doubt [that he] was a profoundly intelligent, switched-on guy who was in complete control of every situation in which he found himself, and he knew how to play that audience, he knew what to say if they were a little bit cooler than he might have expected when he walked out, and the show came out on time to the second every single week – he was very, very disciplined in that respect. But that's the professional Paul was.'

Jayne Tunnicliffe agrees. 'Looking back, the series seems to have been a bit of a hodgepodge of ideas, but we had such fun making it. The celebrity guests and live audiences were amazing. Playing opposite Paul, especially when he was dressed as Lily when he was standing about 7 foot tall, was very daunting. Being on live TV with an excited studio audience all added to the pressure, but I totally trusted his comedic instincts. Years of compèring places like the Royal Vauxhall Tavern had given him the confidence and wit to deal with any eventuality and through it all I thought, "It's just Paul" underneath the wig and the slap, and he was a sweetheart!'

Brenda Gilhooly as Gayle Tuesday also appeared in and wrote for the series. 'People would write lines that they thought sounded like something Lily Savage would say, and it hardly ever worked, so we would loosely have a script and we would loosely know where we were going, from A to B, but if you thought for one minute Paul was going to learn a script and just say it; well, that was never going to happen. He never really liked anything people wrote, because they were doing an impersonation of Lily Savage.'

Arguably, the standout moment from *Lily Live!* took place between the host and regular contributor, Gayle Tuesday, during a segment in which she presented her pick of the week's new film releases. Their conversation soon turned from Guy Ritchie's latest effort *Snatch* to a rant from Lily where she declared that she was sick and tired of hearing about celebrities and their sex lives.

'You never hear me talking about my sex life, do you?' asked Lily.

'It's been a while, hasn't it?' replied Gayle.

Lily looked put out, and the audience roared with laughter.

Lily quickly reassured Gayle that she had enjoyed encounters during her recent visit to Edinburgh, among other places, and asked, 'Where's the most unusual place you've ever had sex?' to which Gayle replies with the killer line: 'Ooh, I dunno, up the bum, I suppose.'

Brenda Gilhooly recalls, 'Paul knew that was a good line, it was about what was good for the show, and it was never about him worrying who would get the biggest laugh. He would just say, "Great, *you* say it." Even though he was the star, he was very generous, he didn't have to have the last laugh; he was too confident for that. Paul was a natural entertainer, a natural comedian, so wanting to entertain the audience was all that mattered. The show came first. How lucky I was! And even when I got pregnant, he kept me on for the second series because he thought it would be funny to see a "page three stunner" in the club.'

One of those watching at home was Alan Carr, who had studied Lily Savage while attending Middlesex University. 'I was a real, huge fan and I had never seen anything quite like Lily, really. The beehive wig and make-up were Paul's armour, and *Lily Live!* was cabaret on prime-time telly. It was a tour de force.'

The series was a respectable hit for ITV and its star, and Paul was delighted when a comedy legend gave him feed-back, as Jayne Tunnicliffe remembers: 'I had met Bob Monkhouse when I appeared on *Bob Says Opportunity Knocks.* He had kept in touch and told me he was a huge fan of Savage. Paul was very flattered. Bob was a TV icon and a comedy connoisseur, and Paul was very touched that he would phone him up after every *Lily Live!* performance and praise him and the team.'

During a break from *Lily Live!* Paul presented a revealing six-part ITV documentary called *Paul O'Grady's America.* The 2001 series was the follow-up to 2000's travelogue *Paul*

O'Grady's Orient. Although both projects had been received indifferently by the tabloid press, they achieved solid ratings. The American series had seen Paul visit New York, Miami, Dallas, San Francisco, Los Angeles and New Orleans. The latter was where viewers witnessed what he later described as 'total anarchy … normally I never drink during the day because it makes me go to sleep.' But in the Big Easy, things were different. O'Grady on a bender, as he often described it, hadn't received such public exposure before, and now it was in a television documentary for all to see. Perhaps his behaviour shouldn't have been that much of a shock as some critics considered it, as the clues had been there at the start of the travel series: dressed smartly in a white shirt and tie, plus waistcoat, his opening link to camera in the first episode saw Paul O'Grady enthusiastically – and uncompromisingly – announce, 'I'm happy as a dog with two dicks, I am! And I'll tell you why, dear viewer, because I'm sailing into the harbour of the most fantastic city in the world. The Big Apple, NYC … oh, show some enthusiasm! I know you've only tuned in to see what I look like without the wig.'

His lairy introduction hid an underlying anxiety. As Amanda Mealing recalls, 'I had never known him so nervous. He was terrified and worried the public wouldn't like Paul, and that they only liked Lily. And I said to him, "No, the world will see what his friends see, which is you – you're brilliant."'

While many of the viewing public agreed with her, some journalists were only keen to see if Paul could make the transition from drag queen to presenter, without the accoutrements of his alter ego. And, ultimately, not everyone was impressed by the brash and garish new 'Paul O'Grady'. In 2001, the man *behind* Lily was still a work in progress.

Juggling travelogues, game shows and complicated variety series meant Paul had a demanding and punishing schedule. He was also still touring and performing on stage. And it was during this period that he suffered his first heart attack. The *Guardian* reported the news on 19 April 2002 explaining the star was doing well following surgery. Paul, who was then 47, described it as 'a life-changing experience'. Things would have to be different, starting with his workload.

In August 2002, Lily hosted her final edition of *Blankety Blank*. The game show had also channel hopped from the BBC over to ITV with its star. Paul's exit wasn't just for health reasons. The series had served its purpose. As his friend Moira Stewart observed, '*Blankety Blank* was a prime example of something that he grew up with and was very excited to be associated with, but after the first flush of fun with it, he was bored rigid by it, and he just couldn't carry on. His brain would revolt – after all, he'd done it, made it a huge success, and he would simply want to be on to the next thing.' It would seem, for Paul, that regular – and well-paid – employment wasn't everything. Boredom was a recurring theme for him, and one, I would suggest, that was root cause of much of his occasional dissatisfaction with people, places and life in general.

He was also bored of Lily Savage.

8.

Front Rooms

'There's a bit more to me than reading an
autocue and being told what to do'
Paul O'Grady

The year 2004 saw the Summer Olympic Games in Athens,
during which a then-closeted Kelly Holmes won her second
gold medal; an openly gay cleric, Dr Jeffrey John, was installed
as the dean of St Albans becoming what the *Guardian*
described as 'one of the most famous – or infamous – gay
clergymen in the world'; and over on ITV, a former sharp-
tongued underground cabaret star who had started out in gay
clubs but who'd fully infiltrated the mainstream, began
presenting a weekday family teatime show.

It was a daring move for both the network and the star, who
only 4 years before had declared to Richard Madeley and Judy
Finnigan on *This Morning*, 'I'm not a teatime entertainer,' but
the transition paid off handsomely for all concerned.

As far back as 1992, Brendan Murphy had told Savage: 'You
need to be seen by a much wider audience, we need to get

you on prime-time telly.' Lily had appeared on numerous Channel 4 shows over the years, including an uncomfortable live edition of Jonathan Ross's *The Last Resort* from the London Palladium in December 1988. The two didn't appear to be on the same wavelength, with the host seeming not to understand that Lily was a character and that Paul wasn't a genuine transvestite. Paul later assessed the encounter as 'a damp, embarrassing squib … [it was] a total disaster.' It did nothing for his confidence; 'I always ended up back in a pub in front of a hundred punters.'

Not anymore.

Often, but not always, broadcast live on ITV, *The Paul O'Grady Show* became a staple of the afternoon schedule for a decade or so, entertaining considerably more than the audiences Lily Savage had delighted at the Royal Vauxhall Tavern years before. It also made its host a multi-millionaire.

Debuting on 11 October 2004, the daily hour-long programme featured a straightforward format originally devised by Granada Television, a factor that would become highly significant in the years to follow.

Paul landed the job thanks in part to Des O'Connor. The legendary entertainer had been paired with Melanie Sykes for a lunchtime series called *Today with Des and Mel*, based on the long-running American morning programme with seasoned entertainer Regis Philbin and his co-host Kathie Lee Gifford. Like the US original, the British version mixed chat with celebrity guests and phone-in competitions, and the chemistry of the two hosts ensured it was a huge ratings winner for ITV. On occasion, Paul O'Grady had stood in for Des and, seeing his effervescent screen presence, ITV ramped up production of a show centred around him.

As with *Today with Des and Mel*, this new programme would be a combination of celebrity guests with live music, but it would also see its presenter doing daft stunts, along with novelty acts, and segments that featured children as reporters and reviewers. It was a throwback to the early days of variety television with the viewing audience at the heart of the action. The first few minutes of the show were devoted to the mail bag, where Paul would attempt to read often outrageous viewer letters and messages – some of which were manufactured – while managing his dogs, who would often sit on the cards he was trying to read. This was a key part of the programme as it demonstrated Paul's ability to communicate directly with the audience at home: it genuinely felt as if he was talking to his viewers. And it was obvious he was having a ball. In a nod to *The Big Breakfast*, members of the production team were seen on screen, including the runner James and tea lady Joyce, along with Paul's own dog, Buster. The new programme would also involve the creative talents of producer Bert Gray, who often received a verbal bashing from the host.

Broadcast in the 5–6 p.m. slot, the first guests on *The Paul O'Grady Show* were Simon Cowell and Jo Brand. 'To be honest, I was shocked,' Jo remembers. 'It beggars belief. I was not really an ITV act because I divided people, so I was surprised to be on teatime telly with Paul. He was so relaxed, so unfailingly funny and just a nice person to be with. People naturally warmed to him. He had a magnetic charm. So many other hosts on television can be a bit standoffish, they had boundaries, but with Paul, people felt they could relax with him. Presenters who are never quite sure how strong their currency is can't let other people shine, they often must top their guest's hilarity, but Paul never did that because he was comfortable knowing he was the funniest person in the room by far. He recognised that the sum of his show was not just him doing well, but it was letting everyone else be brilliant too. That's a fairly rare commodity.'

The programme was an instant success, much to the relief of ITV, which had struggled to find a ratings-winner in the teatime slot since they'd lost the Australian soap *Home and Away* to Channel 5.

Paul embraced the new challenge and, seated behind a desk surrounded by knick-knacks, mementoes and photos, he was right at home. He was a natural. And the audience, both in the studio and those viewing from their own homes, finally got to see Paul as he truly was. The buzz of live presenting reinvigorated him, reminiscent as it was of his stage days. Just like Lily had done on *The Big Breakfast*, he usually disarmed his guests with personal questions and intimate banter. As Jonathan Harvey explains, 'The transformation from bawdy nightclub entertainer to mainstream artist makes sense in retrospect but really surprised me at the time. Lily – especially in pubs and clubs – was so anarchic and sweary, but Paul was able to temper his language and adapt his funniness to play to so many different audiences. That's such a skill. And he had it in spades … Having spent time with Paul, I knew he was so easy to talk to, and you wanted to be his best mate, so I can imagine he was a magnet for some of those reluctant stars who didn't usually enjoy the chat show format.'

Aside from the celebs, regular features included one where Paul 'played' the organ and viewers had to guess the name of the tune. As he would later explain to me on his radio show: 'I studied at the Birkenhead School of Music. If it hadn't been for that ganglion cyst, Malcolm, I could have been a concert pianist.'

His ITV programme was warm, welcoming and inclusive, and, most importantly, fun. And nodding Busters – sent to viewers who were mentioned on the show – became a highly desirable collectible: he even sent one to my mum for Christmas. Paul's teatime renaissance was taking off.

The new series made a sizeable dent in the viewing figures of the opposition, which included his former *This Morning* sparring partners, Richard Madeley and Judy Finnigan on Channel 4, a rivalry dubbed the 'Chat Wars' by tabloids, and which Paul won. In its final week on ITV1 before Christmas 2004, *The Paul O'Grady Show* attracted an average of 3.2 million viewers; on Channel 4, *Richard & Judy* averaged 2.2 million. Talking to Michael Parkinson on his ITV programme on Christmas Day 2004, Lily admitted she didn't watch *The Paul O'Grady Show*, and that she was actually a 'Richard and Judy girl … [because of their] Wine Club. You know Judy can't wait until six o'clock to have a bevvy!'

Paul later confided how embarrassed he was by the supposed 'war' between the two shows.

Paul O'Grady wasn't the first person to present a British TV show five times a week; a couple of years before, Channel

4 broadcast *V Graham Norton* every weeknight at 10.35 p.m. 'It is exhausting,' Graham recalls. 'It's tough, it really is. But the nation felt comfortable with Paul at teatime because *he* seemed comfortable in that slot, and that's all it takes. If he had appeared or looked awkward, it wouldn't have worked. But actually, he seemed happy as Larry behind that desk. And he had a genuine interest in popular culture and terrible television which is what you need when you are doing a five-nights-a-week show because you're not going to be talking to A-listers, so all of that tapped into his sensibility. But essentially, he was a great person to spend an hour with, he was great company. And Paul built a world in his image – all that stuff behind him on the dresser – you really felt that show was *his*, and he wasn't just a presenter that had been wheeled in, he built that show around himself and his interests. And when you were a guest on it, there was very much a sense that you were on *his* show and not something like *The One Show* where any presenter could be opposite you. Paul was a good interviewer, I think, but when you are doing five shows a week, you can't do all the research for all the guests, so they weren't interviews really, they were conversations.'

Paul would occasionally call me to discuss who was in town and who might make a great interviewee, but creating five shows a week sometimes meant the guest pool was a shallow one, and competition to nab big names from other TV chat shows was fierce. After a few months on-air, Paul felt many of his guests were simply there to plug their latest book, show or play, and it bored him, feeling he was just another cog in the media publicity machine.

Watching his show, I could tell which people he was genuinely interested in, as opposed to those who were just there to promote the latest ITV Monday night drama. He'd often tell me he was 'self-mutilating under the desk' because he was so disinterested. And he wasn't shy about sharing his views with the press, saying: 'When a big guest comes into town, the chat show hosts are like a pack of wolves. I think people in the industry are far more interested in the A-listers than we are. I'd rather have someone from *Corrie* than some Yank. They talk bollocks, basically. And they moan. If I was being paid £15 million, I would shag a donkey.' Typical Paul.

Despite the challenges, however, he liked the job: 'I've found a format which suits me. I have trotted around the country, doing stand-up, I've been there, done it. I want to go on doing this.'

Events in June 2005 would force Paul's hand to some extent, when the man who had masterminded Lily's move from drag clubs to Paul starring on mainstream ITV died. An MRI had discovered an inoperable tumour in Brendan Murphy's brain. For Paul, 'life without Murphy was unthinkable'. He told the *Mirror*, 'We were both 49, barely able to believe what we'd achieved – I'd just won a BAFTA for *The Paul O'Grady Show* – and then suddenly bang, he's gone … I'd lost my best mate, someone who'd been in my life for 25 years and saw me through the days when I was lucky to earn £50 for standing on a beer crate in the corner of a pub telling jokes. Murph and I were like brothers – joined at the hip, thick as thieves. It transcended any sexual relationship we'd had. This was a partnership … Nothing could have prepared me for what was to come. To watch someone, you love – a healthy, eloquent man – unable to speak or walk is hideous.'

Going forward, Paul's relationship with life, and death, was redefined by what happened to Brendan. Just two months later he told *This Morning*'s Phillip Schofield and Fern Britton: 'That's it now, nothing fazes me … I'm scared of nothing; I can deal with anything.' Paul and Brendan's good friend, Joan Marshrons, whom Murphy had met while she was a student in Portsmouth in the 1970s, stepped in to manage Paul's day-to-day working commitments.

Towards the end of 2005, Paul told me the ITV show was coming to an end. I was surprised. It had only been on air for a year or so and was a ratings success. 'They haven't sent me a new contract, so I'm leaving,' he confided. This would be a recurring threat from Paul about almost all his telly jobs. Realising the cash-cow that he had on his hands, Paul orchestrated a savvy move, aided and abetted once again by Waheed Alli, and took the show to Channel 4

Crucially, this time, just like Graham Norton, Jonathan Ross, Dermot O'Leary and Richard and Judy, Paul set up his own production company – which he named after his dog Olga – to make the show. As far as the host was concerned, it wasn't just about money: it was also about control of the series, something he felt he didn't have at ITV.

Paul's fans probably didn't know or care what was going on behind the scenes; they were just pleased to read in the press in January 2006 that, 'Channel 4 has poached ITV's biggest daytime star, Paul O'Grady, in an exclusive deal.' The

Guardian suggested the move was, 'a major embarrassment for ITV'.

In an official press release, Paul explained his time at the network with *The Paul O'Grady Show* had surpassed, 'all my expectations, and I'm indebted to everybody who worked on it and watched it, but I work best when I'm set a new challenge and am forced to fly by the seat of my pants. A move to Channel 4 does exactly that and I look forward to a fresh start and feeling sick with nerves again.' In other press interviews, he was somewhat more candid, calling his former employers 'petty tyrants,' saying: 'I'd rather sweep the streets than work for ITV.'

The New Paul O'Grady Show launched on C4 in March 2006. Very little was different from the ITV original – the set looked much the same – and the only noticeable difference was the word 'new' in the title. On moving to Channel 4, Paul said it was 'the only place to be,' and this time he would share the 5–6 p.m. weekday slot with Richard and Judy, with the two programmes rotating every 3 months.

C4's decision to poach Paul paid off, with 3.4 million viewers tuning in to the first edition, compared with approximately 7-hundred-thousand people who strangely chose to watch a repeat of an old edition of his ITV show on 'the other side'. (The broadcaster eventually gave up repeating Paul's old shows, instead airing episodes of *Agatha Christie's Poirot* – something Savage thought was hilarious, especially as back then his agent owned the rights to Christie's works.)

It was a double blow for ITV, as Simon Cowell's production company Syco Entertainment had been developing a brand-new Saturday night series for the broadcaster with Paul as host. A couple of years before, I had interviewed Simon for a series about the prolific American songwriter Diane Warren. In his London office he told me his idea would be a little bit like *The X Factor*, but this new variety-themed talent show would try to find the best magicians, acrobats and dancers in Britain. The programme's title would be *Paul O'Grady's Got Talent*. Paul apparently told the producers that they 'were having a joke if [they] thought I would front a show with that title'. But he filmed the pilot programme, nonetheless, featuring a judging panel of Simon Cowell, Fern Britton and Piers Morgan, with Paul as host. Plans were progressing well until his defection to Channel 4, which meant he was persona non grata at ITV.

Paul phoned Simon Cowell and explained he had to bow out, even though he felt that Syco had a hit on their hands. He wasn't wrong: Anthony McPartlin and Declan Donnelly owe him a lot. Paul later confided, 'If I'd done *Britain's Got Talent*, I could have retired and bought a flat in Venice!'

Over on Channel 4, his teatime show gave Paul the opportunity to meet some of his big-screen favourites, and once in a while he even got to talk to his idols. In 2006, he was joined by the Academy Award winner Lauren Bacall. Their mutual respect was clear to see: she was a star who not only welcomed the chance to discuss her career, but also chat informally about her life, and he was a knowledgeable, informed and polite fan. She was clearly impressed by Paul's insight. And, as Miss Bacall was accompanied by her dog Sophie, Paul and the star also bonded over a mutual love of dogs – something Paul would use to soften even the trickiest of guests.

In August 2006, a bruised ITV hired Sharon Osbourne to host a new series called *The Sharon Osbourne Show* in the slot vacated by Paul. It owed much to his format but when the two went head-to-head in September, he comfortably beat her in the ratings. Sharon's series wasn't recommissioned.

A few months after he started on Channel 4, Paul suffered another heart attack, his second in just 4 years. The channel's executives insisted he take time off work, and Cilla Black and Lorraine Kelly were among those who stood in for him, allowing him time to recover. He phoned me from hospital to tell me he would be back sooner rather than later – it was good to hear his voice, and I was touched he had called.

In 2007, ITV tried once again to find a show to match the one it had lost, this time with *Coronation Street* actor Anthony Cotton as host, and, again, *That Anthony Cotton Show* was short-lived. Having previously piloted another substitution programme for the 5 p.m. slot with Phillip Schofield which wasn't commissioned, ITV didn't give up. It launched a further series, this time hosted by Alan Titchmarsh. Paul was quick to moan to me: 'It's just another copy.' Despite ITV's efforts, Paul continued to win the day.

But it wasn't all channel wars. I recall there was much excitement when Paul told me he was going to be in an episode of *Doctor Who*, and that was down to his teatime show. Russell T Davies remembers, 'He came up to me at the National Television Awards, and I didn't know if he knew who I was. And he said, "I don't want a big part, I just want to walk down a corridor, in a white coat, and say, "I don't know what it is, but I think it's alive!", and then he walked off, leaving me laughing.' That chance encounter resulted in an appearance in the 2008 *Doctor Who* finale, 'The Stolen Earth', which saw Paul as himself sitting behind his Channel 4 teatime chat show desk, naturally accompanied by Buster, talking to his studio audience about some strange lights he'd seen in the sky. Sadly, Paul's longstanding ambition to play a cyberman was unrealised. Russell explains, 'I put him in *Doctor Who* because I loved his 5 o'clock show so much.'

In March 2009, Paul interviewed the American singer, John Legend. Also joining them on the teatime show was Jodie Prenger, who was there promoting her autobiography. It was the first time the two had met. 'I was just a reality kid,' Jodie explains. 'I'd just come off the back of the BBC talent show *I'd Do Anything*, and you just naturally felt at ease with Paul. Quite simply, he was a lot of fun. He gave the impression that, even though he was seriously successful, he hadn't forgotten his roots. And he took me under his wing, and he helped me up; he never put any of his guests down.' Bonding over Blackpool, drag queens and their mutual love of musical theatre (Jodie was now playing Nancy in *Oliver!*), the two clicked, while John Legend simply sat quietly looking both entertained and bemused.

In April, Paul added to his workload: as well as presenting five teatime TV programmes each week, he began hosting his own Radio 2 show. Seeing him on a Sunday over at the BBC, I could tell he was getting tired, even though he was taking regular and carefully managed breaks from the small screen. It was a measure of the affection his audience had for him that they stayed with the programme, trusting he had endorsed his many replacements, who included Michael Bublé, Johnny Vegas, Judith Chalmers and Jackie Collins. Another guest host was Jo Brand. Reflecting on her time sitting in Paul's chair, Jo remembers, 'His were massive shoes to fill, impossible! If the request had come from anyone other than Paul, I probably would have said no. I thought I was a bad fit because I was the "much hated, professional man-hater Jo Brand". I mean, why would you have someone like that presenting a show at teatime? But I enjoyed doing it and I just tried to be interested in the guests [which included the singer Shakira]. For me, it was a massive honour.'

As well as his own absences, the second incarnation of his teatime show had to contend with the loss of his beloved 14-year-old dog, Buster, in November 2009. In the early days of the radio show, Paul used to bring Buster into the studio with him. He never once barked during the live programme and was extremely well behaved – Buster, not Paul. Paul was broken when Buster died. He explained to his television audience, '[Buster] was riddled with cancer. He had cancer in his neck and his face and a tumour in his leg. The kindest thing for me to do was let him go but it was the worst thing I could ever do in my life, but it had to be done because otherwise, it would have been selfish.' The production team compiled a short montage of Paul's canine companion accompanied by the song 'Thank You For Being A Friend'.

Paul would later ask me never to play Andrew Gold's version on Radio 2 because it hurt so much.

The media was now describing Paul O'Grady as one of Channel 4's 'most bankable stars,' so the news there were problems with his relationship with the network came as a surprise to me. This time it was simply financial. Paul's original deal was agreed when there was plenty of advertising money in the system, but by 2009 the market was down and C4 was slashing its programme budget accordingly. In June that year, Paul was reportedly keen to avoid 'fights' with his bosses, hoping instead for 'an amicable agreement'. He also knew he had a responsibility to his production staff. Hopes for a deal soon faded, however, as the two sides couldn't agree terms. In September, the press reported Paul was unhappy with the network, who wanted to cut the show's budget in half. He told the *Daily Mirror* he was 'gobsmacked,' and that he would rather walk away than do it 'on the cheap … You're going to end up with the blandest of the bland and I won't be part of it … I would understand if my ratings were down and the show wasn't performing but it consistently wins its slot and brings in good advertising revenue … Honestly, I'd be mortified to do a show that's third rate.' While I'd never describe Paul as flash, he certainly wasn't cheap, and a low-budget show wasn't something he would be associated with. Privately, he would tell me, 'No cash, no ping pong.'

Reports – and rumours – suggested he was talking to Sky Television, a spokesperson for which explained, 'Paul O'Grady is a very talented and much-loved presenter who would be a great asset to any channel.' Paul later told the *Guardian* that he was wary of moving to a digital station however, having recently witnessed Richard and Judy 'just fizzle out' on the UKTV channel, Watch.

It looked like the teatime fun was over and on 18 December 2009, Paul presented his final Channel 4 show. 'I just wanted to say thank you, all of you. This has been the best job in my life. I've been through a lot. My partner dying, my dog dying, two heart attacks. Becoming a granddad! You've been great with all your letters and emails. My crew, everyone in the office, they are brilliant.' But, as the final credits rolled, Paul was already planning his surprising comeback.

This time it would be on the channel which had helped create Paul O'Grady's titular show in the first place. And in another carefully crafted manoeuvre, he left teatime for prime-time. September 2010 saw Paul back on ITV fronting a starry variety show *Paul O'Grady Live*.

The host wasn't too enamoured with the title – 'It's got nothing to do with me!' he declared – but the 9 p.m. slot allowed him to break through the watershed and be a little more risqué. The new two-year deal for *Paul O'Grady Live* was a lucrative one. Paul was refreshed by the move, and he explained the new show would be bigger and more ambitious, while holding on to the essence of the teatime original. He told *Attitude* magazine in 2010: 'Mary Poppins has turned into Medusa! I've had six years of kiddies and doggies and Snow White where everyone thought I was an absolute saint … but this time it's a bit more adult.'

His guests were impressive, one memorable edition including an early UK visit from Taylor Swift during which she gave Paul some dog biscuits and, in return, he presented her with her first UK gold disc for the album *Fearless*. In June 2011, I paid a rare visit to the London Studios to witness a special edition of the show, devoted to Lady Gaga. This was a major coup for Paul. Gaga (as he called her) was a terrific guest, their show business chemistry clear to see. The singer gave an outstanding performance during which she sang songs from her album *Born This Way*. She bedazzled both the host and studio audience and Gaga was so enamoured with Paul, she gave him a china tea set.

It was a truly special television event, but, to be honest, I never really thought the late-evening format was completely successful. Sometimes Paul looked out of place on 'grown-up' telly, and the fun and informality of his teatime, common-touch approach to hosting felt somewhat off-kilter post watershed. Scheduled against Miranda Hart's popular eponymous sitcom on BBC One, Paul knew he had a fight on his hands and, even though ratings were solid – just under a very respectable 4 million for the first series – he eventually completed a total of 22 editions and decided to quit once again. The last edition was broadcast in July 2011.

It's unlikely ITV would have asked for another series of *Paul O'Grady Live*, as the television landscape was changing fast and an expensive show such as Paul's had to deliver an almost unattainable number of viewers to justify its cost. But Paul just couldn't stay away from the box.

On 11 November 2013, airing on ITV in its traditional slot of weekdays at 5 p.m., *The Paul O'Grady Show* returned once again. Featuring a new theme tune performed by McFly, the host was joined by many of the guests who'd appeared before on different incarnations of the series, including one of his favourite singers, Alison Moyet: 'Paul was unfailingly warm, welcoming and charming. [He was] a prince among men.'

Favourite guests, and those who were there simply plugging something, populated a considerably shorter run of programmes this time, and by 2015, after some fifteen series in total and 769 episodes across two networks in 11 years, Paul bade farewell from his chair behind the desk one final time.

Paul was the first to admit he'd had a good innings, made a lot of money, and given millions of viewers a great deal of pleasure. He'd provided employment for hundreds of people behind the scenes, and proved the once graveyard spot in the TV schedule could be a winning one. As for his 5 p.m. viewing audience – he would be missed.

9.

Dead Pets, 'Triples' and Keeping the Faith

'Don't you dare touch that knob'
Paul O'Grady

Paul and I had kept in touch since the Cilla documentary we'd made together in 2003, and he often popped into Radio 2 to promote his many activities, or to stand in for the likes of Jonathan Ross. But a radio show of his own had eluded him, and it was something he wanted. The station's head of programmes, Lewis Carnie, was a supporter and was on the lookout for a permanent slot for him, but, until then, Paul continued to present ad-hoc programmes and specials. He was a fan of the station and enjoyed the shows of Steve Wright and David Jacobs in particular. He would phone me to see what I was up to, and share the latest gossip, something he did with all his close friends. He rarely had an agenda when he called me, usually simply wanting to chat about something he'd heard on air.

It seemed that very many people Paul worked with over the years – be they a panellist on *Blankety Blank* like Liz Dawn, or

Big Breakfast presenter Gaby Roslin – became fast and firm friends. He might not have seen them that often outside work, but he kept in touch via phone and text, and his network of show business pals extended far and wide. But, if it came to his own radio show, he told me, he didn't want to exploit those relationships; neither did he wish to sit there chatting to celebs about their ghost-written autobiographies. Instead, all he wanted to do was be himself, playing music he loved, hearing from listeners, and saying whatever came into his head. I took note.

In 2004, I had launched a new weekly show on Radio 2 devoted to the music of the West End, Broadway and Hollywood. My first choice of presenter, Tim Rice, had politely declined the offer to host a regular Sunday show, and I spent the next few weeks putting together a new proposal for Elaine Paige, who had found theatrical success in the stage musicals *Evita*, *Piaf* and *Chess*. We recorded a pilot show at her holiday home in Cannes and the powers-that-be back at the BBC were sufficiently impressed to add her to their roster of presenters. Paul called to congratulate me, 'I'll be listening while I cook lunch.'

In September, *Elaine Paige on Sunday* became part of the Radio 2 schedule and we went on to showcase musicals in a way that, back then, was unprecedented and ambitious. As well as playing great showtunes, 'EP', as many people called her, interviewed theatrical luminaries like producer Cameron Mackintosh, composer Marvin Hamlisch and director Hal Prince. And the stars lined up too, including Elton John, Barry Manilow and ABBA's Benny Andersson and Björn Ulvaeus.

The two of us would sometimes chat on-air, regularly having a laugh and a giggle – especially when Elaine introduced the closing number, 'Malcolm's Big One'.

For a few years, EP and I were almost inseparable, something that interested and amused Paul. Elaine was someone who had often been mentioned by Lily Savage in her act, and her radio programme was a subject Paul regularly phoned me to chat about, usually with the request to play more 'bump and grind ... have you done *Gypsy*?' and I had registered that he might make a useful stand-in if ever we needed one.

An opportunity for Paul and myself to work together again came in early 2007, when Elaine had to take a break from her regular Sunday show. Paul readily accepted the offer to stand in for her.

I could see EP was a bit anxious about having him take over, but she needn't have worried. Paul knew it was *her* programme and was extremely respectful, mentioning Elaine throughout. He would go on to host her show twelve times over the next couple of years.

For me, as producer, the main difference between the two presenters was that his editions were broadcast live, which brought a healthy dose of excitement and energy – and a significant amount of nervous anticipation on my part. Paul was always well prepared and informed, though, while Elaine's audience recognised he was a fan of the musical genre and embraced him without hesitation. Radio 2 management was taking notice, but we still had to wait.

Paul and I did an Easter special in 2007, joined by the singer Lesley Garrett. That show was a hoot, as Paul had worked with

Lesley on her 1998 BBC Two TV series, *Lesley Garrett Tonight*, during which she performed a song from Gilbert and Sullivan's *The Mikado* alongside Patricia Hodge and Lily Savage.

Following the death of BBC Television executive Bill Cotton Jnr in 2008, I produced a two-part radio tribute, presented by Paul and written by Brian Sibley. The three of us admired Bill greatly – he had been one of those who helped define the 'Golden Age' of BBC light entertainment. While his life story was a fascinating one, this time it was obvious to me the format of Paul reading short links in between newly recorded interviews, music and archive clips wasn't really what he did best. Reading somebody else's words left Paul little opportunity to be himself and we agreed we wouldn't make another documentary together, although others tried to.

In 2009, Bob Shennan succeeded Lesley Douglas as controller of Radio 2. I was particularly concerned about Lesley's departure for two reasons: it was she who had originally given me the job as producer, and she had been a supporter of Paul's early work on the station. My fears were soon allayed.

In early 2009, in addition to producing *Elaine Paige on Sunday* at 1 p.m., I was finally asked to launch a new, permanent Sunday five o'clock show for Paul O'Grady. He was already busy hosting his teatime telly series, so the fact he committed to presenting a weekly radio programme said a lot about how he viewed Radio 2 back then.

Mind you, he'd often tell me how he and Vera would have a mutual moan about the callers on Jeremy Vine's programme.

Part of a refreshed weekend schedule, Paul's new series would begin on the same day Elaine's programme was being extended by an extra 30 minutes. It was a busy time for me, but as Elaine's show was recorded, it meant I would be able to focus on Paul's live series. Announcing his new schedule, Bob Shennan told the *Guardian* that, 'Radio 2 is committed to offering the very best entertainment, and in Paul … we are bringing [one] of the UK's best loved presenters to our listeners.' Throughout his tenure, Bob was one of Paul's biggest supporters, and he often described his programme in glowing terms.

The message the station was now sending out was one of change, but hopefully in a considered and sympathetic tone. Some listeners might have been alarmed with the prospect of a former drag queen – and an unapologetic and uncompromising one at that – taking over the treasured 2-hour slot, so we were expecting a bit of a backlash.

Given Paul O'Grady had such a successful and prolific television career, often running in parallel with his ad hoc radio work, you might wonder why he was interested in having his own weekly radio show Joan has suggested that he liked the notion of being 'on the wireless,' as it harked back to his childhood, and the 'old-fashioned' medium allowed him to speak to the nation and communicate with his listeners. But speech was only part of it: Paul O'Grady also loved music.

Because of our proximity to Elaine's show, we would have to avoid too many songs from the stage and screen, and as *Sounds of the Seventies* directly preceded us, we would have to be careful with our choices from that decade as well.

Paul and I had very similar tastes, and Paul was keen that we played records that appealed to the audience he knew actually listened to radio on a Sunday afternoon. Historically, the slot had been filled by such Radio 2 stalwarts as Charlie Chester, Ed Stewart and the melodic *Sing Something Simple* featuring The Cliff Adams Singers. Paul told me he wanted an upbeat mix of Motown, kitsch pop, Northern Soul and standards, blended with more obscure tracks from some of his favourite artists like Pink Martini, Maggie Bell, Jools Holland, Mari Wilson and LaVern Baker. I was more than happy to comply, and I went on to build weekly playlists that showcased artists that Radio 2 was beginning to routinely neglect and overlook. I recall he wasn't a fan of pan pipes, though.

To celebrate the impending series, I took my new presenter to the Langham Hotel opposite Broadcasting House in London, and we ordered tea and cakes, and chatted about the format of the show. I remember that I ate the cakes – Paul didn't touch them. I had already planned the first few programmes and talked him through the features. Some he rejected, like a slot to celebrate what made your part of Britain 'great', but others he readily accepted. He was also happy when I told him that, to help create an aural identity for his show, a music production company had been commissioned to compose a suite of Paul O'Grady jingles. As inspiration, I'd asked them to use the iconic theme of Paul's favourite TV series *The Avengers*. My new presenter approved, and we kept them for the next 14 years. When, for his fifty-fifth birthday, I presented him with a CD which included all his jingles, and an extended four-minute version of his theme tune, Paul was delighted.

Unlike Elaine's show, it was deemed there was no need for a pilot, but if Paul was apprehensive about hosting his new programme, you couldn't tell. Looking back to the first edition broadcast on 5 April 2009, it wasn't a given he would be a confident and comfortable presenter; after all, his programme was missing one thing that set it apart from almost everything else he had done – a live audience off which he could bounce. Think about it for a second: at the Royal Vauxhall Tavern, Lily Savage performed in front of a captive and well-oiled number of fans and friends. On tour, Lily would appear in shows and musicals in the nation's favourite clubs and theatres – again, in front of a live audience. And even when Lily was long gone and it was simply Paul hosting his teatime TV show, he did so in a studio often with a group of 'old pensioners, smelling of pee, who had come in out of the cold'. But when it came to radio, it was simply Paul, a microphone and me on the other side of the glass, sometimes with a studio manager and the occasional mouse.

As Jo Brand explains, 'Paul had some sort of ability to imagine his listener at home, and although he didn't get any vocal comeback like you do with a live audience, he was very relaxed, it was as if he was just talking to you, and I think that's a skill because it's very hard to do.' Julian Clary agrees, 'There are people on Radio 2 who come across as cheery and jolly, "we must keep the nation in a good mood", that sort of thing, but Paul wouldn't do that. He had the ability to come across as a real, believable person. And it was very like listening to him on the phone, he was like your friend.' Brenda Gilhooly suggests there's another reason why Paul performed so well on radio: 'He found his perfect producer he could riff with, and it worked brilliantly. Another producer might have asked him to stick to a script, but Paul would have hated that. He was allowed to be himself.' For Michael Cashman, radio also gave Paul the chance to show what a great storyteller he was. 'All he had was his talent to engage with the one person – not the people – listening at the other end. You can't get away with a look, a nudge, a wink-wink, it's about how you *tell* the story.'

The first record Paul played was The Pussycat Dolls' cover of the Doris Day song, 'Perhaps, Perhaps, Perhaps'. It was a simple attempt to illustrate that the show wouldn't be stuck in the past but would make a nod to it. The opening playlist included other tracks from Harry Connick Jr, Pet Shop Boys, Fleetwood Mac and one of Paul's favourites from Loretta Lynn and Conway Twitty: 'You're the Reason Our Kids Are Ugly'.

The *Guardian* reviewed the programme saying, 'Paul O'Grady really suits his slot on the network. His banter is reliably funny and warm, with an occasional top note of comic sourness, and real relish for the music,' while *The Lady* suggested, 'O'Grady's show is a million times warmer, brighter and funnier than (Charlie) Chester's … There's an unashamedly sentimental element to the show, something from which I usually run a mile, but I can take it from O'Grady, because it's balanced by his affectionate sarcasm towards punters and himself. He shares with Les Dawson the ability to mock and knock without causing an iota of offence – a gift. Like all of the best Radio 2 presenters throughout the station's history, he's a communicator, and the show is a conversation.'

On the half-hour, Paul would play a 'Triple' – 'Three great songs from one great artist' – which gave him time to pop out for a fag. He still smoked and often complained he couldn't do so in the studio: 'Dale [Winton] does, he told me!' he would say. But me, being the sort that always sticks to the rules, wouldn't let him, so the 'Triples' stayed. Over the years, he started to smoke less, but the feature had proved so popular we saw no reason to drop it.

An early regular correspondent – Pamela from High Wycombe – gave Paul great opportunities to be outrageous, suggesting she was a man-eater who would stop at nothing to find her next target. Paul often embellished his listeners' emails, and in the case of Pamela, who gave the impression of being somewhat upmarket, Paul explained she actually lived above a chip shop on the high street. Pamela wrote back saying she was delighted at being sent up in the programme (her real name wasn't Pamela, and she didn't live in Buckinghamshire). Another frequent contributor was Elsie the studio mouse. I have been asked on more than one occasion if she was real, and the answer is yes – and no. One evening, Paul and I were in a studio at Western House recording that week's programme. He was going away that weekend and so, rather than letting his listeners down, he'd opted to pre-record the show, but we could only get a vacant studio at 9 p.m. So, there we were, Paul behind the mic, with me next door in the control booth and a thick wall of glass between us. Suddenly, I saw him jump up and clamber onto his chair – which wasn't easy because it was on casters and started rolling across the floor.

I ran into the studio and asked him what on earth he was doing.

'There's a bloody mouse in here, for fuck's sake!!!' he screamed.

'Where?' I asked, laughing.

Paul pointed to a small hole in the skirting board. And so, Elsie the studio mouse made her debut appearance.

Western House did have a problem with rodents in those days and the studios and production offices were littered with humane mouse traps. Although we never saw her again, she continued to participate thanks to a somewhat squeaky pen lid which Paul would twist to represent her answers to his many questions. His imagination was vivid at the best of times, and he didn't need any help from me to make Elsie's appearances funny and memorable. Her story, and involvement, grew by the week; later, Paul would announce that *Elsie the Musical* was in development and the search was on for a star mouse to play the title role. Paul also revealed Elsie had duetted with Andy Williams and was planning on recording an album featuring her own interpretations of Jethro Tull's 'One Brown Mouse' and Megadeth's 'Of Mice and Men'. Elsie even got fan mail.

However, fearing her fame might eclipse his own, Paul eventually announced she had moved abroad and died. Only to be later replaced by her sister, Conchita.

Another regular character was Mrs Bala Clava, who came into the studio to play the piano, despite wearing thick woollen mittens. Paul objected to her involvement because he didn't enjoy the way she played, nor the smell she left in the studio after her sweaty performance. Spoiler alert: there was no such lady – she was simply a CD with some random piano music on it. But Paul had created a fully rounded character, complete with a back story. It was so convincing that, at times, I thought I could smell her repugnant signature scent from behind the glass. Listeners would email the show offering their support for her, complete with suggestions as to how Paul might broach the touchy subject of her lingering BO. They also wrote in about their ironing boards, cooking utensils that didn't work properly; some even telling us they managed to tune in while vacuuming. They'd ask for help in locating old friends, or share memories about pubs, shops and cinemas that had long since closed.

And then there was the weekly 'Cocktail Recipe'. This started out as nothing more than an excuse to play something you'd might hear in a 1960s cocktail lounge, but, like so many of the items on the show, it evolved, and Paul suggested I create a recipe for a cocktail each week to go with the tune. He thought, as I was teetotal, it would be funny and he was right – I'd often get the ingredients and their quantities wrong. Resultingly, he nicknamed the slot 'Muck in a Bucket', explaining that it came with a health warning. As he read out the ingredients, he would often retch as he attempted to complete the recipe: 'Malcolm, me mouth's gone dry just reading that.'

A particularly memorable recipe is included at the end of this book.

Paul never wanted his radio programme, aka TeamPOG, to be too sanitised or saccharine and, for a while, we included a music slot called 'Death Is Just Around the Corner', where listeners nominated a song which they would like to have played at their funerals. When I asked him what he'd planned for his own, he went into vivid detail, even down to the horses he wanted to draw his glass coffin, much like Snow White's. I replied, 'Sounds perfect, I'll be on the front row.' On another occasion, when I asked him how he'd like to be remembered, he simply replied he wasn't bothered because he wouldn't be there to hear what people said about him. And he regularly told journalists much the same.

Paul never knew what was coming next on the show, there was no rehearsal, and the listener at home never knew what Paul was going to talk about either, so his conversation with them was often a huge surprise: one minute he'd be gushing about the delights of Isle of Man tea-towels, and then he would change tack to share tips on how to grow a lettuce. He would explain in detail the best way to deal with snoring pigs and then ask if anyone had any spare donkey stones so he could wash his front doorstep. I would just sit there, laughing, as he began a rant about spa breaks and why men shouldn't have hairy backs – 'They're even worse on a woman, Malcolm!' – or why he felt the time was right for ITV to televise lady wrestlers on a Saturday afternoon. I never worried. Yes, he would talk nonsense, but he always returned to my running order – eventually.

Over the first few months, the response from those tuning in grew and grew. And Paul would delight in hearing about his listeners' lives, loves and pets. He would regularly stumble when reading their contributions on-air and once thought the abbreviation 'LOL' for 'laugh out loud' was someone's name listening at home. We never took their involvement for granted and, unlike other shows on the station, we weren't embarrassed to recognise we had older listeners, Paul taking great pride in announcing someone's age, be it 25 or 95. And whenever we received something in the post, we tried to mention the sender on the programme, because, as he explained, 'They've spent money on a stamp, Malcolm', which was true.

It wasn't only listeners who seemed to appreciate what we were doing: the critics approved as well. The *Spectator* declared Paul to be 'a splendidly warm and welcoming [presenter] with a superbly eclectic playlist', while esteemed radio critic Gillian Reynolds, writing in the *Telegraph*, described the programme as, 'like being at a party with the best host in town'.

In the early days, we also offered a monthly prize which included the chance to have 'tea for two' with Paul in the studio. He would announce, 'The prize consists of the opportunity for you and a guest to have afternoon tea here with me and the team. You'll get to meet our friendly security guards on reception, enjoy a ride in the ever-so-reliable lifts of Western House, and then settle into the green room for a cup of instant and some buns from the shop across the street. No expense has been spent, as you'll see.' Quite a few lucky listeners came to Western House for the opportunity to meet the man himself. As one winner put it: 'It's like being Charlie Bucket meeting Willy Wonka!'

Following several scandals at both the BBC and ITV about other competitions being fixed, Radio 2 instigated a station-wide axe to all such contests, and so we had to drop the feature – much to Paul's relief. He had been slightly embarrassed to be in such proximity to his adoring fans.

One item that endured until the final programme was 'Dead Pets'. We always struggled with the name, but the weekly feature was hugely popular with listeners who wrote in to ask Paul to remember their beloved dogs, cats, rabbits and the occasional horse on the programme. Paul never made a joke about it: this was a solemn business, because 'pets are family' as he would say; and the audience knew he took it seriously. Another feature that also stayed the course was the 'Thank Yous', in which he helped to recognise people and places that had made a difference to everyday lives. Other programmes on radio and TV have now adopted the idea, but Paul was there at the beginning and, over 14 years, we must have acknowledged hundreds of teachers, vets, bus drivers and Good Samaritans. He loved that part of the show and was very happy to sign an official Certificate of Thanks, which we posted to those he mentioned.

Sometimes, I would also – deliberately – pick a song that was unsuitable for the occasion a listener was celebrating, and this became a regular feature: 'The Inappropriate Song for a Wedding Anniversary.' Paul would bemoan my choices on air, which only encouraged more listeners to ask to be included. Apparently it was a badge of honour to have a track like Tami Lynn's 'I'm Gonna Run Away From You' played as you remembered your special day.

Long before other radio shows realised their worth, we also played forgotten television themes, which gave Paul the chance to reminisce about his favourites, including *Stingray*, *Crown Court*, *Bewitched* and *The Prisoner*. He loved the box: 'As a child, there was always the telly for consolation. Like every other kid, I lived for television.'

The challenge with some TV themes is that they were never released commercially, which meant we couldn't play them on air, and this was the case for a series Paul mentioned almost every week: *Tenko*, the popular BBC drama set in a fictional Japanese internment camp following the fall of Singapore in 1942. Paul was thrilled when the series' composer James Harpham, who also happened to be a loyal listener, re-recorded his music especially so I could play it as a surprise on our first show of 2012. I can still see Paul beaming, wearing his headphones in the studio as the music played.

For Russell T Davies, the regular features gave the programme a 'beautiful repetition. It would be the same rhythms over and over again and there was a lovely regularity to it. It was beautiful. And because there was nothing fake about it, Paul was talking to *you*, it was intimate. I would have the show on in the background … and I'd be laughing away at him and Malcolm. And not a single "Lost TV Theme" ever defeated me! You know, the show made me happy, it's as simple as that, Paul O'Grady made me happy.'

The early editions were broadcast from the sometimes unreliable studios on the sixth floor of Western House, and, one week, my talk-back unit failed and the instructions I had intended just for him to hear in his headphones were broadcast on air. Paul thought it was hilarious and said to his 'other listener', 'Ooh! Malcolm speaks! Did you hear him?' and the show changed there and then. Paul openly encouraged me to chip in and, judging by the emails and letters we received from the audience, his listeners were happy to hear the two of us bickering away. He would send me up something rotten: 'I still have the negatives of those holiday snaps of you, Malcolm, you know the ones, when you were on the beach in Talacre wearing your mankini', or after reading an email from a listener: 'I should thank Susan for her kind offer of complimentary haircuts for us both at her new salon in Penge, though I don't think Malcolm will be joining me when I pop round,' – he always found the fact that I am follicly challenged to be a source of great amusement. He would also poke fun at my ever-increasing waistline, my failing eyesight with resulting bad typing, or my dodgy back or knees. Basically, I became Paul's straight man – a first for me.

For the actor David Ames, 'When he chimed in every so often, Paul was playing it to him; Malcolm was us, Paul's audience. They had such a gorgeous relationship, and it translated so beautifully to radio.' Amanda Mealing agrees: 'Paul needed someone to bounce off and he needed someone who could match him, you had to be able to keep up and hold your own – and Malcolm did.' As Julian Clary observes, 'Paul had a similar thing on the teatime TV show with his producer, Bert – he enjoyed having someone to diss.'

When I mentioned to Paul that some in BBC management weren't so keen on me playing his foil, Paul only increased his verbal assaults on me and encouraged my involvement even more. That was Paul all over: if he knew *they* didn't like something, he'd turn the dial and do it more. 'Malcolm was his audience,' explains Graham Norton, 'he was talking to *him*. And that's how the show existed for Paul. If he had been alone in a room talking to a microphone, I don't think he would have enjoyed it … But Paul loved to make Malcolm laugh, he loved having jokes with him, and as an audience member, we listened to it and loved it, and it was like he was talking to us as well. I think for Paul, Malcolm was the thing that made it work for him.' ITV News presenter Sangeeta Bhabra agrees: 'He told me it was because of his relationship with his producer that the show worked; he loved how he made Malcolm laugh. And for me, it was that chemistry combined with great music and genuine warmth. That's so hard to convey, especially on radio. On TV it's different, you can *see* someone smile, you can see it in someone's eyes, but how do you convey warmth on radio? That's a real skill.'

Occasionally, we broke self-imposed rules and devoted the show to a theme or special date. One stands out: the fiftieth anniversary of the first broadcast of the soap opera *Crossroads*. Even though some of my younger colleagues at Radio 2 were bemused by my decision to devote an hour of radio to an old television series that hadn't been on air for years, I knew our audience would enjoy a nostalgic tribute to a programme which we seemed to mention or reference with affectionate frequency. Paul and I had been long-standing fans of the famous 'motor-hotel' for years. As a youngster, he had imagined welcoming guests to the motel from behind the iconic green reception desk, and he was impressed when I told him I'd met Noele Gordon – the show's leading lady, affectionately known as 'Nolly'.

With the help of some serious superfans, and the resourceful Crossroads Appreciation Society, in November 2014 we managed to track down Jane Rossington (Jill Richardson/ Harvey/Chance), Susan Hanson (Diane Lawton/Parker/

Hunter), Paul Henry (Benny) and Tony Adams (Adam Chance). All were invited to join us for a radio reunion. Paul was in his element: yes, there was laughter – plenty of it – but he was also respectful, not just towards his guests, but also to the memory of the series itself, and in turn to the memories his listeners had too. For many people, *Crossroads* had been important, and Paul didn't forget that. As he explained during the programme, 'I don't think soaps work unless you care about the characters, and *we*, the audience, really cared about them. You didn't have to *like* them, that works as well, as it makes for a good villain, but you had to care about them, and we really did, we wanted to know what happens to them tomorrow.'

Honouring the fiftieth anniversary of the motel was a truly wonderful experience for all concerned. Afterwards, as we had no programme budget to speak of, Paul took his guests for a drink and some nibbles at the Langham Hotel at his own expense.

In an interview on the ITV show *This Morning* back in 2001, Paul told hosts Richard and Judy: 'I watch television as a viewer [and not someone who works on it],' and that was true. He wasn't a cultural snob. He understood the importance of having soaps and key programmes at recognisable and permanent times in the schedule, explaining that if *Coronation Street* or *EastEnders* were moved because of football it was unfair to regular viewers. He felt the same was true when his own Radio 2 show was bumped in favour of coverage from Glastonbury music festival. Paul recognised the value of serial dramas and, in the case of ITV, how much money they made for the network. 'Soaps, Malcolm, are the pillars on which ITV is built.' For Paul, television was important because it was both nostalgic and reliable company. He was a loyal viewer too and, for me, also a self-confessed telly addict, his passion for series past and present was a joy to witness.

For his radio audience, hearing him talk about a programme he'd watched that week, or another he remembered from his childhood, was a shared experience, and it bonded him with his listener. 'Do you remember a detective series starring Hattie Jacques?' he once asked. Some in his audience did and they emailed the show to tell him. 'Yes! It was called *Miss Adventure* in 1964.' It would annoy him sometimes that I didn't recall some of these vintage series, and I was keen to remind him that he was much older than me. He would counter, 'Oh, shut up, or I'll throw a wet flip-flop at you.' Thankfully, he never had one to hand.

The Sunday programme went from strength to strength and, with a few exceptions, the format stayed the same: Paul, a box of records and a pile of messages. It sounds simple, and good radio always is. Another constant was Lucozade – he often seemed to have a bottle with him, and it regularly caused him to burp during the show, much to my annoyance. Belching aside, we were both pleased that, on the whole, we were left to our own devices by BBC management, and the programme was never once on the agenda of an internal review panel.

One bit of feedback Paul did receive was from Cliff Richard, who would text to thank him for playing his music – and to say how much he enjoyed hearing the two of us take the mickey out of each other.

After a change in network management, I had to introduce Paul to the latest in a long line of 'new' editors. Unlike in film, these people didn't physically edit the programmes they oversaw; instead, their role was to guide a small number of producers and assistant producers. I tried to have as little to do with them as possible as I didn't need someone telling me which music to select, or which features would appeal to Paul's audience. On this occasion, the new editor attempted to crack a few jokes with Paul – never a wise move – and then tell him, in all seriousness, 'Hey, you know, I never listened to your show, but I heard it last Sunday for the first time and, you know what, you're really funny.' Paul smiled and crossed his arms, making it quite clear the editor was free to leave the studio, describing them afterwards as 'yet another BBC management buffoon'.

Thankfully, managers were seldom in sight at Christmas. Paul presented 14 or so editions of a Christmas Day radio show and, for me at least, it was an annual highlight, full of traditions, much like *Blue Peter* when they finally lit the fourth candle of their flame-retardant-tinsel-covered advent crown. Judging by the response we received when Radio 2 neglected to include us in their festive line-up one year, I wasn't alone. Apparently, many listeners had come to enjoy and look forward to the rituals we observed as well, and the Christmas special became a bit of an event, a 'must listen' if you will, and one which regularly received praise in the press. Paul played up to his reputation of being a festive grump and encouraged the use of jingles that sent him up, including one which announced, 'You're listening to Paul "The Grinch" O'Grady.'

Despite his on-air protestations, he thoroughly enjoyed celebrating the big day with some of his favourite Christmas tunes.

When it came to his weekly programme, Paul wasn't afraid to foster emerging musical talent; in fact, he would often encourage and support artists, both old and new. It meant the show's playlist was a microcosm of Radio 2 itself: we would play Motown and country, classical cuts and big hits, forgotten gems and a smattering of brand-new releases, sometimes from emerging artists. Harriet, like Lulu, is only known by her first name. Harriet explains, 'Paul was the first to play one of my songs on national radio, and I'll always cherish that moment. Breaking onto national radio is tough for independent artists, but Paul was a passionate advocate for new music. His rapport with listeners was wonderful, and his enthusiasm was contagious; they trusted his taste. Opportunities like that are rare for unknown acts … Honestly, I don't think I would be where I am today without Paul.' Harriet has since supported Michael Bolton in concert, performed at London's Royal Albert Hall, and played to sell-out audiences on her own UK tours.

And it wasn't just new artists who appreciated the show, as Ian 'H' Watkins from Steps explains: 'Paul always played our songs on the radio and was a big supporter when we came back with new music after many years away. We'll always be grateful for that. All of us in Steps were fans of Paul's Sunday programme. His bonkers, eclectic choice of music and hilarious chat with his producer Malcolm made it like no other show on the radio. It was like a big warm hug that you could lose yourself in at the end of the weekend … [Paul] used to complain about how cold it was in the radio studio, joking that the BBC was too mean to pay the heating bill. We thought it would be funny to send him something to warm him up ahead of the following week's programme … [and] from there the jokes about the Steps' fan heater became a regular source of chatter on the show. We followed up at Christmas with knitted hats and scarfs for both Paul and Malcolm! There wasn't another show like it. It was unique, special and hilarious – just like Paul himself.'

Sunday afternoons on Radio 2 also gave Paul the chance to tap into his comedic arsenal and revisit some of Lily Savage's finest material. He wouldn't acknowledge he had used the gags before; he would just somehow find an appropriate moment to slip something in. Listeners who'd seen Lily at the Tavern were delighted to hear him explain my surname was Goebbels, or the reason why he struggled with his mobile was because 'it's riot gear and I don't have the instruction book'. Another favourite 'Lilyism' of mine was the story of when he visited Skippy in Australia who, now long retired from television, was found at Waratah Park wearing a turban and a dressing gown *à la* Norma Desmond. Paul explained that he had gone up to her in her cage and said, 'You're Skippy the bush kangaroo, aren't you? You used to be big.' And she replied, 'I *am* big. It was the bush that got smaller.'

Paul and I didn't socialise a lot in the early days, but there was one occasion that I will never forget. Following a major leap in our listening figures, he announced he wanted to take me and my assistant, also called Paul, for a celebratory snifter at his favourite restaurant. There, he insisted I had a Black

Velvet cocktail – a combination of Guinness and Champagne. I complied and, because I'm teetotal, was soon under the table. Both Pauls had to escort me out of the refined eatery and into a taxi, and this one-off event quickly became something Savage would mention on the show, much to my embarrassment.

When Paul needed a short break, finding the right stand-in for him wasn't always easy: audiences responded favourably to the warmth of Jodie Prenger, Paddy O'Connell, Martine McCutcheon and Nicki Chapman, but other hosts, including Matt Lucas and Len Goodman, struggled to connect quite so well.

I was a bit picky too and I usually arranged to be on holiday at the same time as Paul. But one stand-in really stood out when, in August 2009, impresario Bill Kenwright was booked by Lewis Carnie to host three shows. Bill was an excellent choice, effortlessly linking the music while sharing his many showbiz stories. Lewis asked me to produce, and I was impressed with Bill. I hadn't realised Paul had been listening at home until he phoned me after the second programme to say he had decided to come back a week early. It was the only time I had ever seen Paul concerned that someone else could present his show just as well. Lewis paid Bill off, and it was business as usual.

As far as Paul was concerned, Sunday at 5 p.m. was *his*.

10.

Cuddly Toys and Weatherfield

'Let's not keep in touch'
Paul O'Grady

In the early days of his Radio 2 programme, I recall a conversation with Paul about which television themes we might revisit on the show for the 'Lost TV Theme' slot. One of my personal favourites was *The Generation Game* and I was keen to include Bruce Forsyth's iconic signature song, 'Life is The Name of The Game'.

'Oh, Malcolm, not the bleedin' *Generation Game!*'

I had forgotten Paul O'Grady had narrowly escaped being the show's new host. Back in September 2003, the BBC reported Paul would be filming a not-for-broadcast pilot episode of the famous family game show following Jim Davidson's departure some eighteen months prior. Paul later discussed his new job with Sue Lawley on Radio 4's *Desert Island Discs* where he explained it was he, and not Lily Savage, who would be hosting the new series. A decade or so later, naively, I asked Paul how he had found the experience and why his version of the TV classic had never materialised.

His short reply was: 'It was torture, Malcolm, torture.'

On paper, Paul O'Grady and *The Generation Game* had looked like the perfect fit – if you had watched Lily perform with the Sixties Tiller Girls on the 1995 home video *Lily Savage: Live and Outrageous*, then you couldn't have failed to see how suited he was to physical comedy, something which was at the centre of the television game show's format. But the reality was the whole process had been an unpleasant one for him. The opportunity to find comedy had been there for him in the pilot, especially with one game: a James Bond spoof featuring Brian Blessed as director, Dermot Murnaghan as the villain and Paul's good friend Barbara Windsor dressed as a pink squid called Octopussy Galore. But watching the pilot now, it all feels rather laboured. While Paul looked very smart in a tuxedo as he introduced the pilot, acknowledging he was pleased to be following in the footsteps of some enter-tainment giants, there wasn't much chemistry between him and his 'Girl Friday', Colette Bibby, even though they had worked together in pantomime a few years before. Paul also struggled with the length of the recording process: 'People were leaving because they were worried they'd miss their buses home,' he later revealed.

Throughout the pilot episode, which was one of Paul's first television appearances not in the guise of Lily Savage, he looked distinctly awkward and uncomfortable. During another game, Paul injured his back and was in pain for the rest of the recording: as he bid farewell to the studio audience at the end of the show, his face said it all. He later told his producer he had no intention of signing up for a series. Key to making Paul happy on any job was surrounding him with a team which could support him, and from what he told me, during the reboot of the much-loved game show, that hadn't been the case.

In May 2004, while appearing on *This Morning*, Paul told presenters Phillip Schofield and Fern Britton he had decided against presenting *The Generation Game* after finding the whole experience physically exhausting. Even though Larry Grayson and Jim Davidson had managed to host successful reboots of the series in 1978 and 1994 respectively, other well-known names would also think twice about taking on the iconic entertainment behemoth. Graham Norton turned it down, as did Miranda Hart, who had been in talks to host a revival in 2014. And I'd suggest Mel Giedroyc and Sue Perkins wished they had said 'no' after their 2018 version of *The Generation Game* became a notorious flop, *The Times* noting: 'You could almost smell the desperation to make it work.' So, Paul wasn't the only one to lose that particular game and, perhaps his decision to pass had been a lucky escape for him. As he later told me, 'Brucie made it look too easy.'

The family game show wasn't the only time the BBC asked Paul to take on Forsyth's mantle. In 2008, he told the *Guardian* the Corporation had proposed he host *Strictly Come Dancing*. 'I don't want to take over,' he explained. He also said that he would find it hard to stand back and let the judges rip contestants to shreds when really he would want to lean over and say, 'Come on, you shower of clattery old ghosts, let's see you do it.' As he put it to me: 'I'd rather stick needles in my eyes than do *Strictly*.' Even as a contestant.

There was another project, again related to a much-loved television staple, which saw history repeat itself. Once more, on paper, it looked like a sure-fire hit, but just as with *The Generation Game* reboot, the much-needed chemistry between star and producer simply wasn't there, and what Paul had hoped would be an enjoyable and significant success became one of the biggest embarrassments of his career.

In late 2011, he arrived at the radio studio for another Sunday show, announcing with great gusto, 'Hey, you'll never guess, I'm going to be in *Corrie!*'

Paul was a lifelong fan of *Coronation Street* and had appeared on a 1995 edition of *The South Bank Show* discussing some of his favourite moments from the cobbles. In *Open the Cage, Murphy* he explained, while on tour in Australia, 'Suddenly I missed everything about the UK. My flat, the cats, friends, family … *Coronation Street*, just about everything in fact.'

Jonathan Harvey, who has written more than 330 episodes of the *Street*, explains, 'Lily wouldn't have been out of place rowing with Ena and Elsie on those cobbles about the latest poison pen letter! In the early days it was ruled by those cracking matriarchs, in a show created by a young gay man. Nobody had seen anything like it on TV before, so it was arresting. But those women would be what Paul tuned in for.'

Created in 1960, *Corrie* – as millions of its faithful viewers often call it – has been the nation's favourite continuing drama for over six decades. There was a time when ITV didn't like to associate the serial with the genre and wouldn't even use the word 'soap' to describe it, unlike its original competitor, *Crossroads*, and the BBC upstart *EastEnders*. But, eventually, the commercial channel was happy to acknowledge it had two of the most successful and long-running soaps in its stable, the other being *Emmerdale*, and they had an awful lot in common. Even though one was set in the Yorkshire Dales and the other in the back streets of Salford, both were created by highly professional and committed production teams, with actors who were, in the most part, widely recognised across the country.

In 2010, *Corrie* was celebrating its fiftieth birthday. To mark this, there was a dramatic live episode which saw a Weatherfield tram crash from the viaduct onto the Corner Shop and The Kabin. That ambitious hour-long instalment of the *Street*, complete with computer generated stunts, was just part of a week of episodes broadcast that December under the promotional banner 'Four Funerals and a Wedding.' Almost 15 million viewers tuned in, the show's highest audience for 7 years. Cashing in on the significant anniversary, ITV authorised a commemorative one-thousand-piece jigsaw, numerous ceramic mugs, gold-plated medals and a box set of classic episodes on DVD.

Completing the celebrations, there was a TV gala quiz show called *The Big 50*, presented by Paul, who was happy to be associated with his favourite soap, writing of the programme: 'Watching *Coronation Street* was like watching the inner workings of the lives of people we knew.'

And it wasn't only on the small screen where the *Street*'s golden jubilee was marked: numerous characters from the cobbles were brought to life in Jonathan Harvey's comedy stage play *Corrie!*, presented at The Lowry in Salford and with a six-month UK tour the following year.

After the release of yet another official golden anniversary project – an album featuring newly written songs all about Weatherfield's most famous inhabitants in December 2011 – the BBC News website carried a story about a second theatre-related project: '*Coronation Street* musical to hit the stage.' It would be the first and probably only time the word 'hit' would be used to describe this new endeavour.

It seemed an unlikely departure for ITV, but the credentials were there: the production would feature choreography by the multi-award-winning Stephen Mear, and a cast that included some of the soap's original actors. And there was 50 years' worth of drama to draw upon; ask anyone who works in musical theatre what the most important thing when it comes to creating a new show is, and the answer is always 'the book', i.e. the story material on which the musical is based. When it came to it, Trisha Ward, the composer who came up with the idea of turning *Corrie* into a stage show, would have more than enough to inspire her. And therein lay the problem.

A production team was established, and casting decisions were made. Hopes were high and belief was strong that the transition of the TV brand from the screen to stage was not such a strange leap. But the proposed format was a complicated one from the off: the live stage show aimed to celebrate and replicate some of the soap's iconic stories, there would also be archive clips shown on big screens, and an impressive replica of the famous street, with the Rovers and the Corner

Shop. All of which would be accompanied by brand-new songs.

The project was called *Street of Dreams – The Official Live Music Event*. On posters, Paul's name received star billing, above the title. Despite some misgivings about the idea, Paul had agreed to play a milk man/narrator, telling *MailOnline*, 'I feel like a child on their first visit to Disneyland … Oh my God, I'm on *Coronation Street!*' I suggested to Paul it was all meant to be, as he had actually been mentioned in an episode of *Corrie* back in 2008 by Deidre Barlow's mother, Blanche Hunt, who, in conversation with her daughter, shared, 'I have no problem with the gays. You know I'd walk on hot coals for Paul O'Grady.'

Joining Paul would be *Street* legend Julie Goodyear, meaning fans would be able to see Bet Lynch back on the cobbles for the first time in years, while other key *Corrie* cast members had also been persuaded to take part, including Kevin Kennedy (Curly Watts), Katy Cavanagh (Julie Carp) and Brian Capron (Richard Hillman). Understandably excited by the prospect of working with some of his *Street* heroes, Paul would arrive for his Radio 2 show with updates about how it would be staged, the scale of the set, and who had joined the cast.

I remember saying to Paul, 'With a brand like *Corrie* and all these star names, what can go wrong?'

Publicly, Paul was very positive, telling BBC News, 'To relive it all alongside unforgettable characters and talent on the stage, revisiting such iconic scenes from across the years, is just brilliant. I can't wait to watch it all come together and the reaction it receives.'

But there was trouble on t'street. As the preparations continued, Paul's updates were becoming less positive, and I could see he was frustrated with what was going on behind closed doors. There were problems with the script he explained, and he was rewriting it, much to the annoyance of the show's creator. This wasn't a surprise, to be honest. Paul was prone to a bit of rewriting, be it a panto script or a listener's email.

The planned opening performances were postponed from March to May 2012, and the frustratingly slow rehearsals at Shepperton Studios continued.

Speaking to the press a few weeks before the rescheduled first night, Jodie Prenger, who had been cast as Elsie Tanner, was as positive and upbeat as ever, but even she struggled to explain what *Street of Dreams* now was: 'I say it's a show, but it's like a total spectacle with the way the set has been created, and there's a big orchestra. It's hard to describe and it's something that you really do have to see for yourself. But it's going to be really big. If you're doing something like *Corrie*, you've got to get it right.' How prophetic. By the time it arrived at the Manchester Arena, the production boasted an impressive 38-strong West End–style chorus, a 25-piece orchestra and a 26-metre-long set recreating the familiar façade of the famous terrace street – which was probably the main issue with the whole project: TV soaps are meant to be viewed intimately, in the comfort of your home, and not in a vast sporting arena.

Behind the scenes, members of the cast were calling the project *Street of Screams* and it was Paul, according to Jodie, who kept spirits high. 'It was shabby, but it had a brilliant cast. It takes a lot of time for a show like that to be staged, hours.

But people were given not minutes but mere seconds. People were crying, the make-up girl walked out. I was using my own dresses to dress the drag queens in one scene – I went to *Funny Girls* [the drag burlesque bar in Blackpool] to get shoes for some of the lads in the cast; everyone just pulled together and a lot of it was down to Paul, he was a great company leader. The show just wasn't produced properly, and there was a lot of tension. It needed to be run a few times before we opened, but there just wasn't the time. Russell Watson came in to sing a song at the end, and he didn't know the words: he'd requested an autocue, but they'd run out of budget. So, Paul put three A4 pages with the lyrics on the floor of the stage and told him to read that instead. It was Paul doing things like that to keep the show going.'

Paul invited me to the opening night in May 2012, and I went with some trepidation as he'd already warned me things weren't going well. Still, the idea of being with thousands of fellow *Corrie* fans was an appealing one and I was intrigued to see how a show based on a small-screen soap had been turned into one that could play in a huge arena.

Street of Dreams turned out to be an unashamedly self-indulgent and well-intentioned tribute, but, for me, the key issue wasn't about the scale of it, nor the performances – many of which were hugely compelling – nor was it that the catchy music was, overall, somewhat forgettable, even though it was splendidly played by the on-stage band. No, the problem was the show didn't know what it was supposed to be. Was it an homage or a send-up? Paul's on-stage narration certainly didn't help clarify the issue. His lines were often self-referential, and his innuendo did seem a bit out of place at times, especially for the pre-watershed soap. Undoubtedly he was a fan of the source material, but it was also clear to me he wasn't comfortable playing a milkman trying to connect random scenes from the show's 50-year history.

The opening–night critics happily found fault. The *Guardian* suggested the evening was simply 'another vehicle for the Scouse comic [Paul]'. The journalist ended his scathing review complaining it was a shame that the serial murderer Richard Hillman didn't 'quietly claim another victim and bump off Paul O'Grady'. The *Mirror* was a tad more generous: 'Paul O'Grady was a masterful MC … but it's not all happiness and hot pot. Repeated sound problems and a script that seemed more cobbled together than constructed gave the whole thing a disappointingly disjointed feel.' A month after the opening night, the *Daily Star* newspaper was forced to apologise after printing a story which claimed Paul 'caused chaos behind the scenes and was a nightmare to work with'.

For Jodie Prenger, who was actually there, such accusations were ludicrous. 'If Paul was complaining, he wasn't doing it in public. And on opening night, it wasn't the producer who was backstage helping me push parts of the set onto the stage because bits of it weren't working, it was Paul!' The newspaper later said it accepted the allegations were incorrect.

After just two performances, future dates in Dublin, Belfast and Newcastle were all shelved. Reports soon appeared suggesting many of those involved hadn't been paid, and Paul accused the producers of being 'incompetent, inept and unprofessional'. In September, his team launched legal action and by November 2012, the *Guardian* reported *Street of Dreams'* two production companies had been put into administration.

For such a high-profile project, the stage show was a huge disappointment and one that left a bad taste in the mouth of everyone involved. A year later, Paul told the *Radio Times* that he couldn't even listen to Eric Spear's iconic theme tune following his involvement in the ill-fated production.

Despite a 2014 cross-over episode with *For The Love of Dogs* – when a Battersea stray called Krystal appeared in an episode outside the Rovers – *Coronation Street* soon became one of the few subjects we tried to avoid mentioning on the radio show. By 2018, when Paul surprised his beloved Barbara Knox in *Rita & Me*, a special ITV tribute programme for her, he told reporters that he'd stopped watching the series completely. For him, the ongoing story had come to a permanent end.

11.

On the Box

'I ran away from school on the first day.
I'd reminded the teacher that it was nearly
time for *Watch with Mother* on TV'
Paul O'Grady

Telly always played a large part in the life and career of Paul, and he never hid the fact he enjoyed a lifelong affection for the small screen. Perhaps that's why he was such a natural presenter. He knew how the medium worked. He was also proud of the fact he'd provided the voice of a WC for a television commercial promoting a toilet cleaner: 'Pop a blue in your loo,' and another as a cat litter tray: 'Empty me, empty me.' Talk about versatility.

Watching television was one thing, but *acting* on it was something else. It might be a controversial thing to say, but I wasn't a huge fan of Paul O'Grady the TV actor. His own personality was so fervent, so formidable, that I often struggled to see his performance because the Paul I knew was never that far away.

This might have come as a surprise to Lily Savage, though, who once said, 'Some of us spent a year in drama school, at the RADA … I was cleaning it, but still.'

While performing as Lily in clubs and pubs, Paul O'Grady started to get work as an actor on the small screen. Using his mother's maiden name, Paul Savage played the transvestite prostitute informant Roxanne, in three episodes of the popular ITV police serial *The Bill*. Broadcast in 1988, 1989 and 1990, the trilogy saw Roxanne help to uncover a rent boy business. He filmed his first scenes just a couple days after he'd buried his mother, Molly. The following year, this time under his own name, Paul played Donaldson, a social worker who used sign language to talk to chimpanzees in the 1991 science-fiction horror drama *Chimera* based on the Stephen Gallagher novel about genetic engineering. Both performances are interesting to watch now, some 30 or more years later, but Paul doesn't exactly light up the screen.

Undeterred, in 1993, he appeared in the Oscar-nominated film, *In the Name of the Father*. Based on the true story of the Guildford Four and their wrongful convictions following the 1974 Guildford pub bombings, Paul played an inmate at the prison where Gerry Conlon, one of the wrongly accused, was held. Unlike *Chimera*, Paul was again credited as 'Paul Savage'. Even though he spent 3 weeks filming in Kilmainham prison, it's a blink-and-you'll-miss-him role, as much of his work ended up on the proverbial cutting room floor. Paul told me later he had enjoyed the experience of movie-making with director Jim Sheridan, who promised to work with Paul again. Sadly, the phone never rang.

For the next 10 years or so, Paul focused on Lily Savage, but, following his first heart attack, he decided it might be prudent to explore other opportunities which wouldn't require him to wear high heels. He was relieved to be saying farewell to his alter ego, but he also recognised she'd been his passport to what was fast becoming a career full of possibility; he later told the *Mirror*, 'I feel very grateful for the opportunities she gave me … and the friends I made through her.' In 2003, Paul joined the cast of *Eyes Down*, a new BBC television sitcom. The situation in question was a bingo hall and the official press release promised the comedy would come from 'the lives, loves, hopes and disappointments of the staff and customers of the Rio Bingo Hall in Liverpool'. Paul was in great company as the cast included Edna Doré as cleaning lady Mary, rising star Sheridan Smith as Sandy and Tony Maudsley, who played co-worker Martin. Paul O'Grady was cast as misanthropic Ray, the Rio's biting bingo caller, who regularly dipped his tongue in vitriol before welcoming punters to his Liverpool lair.

Speaking at the launch of the series, Paul explained: 'Ray hates humanity, pensioners in particular – but when you look at what he's got to deal with, you're not surprised he's wicked and snide. He's a deeply frustrated man. The things I say to the customers in the bingo hall are dreadful because I hate them all; I loathe them.'

Paul's own irritation sometimes filtered its way onto the set. Co-star Tony Maudsley remembers the early days working with Paul: 'It was his first time doing scripted comedy. As Lily, he'd always had free rein over what he said and when he said it. But with a sitcom like *Eyes Down*, he was working alongside five other actors and had to stick to a script. In the beginning, he would get so frustrated when he had to film something again. He didn't understand why he had to repeat the same scene, even though he had got his lines right first time.'

Discussing the series with me during one of his Sunday radio shows, Paul admitted that he loathed having to do his scenes over and over again because it simply bored him.

Vera, however, has suggested it wasn't just about getting the right performance. Paul hadn't been impressed with the scripts for *Eyes Down* and would often argue for changes he proposed. 'It just wasn't good enough,' explained Vera. 'It wasn't a completely happy time for him.'

Someone who worked with Paul many times over the years, the BAFTA award-winning hair and make-up designer, Vanessa White, agrees: 'I first met Paul at the read-through for the first episode of *Eyes Down*. Everyone had told me he was quite scary. He had a reputation. He thought he could do better than the writer had done, which he probably could.' During a particularly challenging scene, Paul stormed off the set. Tony Maudsley recalls he chased after him, explaining: '"Paul, there's no car to pick you up till 4 p.m.!"' Next thing, Paul had stuck out his hand and flagged down a double-decker bus. "Take me to Tower Bridge," he said to the driver. "I can't, mate, this only goes as far as Cricklewood." "Oh, then I'll go as far as Cricklewood, and I'll get a taxi."' His dramatic and sudden exit meant the production had to stop filming, but the following morning Paul O'Grady returned with his tail between his legs and apologised to everyone. 'Interestingly,' recalls Vanessa White, 'when *Paul* told that story, he said he'd flagged down the bus with two dogs under one arm and a bird cage in the other. We never knew where that cage came from!'

This was typical of Paul. His stories, though usually based in truth, would often be embellished for comedic effect. The challenge for those on the receiving end was to work out what was true and what was O'Grady.

Running for 15 episodes, *Eyes Down* wasn't a spectacular success, nor was it an embarrassing flop. But in a survey commissioned by digital TV channel UKTV Gold in 2008, it was voted as one of the 'worst programmes of all time'. I wouldn't go that far, but when I got to know Paul well, even though he would acknowledge the series, usually telling me wild stories about Edna Doré or Tony Maudsley, the sitcom didn't seem to be something he was particularly proud of, despite the friendships he had forged with the cast. Sheridan Smith had fond memories of what was one of her first jobs for the small screen: 'Paul was a friend till the end ... As real and genuine as they come. [I] will never forget his kindness, fun and constant support.'

Acting on the small screen might not have been where Paul O'Grady truly shone, but as a guest on TV chat shows, he – and Lily – were comedic gold. His appearances on *Parkinson* are fascinating to see – as Lily Savage he was outrageous, confident and relaxed; as himself, though, Paul initially seemed slightly less assured, albeit equally as entertaining.

By the time he sat down with Alan Carr in 2010, Lily was almost a distant memory, and it was Paul O'Grady the audience wanted to see. Paul was a regular guest on the Channel 4 talk show *Chatty Man*, which usually employed a one-on-one interview format. This suited Paul as it allowed him to be the centre of attention, something he revelled in, and he thoroughly enjoyed having a glass of absinthe or Blue Nun wine on screen, while simultaneously regaling Alan Carr and the studio audience with stories and anecdotes. As Alan explains, 'When you get a master like Paul on, talking with him was just like being round his home, having a chat, not an interview, and that's what people want. And when you knew he was going to be on a talk show, you knew you were going to be entertained.' Graham Norton agrees: 'He was an excellent guest, and I think he liked it because he didn't have to bother with the business end of it. You know, "Oh, we've got to go to music now," or, "I have to introduce the next guest." As a guest himself, Paul could properly relax, facing that audience and having fun. He was never happier than when he had an audience.'

In 2012, television gave Paul the chance to try something new, and it was an opportunity he relished. Broadcast that April, *Nellie and Melba* was a short film shown in Sky Arts' anthology series *Playhouse Presents*, curated by Sandi Toksvig and Stephen Fry. It starred Sheila Hancock as the mother, with Paul playing her closeted son, Neville. Significantly, the comedy-drama was co-written by Sandi and Paul. It was full of references from his own life: Miss Flaming Nora – a character who did fire-eating, just as Lily had done; a reference to *Skippy The Bush Kangaroo*; and then there was Neville himself, who worked at the local social security office, again something Paul had done in the past. The biggest similarity was that Neville loved stage musicals, especially *Gypsy*, and wanted to follow his dream of a life on the stage. Sandi Toksvig told the *Guardian*, 'I have co-written with many people but never like that, he would send me handwritten scribbles of thought … Sometimes we met and he just talked at me as I hurried to dash it down before going home to try to make some kind of sense of it in the form of a script.'

Paul had obviously enjoyed the new challenge, and a few months later he received sole writing credit for another Sky TV short film called *Boo! A Ghost Story*. He was the first to acknowledge the challenge of making the project, though: 'Brevity is not in my vocabulary. I've got a wealth of them [stories]; I could churn them out. I find the past more interesting than the present when I'm writing.' *Boo!* was filmed in 3D – it was all the rage in 2012 – and told the story of an adolescent Paul, played by Robin Morrissey, who is left more than a little spooked after seeing *The Exorcist* at his local cinema. A series of encounters with several unsavoury characters on his journey home forces the young man to seek comfort from his sleeping mother, played by Alison Steadman. As well as writing the piece, which again was inspired by events in his own life, the adult Paul O'Grady played a scary rough sleeper, and a ghost who was looking for her son.

He also managed to coax Lily Savage out of retirement. In a behind-the-scenes featurette, the star explained that she'd thought Paul O'Grady had described the project as, '*VD*, not *3D*. I've got some penicillin in my bag. I had no idea it was 3D! Anyway, it's only a fad. I've still got the telly I bought in

Lily

TOP LEFT: A gay icon. Paul Massey's celebrated 2003 portrait of Lily Savage on Blackpool's North Pier.

TOP RIGHT: Miss Savage with Julian Clary at the 1993 London Pride festival.

ABOVE: Two legends on the bed in *The Big Breakfast* house: Cher and Lily, 1996.

BOTTOM RIGHT: Dragging Lily onto prime time telly – as host of *Blankety Blank*.

Chatting with Jo Brand on Paul's ITV chat show in 2010.

On the cobbles with the 2012 cast of *Street of Dreams*, aka *Street of Screams*.

Paul, a corgi and Ali Taylor entertain HM the Queen during a 2015 visit to Battersea Dogs and Cats Home in London.

With human rights campaigner Peter Tatchell, launching the campaign to get British police forces to apologise for their past homophobic witch-hunts, 2023.

What an entrance! Paul in the London Palladium panto *Cinderella*, 2016.

Full circle: Paul's final starring role in Michael Harrison's production of *Annie*, 2023.

Pals

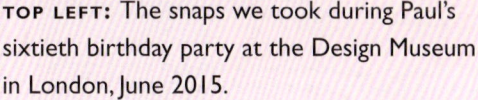

TOP LEFT: The snaps we took during Paul's sixtieth birthday party at the Design Museum in London, June 2015.

TOP RIGHT: Having a cuppa in the kitchen of Knoll Hill House, just before the return of TeamPOG on Boom Radio, December 2022.

BELOW LEFT: My wedding day and smiles all round: (*left to right*) Graham Norton, Jodie Prenger, René, me, Nicki Chapman and Paul, 2016.

BOTTOM RIGHT: Our last photo together, taken at my home in Sandgate just two weeks before Paul died, 2023.

Radio

With Paul and Cilla Black in studio 6A, Wogan House, Christmas 2011.

Paul loved *Doctor Who*, and my dalek! In my office at the BBC, 2013.

ABOVE: This was the photo I chose for Paul's caller ID on my phone, 2014.

LEFT: Paul, the rulebreaker, in the lift at Wogan House, 2017.

TOP LEFT: Happy days. In studio 6A, Wogan House, home to TeamPOG for over a decade, 2017.

TOP RIGHT: Paul with Elsie, one of the regular contributors to his radio show, 2018.

LEFT: He seldom said no to a selfie, 2018.

BOTTOM RIGHT: Celebrating ten years of the Sunday show, 2019.

Family

LEFT: Paul with Sharyn on her wedding day, 30 July 2005.

ABOVE: The family: Phil, Sharyn, Paul and his grandson Abel, 2010.

BOTTOM RIGHT: With Sharyn in front of Adam Brezaux's impressive mural in Birkenhead, 2024.

1965; it doesn't have a remote, but it's got a big knob, it's handy.' Lily continued, 'I find filming very easy – well, it depends what kind of films. Swedish films are usually more difficult for me at my age, but this kind of thing – it's only a walk-on, a cameo, I'm doing him [Paul O'Grady] a favour … and if I forget it, I make it up. Bugger the writer … It's crap, but times is hard, friends are few, and I need the money.' Retirement, it would seem, hadn't changed Miss Savage.

Boo! was the first television job for actor Robin Morrissey, who was somewhat more positive about the project. 'I was fresh out of RADA … I felt pretty intimidated from the get-go – not only playing the iconic man himself but also playing opposite Lily Savage! I buried myself in all I could get my hands on about Paul's early life, and sort of fell in love with him before I'd even met him. Stepping into his shoes was genuinely a privilege. Any fears I had were quickly dismissed when I met him, cracking jokes and laughing at all my lines in the first read-through in Soho. He put me totally at ease. He'd written such a funny little film … I remember it so fondly … his warmth and his humour, and the twinkle of mischievousness he had in his eye.' Paul thought the casting of Robin was perfect.

Lily Savage agreed, and suggested Robin should 'go on the game'. Tut.

It was another 'honourable profession' (his words) that was the focus of Paul O'Grady's next television project. In 2013, he returned to New York, where a decade before a nervous and boorish Paul had introduced one of his travelogues for ITV. This time, more confident and polished, he was fronting a documentary for the channel called *Perspectives*. In this pilgrimage, produced by Paul's own production company, he charted the story of his beloved Gypsy Rose Lee, and illustrated how the most successful burlesque star of her day had singlehandedly elevated striptease into an art form. In the compelling programme, Paul noted that, 'When you look at pictures of her [Gypsy], although she's got a very beautiful face, she actually hasn't got the equipment – if you pardon the expression – the boobs.'

He interviewed Jo Weldon, of the New York School of Burlesque, who explained that the secret of the stripper's success was down to her gimmick: 'Her personality was hers; her intelligence, her playfulness, her openness; she spoke directly to the audience' – much like Paul O'Grady himself.

Later in the programme, Paul travelled to San Francisco to meet Gypsy Rose Lee's only child, Erik Lee Preminger. 'What was your mother like?' enquired Paul. When Erik replied, 'She was an acquired taste,' Paul cracked back: 'But *I* am an acquired taste, Eric!' The fan, it would seem, had much in common with his idol, and he later told me he had greatly enjoyed making the programme.

While the subject of a superstar stripper might be considered 'adults only', Paul also had a strong interest in family-friendly animated films, which he was always keen to explore. His kitchen at Knoll Hill House in Kent was home to figurines from *Sleeping Beauty* and Walt Disney's first full-length animated feature, *Snow White and The Seven Dwarfs*. In 2016, Paul's fascination with fairy tales led to another television documentary which promised to reveal the 'gruesome truth about Snow White'. In the ITV programme, he travelled around the chocolate-box schlosses of Germany to uncover the origins of the Grimm tales. The result was a far cry from the family-orientated fare of the Disney studio. Promoting *Paul O'Grady's Favourite Fairy Tales*, he explained, 'I've always found fairy tales intriguing – stories of cursed princesses, evil queens, charming princes, and above all, a happy ending. For years I've been playing those well-known characters on stage in panto, and children love them. It's only when you get older that you wonder, "Where did this come from? How did you invent a magic mirror, seven dwarves in a diamond mine, and why do children today, hundreds of years later, still find them fascinating?"' I remember Paul bounding into the radio studio a few weeks after he'd completed filming the project. He had thoroughly enjoyed the process of making a programme in which he could flaunt his knowledge and appreciation for the genre, something the press was quick to acknowledge.

The documentary was reviewed by the *Independent*: 'Our favourite drag artiste … looked perfectly happy splattered in blood and engaged in cannibalism … the story was told with wit and affection … Paul O'Grady is an underestimated broadcaster confined to the fluffier end of the market; this incursion into horror will, I hope, help him evolve his repertoire.' While it's a glowing endorsement for the host's skill in the documentary genre, it's interesting to note that the reviewer was still citing Paul O'Grady's former career, even though Lily Savage was by 2016 long retired, and Paul was by then associated more with his own television programmes about unwanted dogs than drag queens.

In 2021, in the midst of the Covid pandemic, Paul launched a new game show, *Paul O'Grady's Saturday Night Line-Up* on ITV. Piloted a couple of years before, the series was a return to his entertainment roots. Filmed at Elstree Studios, Paul's celebrity guests would guess what the British public really thought of them, lining up in order of most loved to most disliked. It wasn't a huge hit like *Blankety Blank*, but it was good to see him sending up the likes of Joan Collins, Boy George and Jack Dee. *Saturday Night Line-Up* was, he told me, a 'doddle' and the six-part series was followed by a Christmas special which had been shot in the height of summer – something he loathed to do. When the *Daily Mail* later reported: 'Paul O'Grady's Saturday Night Line Up is AXED by ITV after failing to wow audiences', Paul wasn't bothered in the slightest.

That same year he agreed to give acting another go in the cosy crime drama, *The Madame Blanc Mysteries*. Paul had filmed a short cameo role for the finale of the first series, playing a character called David, an eccentric antiques dealer. Shown in a Zoom call, which was filmed in his home in Kent, Paul's character was seen chatting with Jean White, played by Sally Lindsay who had co-created the show with the writer Sue Vincent. Discussing his appearance, Sally Lindsay said: 'I wanted David [Paul's character] to be really outrageous and always looking pristine – he was based on an amazing antiques dealer that lives on the King's Road.' Later, Sally was delighted when Paul accepted her invitation to guest star in the second series, and she began writing an episode which had him front and centre of a new mystery for Jean to solve in her home in the south of France.

Sally and Paul had been pals for years. I remember she was one of the guests of a very starry edition of his Friday night chat show, *Paul O'Grady Live* in 2010, alongside Victoria Wood and Barry Manilow. As with all his close friends, Paul kept in regular contact with Sally by phone and text. 'He was a dear mate,' she later explained. A great example of their friendship was when he made a surprise panto appearance as an angel, complete with wings, in *Cinderella* at the Marlowe Theatre in Canterbury, in which Sally was starring. 'Paul came to see me. He went on to the roar of a loving crowd.'

Being a guest star on *Madame Blanc* would be one of the first jobs Paul had agreed to since the Covid lockdowns, and he was looking forward to the filming. The episode would see his character, David, and his new, much younger, husband George (David Ames) visiting Jean in the French village of Sainte Victoire. Paul had told Sally, who wrote the episode with Sue Vincent, he didn't want any 'bedroom scenes' as he was old enough to be his co-star's grandfather. Instead, the newlyweds would take in the region's beautiful scenery while George would try to murder his new, wealthy husband.

Despite being set in France, the series was shot in and around Malta. However, almost as soon as work got underway in 40° Maltese heat, Paul tested positive for Covid. He later told the press that he had been coughing like a 'sick donkey' and had been laid out in his hotel room. He messaged me from Malta to say how guilty he felt, letting everyone down. 'We got one day's filming in the can and that night I felt a bit off and the next day I felt like I was dying,' he explained.

Paul spent over a week isolating in his hotel, 'going slowly around the bend' before Joan Marshrons was able to get him back to Kent, where he spent two months recuperating. Actor and comedian Les Dennis took over the role intended for Paul and the completed episode was eventually broadcast in January 2023. It was a shame we didn't get to see the on-screen partnership of Paul O'Grady and David Ames, who'd been pals since their first meeting back in 2013. The two had met on the set of the medical drama *Holby City* when Paul had played cancer patient Tim Connor for three episodes. 'Paul was a great orator,' explains David. 'He was someone who could command a room with his tales, with his stories, and while he didn't tell jokes per se, the entire story he'd be telling was like a punchline.'

A few weeks after the aborted filming, Paul phoned me. He explained that although he was still not feeling 100 per cent, he wanted to keep busy and even though his trip to Malta had ended in disappointment, he had plenty of other travel plans. And he was, he told me, about to start work on a new adventure for the star of his children's books, Eddie Albert, plus he was also in discussion to turn his first two autobiographies into a TV drama, and there was talk of a stage musical based on his formative years in Birkenhead. He additionally revealed he had created a brand-new television series. This was unexpected. 'I wrote the first episode while I was stuck in that bloody [Maltese] hotel bedroom.' For the next hour or so, he enthusiastically shared his format for *Kelly and King*, in which he would star as Francis Kelly, an old and unkempt secret agent brought out of retirement to aid a handsome young rookie spy, Charles King, played by David Ames. Think *The Avengers* – John Steed and Tara King era, obviously – meets the Ian McKellen and Derek Jacobi sitcom *Vicious*, combined with a whiff of Gary Oldman and Jack Lowden from espionage drama *Slow Horses*. Paul was so good at painting stories with his words, it honestly felt like the show was already in production. He spoke about filming locations, potential guest stars, and hoped that Vera would be in it too, along with the actor Celia Imrie. 'I'll get Amanda [Mealing] to direct and, yes, before you ask, Malcolm, you can have a non-speaking cameo part serving sandwiches or playing a corpse.' Clearly, he already knew my limits as an actor.

After listening to his plans, I could easily picture *Kelly and King* on a Sunday evening on ITV in the slot traditionally held by *Midsomer Murders*. Sadly, though, it wouldn't be the only Paul O'Grady-penned project which wouldn't see the light of day.

12.

A Blind Date with Cilla

'We used to get invited to dinner parties as the entertainment, of course we didn't mind. We were just being ourselves ... We had the same roots, you see, that's how we connected'

Paul O'Grady

By the time I knew him, Paul was an extremely well-travelled man, and when it came to going overseas, luxury was important: Paul O'Grady always turned left on a plane, and he stayed at the finest hotels and resorts. Fair play – he had worked hard for it, and he was happy to share his love of extravagant travel with those closest to him, be it a first-class trip to Venice aboard the Orient Express, or a five-star break in the Big Apple.

In 2009, Paul enjoyed an adventure from Siberia to Vladivostok and back with his pal Vera who remembers, 'It was fabulous, a steam train with five gold cabins and you had your name on the door. It was the journey of a lifetime. And we were on board with Lady Solti and Leo de Rothschild. We had a ball.' No surprise really, as Paul once told the *Daily Express*, 'Alan/Vera is my best friend … we've been through thick and thin together.' As a souvenir of their adventure, Paul gave me a Siberian woolly hat.

Paul wasn't the only one who enjoyed rail travel; Lily Savage did too, though perhaps hers was second-class: 'I used to look forward to a long train journey. It was an expedition, sat in a comfortable seat, a can of lager in one hand and a *Woman's Own* in the other.'

While Paul and Lily enjoyed going places, getting there could have its challenges. Alan Carr recalls bumping into Paul at London's Heathrow airport. 'I heard someone behind me complaining about the touchscreen check-in: "How the fuck do you use this fuckin' thing?" and I turned round, and it was Paul O'Grady. I asked him where he was off to and he told me Vienna, and I was going there too! And so we spent the most glorious weekend together, and he had everyone in fits. He was such a great storyteller. He knew everyone and it was like going away with Oscar Wilde or Truman Capote. He collected anecdotes like other people collect stamps.'

When it came to good stories, Paul's friendship with Cilla Black generated plenty. Many outrageous tales stemmed from their travels around the world together, be it to her home in Barbados, visiting mutual friends in New York, or celebrating a birthday aboard the Orient Express. Theirs was a very special friendship based on similar backgrounds, mutual respect and a lorra, lorra laffs. The parallels are clear: they both had huge personalities, they were good with people and were naturally relatable. They trusted each other, and shared a bond forged by their Merseyside working-class roots. As the broadcaster and chat show host Michael Parkinson explained, they had 'rags-to-riches stories, both coming from what used to be called humble beginnings to achieve stardom'.

It was on an edition of Parky's legendary chat show broadcast on BBC One in February 1998 where the two stars clicked; though, to be accurate, Cilla met Lily Savage. This was the first time Cilla had appeared on Michael Parkinson's talk show, and she was both apprehensive at being back at the BBC and intrigued by the prospect of meeting Paul. There were three guests that Saturday night: the actor Liam Neeson was interviewed but didn't stick around to share the stage with Lily (who came on second) and then Cilla. Lily told the host it was 'an honour to be … [seated] in Parky's swivel chair'. Miss Savage was there to promote the return of *Blankety Blank* and confided she couldn't master the autocue – a vital tool for a television presenter – instead opting to 'wing it'.

When Parky asked Lily if she knew Miss Black, she replied they'd been speaking before the show in the dressing room. 'She's got fabulous legs, you know,' declared Lily, a description Cilla would use to describe her fellow guest as she joined the conversation moments later. Even though Cilla was 12 years senior to Lily, it didn't take long for the two guests to bond over their mutual appreciation of net curtains, and, as Lily explained, 'We both had outside lavs.'

I was one of many who enjoyed that edition of *Parkinson*; what struck me at the time was how Cilla addressed Paul as 'Lily' and not 'Paul', who stayed in character the whole time.

More than two decades later, it's very clear to see that the chat show was the perfect place for the two Scousers to connect and reminisce, while Parky did what he was best at: he let them talk. That night, something very special happened: two stars – one firmly established, the other rapidly ascending – became fast friends. Paul later explained that Cilla 'would say awful things about me and I'd say terrible things about her. It was a good double act we had going.' For almost 20 years, Paul and Cilla would continue to socialise together, becoming what *The Big Issue* described as 'a Scouse Will and Grace'.

When I interviewed Cilla for the Radio 2 documentary in 2003, she told me that Paul had taught her how to laugh again after the death of her husband and manager, Bobby Willis. In her autobiography, *What's It All About?* she admitted, 'Savage and I were like brother and sister.' Along with Christopher Biggins and Dale Winton, Paul was one of a small number of pals she would socialise with. The tabloids might have been surprised that Cilla was hanging out with 'a former drag queen,' and she told me her son, Robert, 'asked me not to bring the Willis name into disrepute!' But Cilla Black was grateful for Paul's friendship and companionship, and he was publicly proud to be associated with her, even if he did share some concerns about it: professionally, he didn't want to be seen to be riding on Cilla's coattails in any way.

In 2010, when Cilla was doing her 'part-time' job as one of ITV's *Loose Women*, Paul agreed to be a guest, and his rant about his frustrating and annoying journey to the studio caused much amusement with the viewing audience and panellists.

Whenever the two friends appeared together on screen, their chemistry and mutual respect shone through, to such an extent that in 2013, Laurence Marks and Maurice Gran, the creative geniuses behind the hugely successful British sitcom *Birds of a Feather*, were approached to create a vehicle for Cilla and her pal. That project became a comedy called *Led Astray*, in which Cilla played Tanya, a has-been TV host in need of a career boost, with Paul as her long-lost half-brother Arthur, who was serving time in prison. With some skilful forging, Arthur fixes his release from HMP Wymott – the only conditions: he must wear an electronic tag and stay with his newly found half-sister.

A pilot script was commissioned, and a production team was assembled. As preparations for the sitcom progressed, Paul continued to host his Sunday radio show. During one broadcast, he eagerly revealed a photo on his phone, 'Have a look at this, Malcolm … look at the state of me!' It was Paul, in character as Arthur, dressed in a prison-issue grey tracksuit, with shocking dyed red hair. He looked terrible, especially as another picture had him standing next to a very glamorous Cilla as Tanya.

Paul couldn't stop laughing when he saw my reaction.

'You look awful, what will people think?' I exclaimed.

'Exactly!' came his delighted reply.

'He did look absolutely dreadful,' recalls the actor, David Ames. 'The first time I met Paul was in the canteen at Elstree Studios. I was a series regular on *Holby City* playing the junior doctor Dominic Copeland. I was ordering a coffee, and I heard someone say, "Well, I see you're back then, causing trouble on the wards," and I turned and froze for a moment because there was Paul O'Grady with the most ridiculous ginger hair. And he started telling me he was doing a pilot with Cilla, and then, after chatting for about fifteen minutes, he said, "Anyway, I'd better get back, she'll be wanting her coffee." And he turned around, and Cilla was behind us. I hadn't even clocked that Cilla Black was there!'

The writers Marks and Gran were understandably optimistic about *Led Astray*. They wrote in a blog, 'It is fair to say that we all had enormous fun in the rehearsal room and studio working with Paul and Cilla … They are very good … much better than we expected them to be. Our audience in Elstree Studios appeared to love the comedy.' According to Vanessa White, Paul and Cilla's relationship and their chats with the studio audience between takes, really made the day.

The same month the pilot of *Led Astray* was filmed, Paul presented *The One and Only Cilla Black* on ITV. Broadcast to mark Cilla's fiftieth anniversary as a star, the programme saw various celebrity tributes and musical performances, while Paul chatted to his friend. As the programme came to a close, he asked the audience to show their appreciation for, 'the wonderful, the brilliant, and I'm proud to say a very good pal of mine, the one and only Cilla Black!'

Back at HMP Wymott, Laurence Marks and Maurice Gran were still hoping the BBC would commission a full series of their new sitcom. It didn't. Afterwards, Paul told me the pilot had been hard work for him and Cilla, and he was concerned they wouldn't have been able to cope with the demands of making a whole series. 'She's 70, I'm 58, it was knackering,

Malcolm.' Later, it would be reported that Paul had been hospitalised shortly after the filming, suffering from an angina attack. Cilla told the *Daily Mirror*, 'I was looking forward to the sitcom but the week after we filmed the pilot, he had heart problems again and we talked it over and just thought it wasn't worth the long hours. He put the kibosh on it. We just agreed that it was too much of a risk.'

Knowing Paul as I did, I wasn't surprised to hear his heart wasn't entirely in it – no pun intended – and it was obvious to me at least he'd only agreed to do the sitcom out of loyalty to his friend. It's clear the premise for the show was a strong one, and its starry cast would have proved a draw, at least for the debut episode. But in the mid 2010s, television times were changing: successful home-grown studio-based comedies were rare on British TV screens, and perhaps Paul's reservations about *Led Astray* had as much to do with it appearing dated as much as the slog it would have been to make it.

The disappointment of the failed sitcom pilot did nothing to diminish the stars' friendship though, and Cilla was a frequent guest on Paul's TV shows to the extent that, for some viewers at least, they now went hand-in-hand. To witness them send each other up was a delight. On one occasion, Cilla popped into our radio studio, and I reminded Paul that Cilla had told me she would often turn the radio off if she heard herself singing because she didn't like to hear her own music. 'She's not the only one,' he quipped, much to her amusement. Cilla also joined us on a Christmas Day edition of the Radio 2 show, reading out messages and eagerly sharing tips with Paul on how to prepare roast spuds for a perfect festive lunch. The photo of the three of us in studio 6A that day is one I now treasure.

One of the last times I saw the two of them together was at a party for Paul's sixtieth birthday in June 2015, held at the Blueprint Café in Butler's Wharf, minutes from Paul's London pied-à-terre. In a spacious room overlooking the River Thames and Tower Bridge, Paul's friends and family gathered to wish him well alongside an impressive guest list from the world of entertainment. I remember chatting to Barbara Windsor who was there with her husband Scott, and laughing with the actor Ann Mitchell (Dolly Rawlins in *Widows*) when one of the heartfelt speeches given in Paul's honour went on a bit too long. Paul's pals from his early Lily days were there, including Jayne Tunnicliffe and Brenda Gilhooly, not forgetting Vera of course. The party featured a photo-booth where guests could take a set of four passport-style pics – I still have the ones of Paul and me – and there was a colourful wall display covered in photos of Paul, from a young child to the star he'd become. Cilla was there too, but at 72 she was a shadow of her former self. She looked frail and walked slowly around the room, escorted by her son Robert. I was upset to see her in this way, and I know Paul was too. He did have a dance with his friend that night, their last, and she died just 7 weeks later at her holiday home in Spain.

When the news of Cilla's death was announced, Paul phoned me. It was a Sunday morning, and we had already recorded that day's edition of his radio show. 'I'm gob-smacked, Malcolm,' he said, as we reminisced about his birthday party and the many other happy times he'd spent with her. The following week, in the final hour of Paul's Sunday show, he paid tribute to his chum. 'We lost the queen of showbiz herself, and I lost a very good friend,' he told his listeners. He joked about Cilla's wish to be remembered as a vocalist rather than as a presenter, explaining: 'She said to me, "I want 'singer' on my headstone," and I said, "Why do you want to be known for being a sewing machine?"' After playing her 1966 hit 'Alfie', Paul appeared to be overcome with emotion and he paused, saying, 'Malcolm, you'll have to give me a minute.' I told him, 'You start when you want to,' and he blew his nose, and tried to carry on, later explaining that 'Alfie' always 'does me in … it completely finishes me off'. It was one of the only two occasions I saw him be emotional; the other being some years later, when we played John Williams' theme from *Schindler's List* on the radio show, performed by Itzhak Perlman.

On 20 August 2015, Paul attended the funeral of Cilla Black at St Mary's RC Church in Liverpool. He gave a touching and humorous tribute in which he declared, 'I firmly believed that Cilla was indestructible and that I would go first, the state of my heart. In fact, we discussed my funeral at length, me and Cilla, and she had a major role in it which involved a mantilla and lilies.' He continued, 'I've got fabulous Cilla stories, 'cos we had such a good time together. Whenever we went on holiday, or even if we went for a simple meal, something always happened, usually to me … We got into a lot of trouble … but we laughed while we were doing it … We were soul mates … After Bobby died, I went down for dinner at the house in Denham [where Cilla lived] and we sat up until five in the morning and decided to go and stay with Peter Brown [Cilla's good friend] in New York, which we did. And I introduced her to the finer things of New York: bars, burlesque shows and nightclubs with such a reputation that taxi drivers were reluctant to drop us off … She loved life! And I loved this lady dearly … she was one of my closest friends … and I'm just so grateful that she allowed me into the whirlwind of her life, and we spent nearly two decades together, hellraising.' He also mentioned how, while staying at her home in Barbados, he had managed to break his nose in her jacuzzi. He then repeated a story which he had seen in the press: Cilla had said that, 'Bobby had sent [her] a guardian angel, only this one had hooves, horns and a tail.' Paul's heartfelt eulogy was featured prominently in the media coverage of Cilla's funeral, and quite right too: it was a masterpiece, and delivered with sensitive aplomb.

A couple of months after his friend's funeral, Paul's autobiography – *Open the Cage, Murphy* – was published. In the introduction, he explained that Cilla didn't appear in his memoir because a mere chapter or two simply wouldn't do her justice. He wasn't wrong, and Cilla even continued to play a part in Paul's life after her death.

In 2017, 14 years after Cilla quit *Blind Date* live on air, Paul was invited by Channel 5 to present a reboot of the popular dating show. At its peak, the series on ITV had attracted 18 million viewers, and it became one of the most valuable properties on commercial television.

When he was first approached, Paul apparently declined the job because it was synonymous with his late friend. But he later changed his mind, and the new series launched to solid praise from fans and critics, even though Paul initially admitted to feeling uncomfortable about it all. 'When we did the first recording it felt wrong,' he told the press. 'I heard the music, and it felt like it shouldn't be me.' Introducing the first programme, he announced, 'The reason I'm doing this show is because a certain person left this to me in her will.'

Just like Cilla, Paul was there to help singletons find love by asking their potential partners a few very random questions from behind a screen, though in this reworked version, the series would see same-sex pairings for the first time. While some noticed the new budget didn't match the original's, with winning contestants being more likely to share a game of table tennis or junkyard golf than to fly off to the Maldives for their date, many watching conceded that Paul was the ideal person, indeed the *only* person, who could have taken up Cilla's mantle. Promoting the series, Paul was quoted in the online edition of the *Radio Times*, 'There's a definite skill, because you're not interviewing celebrities, like I used to. You're interviewing the public, so they're not as confident. The last thing they need is for me to devour them, so I'm very avuncular with them, I'm very kind. I'm like a brothel madam, really.'

The *Daily Telegraph* gave the new *Blind Date* 4 stars out of 5, suggesting, 'Cilla would have approved of this disarmingly faithful reboot.' But there was a problem: boredom. It was *Lily Savage's Blankety Blank* all over again. And while Paul was paid handsomely, just as Cilla had been, he struggled to find the contestants interesting. In June 2019, he quit the hit after

33 programmes, bringing the revived series to an end. It would seem with *Blind Date*, Paul O'Grady hadn't met his match.

Four years later, I remember talking to Cilla's son, Robert, and I told him that if it hadn't been for his mum, I might never have had the opportunity to work with Paul. I still thank my lucky stars.

13.

Puppets, Plays and Pantoland

'I don't go for glamour roles'
Lily Savage

For every person who discovered Paul O'Grady through the small screen or radio, and there were many, there will also be others who first saw him on stage. And for thousands of people, that was probably in a panto.

The stage book-ended Paul O'Grady's life and career. As a youngster, like so many before him, he had a toy theatre – constructed by his dad – and often put on puppet shows. But one of my favourite stories about the young Paul was why he later joined an amateur dramatic club in Birkenhead, the Carlton Players, in the early 1970s. He was 16 years old or so, and he explained it was to enable him to 'scratch the acting itch', as they welcomed anyone interested in the theatre. For Paul, it wasn't just a life on the stage that appealed to him: it was the prospect of meeting fellow gay men. 'I'd read some-where that the theatre was absolutely teeming with homosexuals,' he wrote, many years later.

The great parts, of both stage and men, initially eluded the young Paul; his first job was being given the responsibility of looking after the stage props. But, when he finally landed a non-speaking role in a Christmas show in 1971, he realised he was genuinely smitten with showbiz, loving the sense of community that theatre offered.

While Lily Savage began to entertain audiences in the 1980s, Paul still hankered after a significant role on the theatrical stage, and that eventually came in the form of the musical *Elegies for Angels, Punks and Raging Queens*. A response to the AIDS crisis, it was originally called *The Quilt*, in honour of the NAMES Project AIDS Memorial Quilt, and the piece featured a collection of heart-wrenching monologues and songs set to a blues, jazz and rock score.

With its new name, the immensely powerful song cycle debuted in New York in 1989 and was later staged in Islington in 1992 at the King's Head Theatre, the oldest pub theatre in London. The 30-piece ensemble cast included Paul O'Grady and Amanda Mealing. The two hit it off the moment they met in the rehearsal room. Paul thought Amanda was stunning, 'like a young Liz Taylor' and 'had a real whiff of trouble about her'. Each of the cast had a 2-minute monologue about the ghost of someone who had died of AIDS. For Paul, in particular, it was a moving experience as he had lost so many friends and acquaintances to the disease. 'For a time, I was forever at a funeral', he said. At the end of the play, the cast came together to sing 'My Brother Used to Live in San Francisco'. Amanda remembers, 'Savage and I only came on halfway through the second act, so we'd sit in the dressing room after the others had gone, gossiping away. What the audience didn't know was that the performers all had to crawl through this small space to reach the stage. I recall one night, I had done my monologue and then I had to go and sit with the other members of the cast at the back of the stage. Everyone there was supposed to be still and silent. But all we could hear was Savage kicking off backstage, because Lily's wig had got caught on a nail!'

Paul later described the cramped environment as being worse than *Tenko*.

The following year, in a benefit in aid of the King's Head Theatre, which had staged *Elegies*, Lily Savage joined forces with Victoria Wood at the London Palladium. He later told me, 'Vic was a bit moody, but friendly and businesslike … I admired her as she had a brilliant mind and an enviable ability to consistently produce a wealth of astounding comedy material.' Paul was back at the Palladium later that year, when Lily appeared in another fundraiser in October – *The Equality Show* alongside Julian Clary, Stephen Fry and Pet Shop Boys. Paul wrote that the London Palladium was where he felt 'at home'.

On Easter Sunday 1994, Lily held court in her own show at the famous theatre. It featured special guests: Bob Downe, with whom Lily performed the Bolero; loyal friend Vera; and a heavily pregnant Gayle Tuesday. 'It was one of the best nights of my life!' remembers Brenda Gilhooly. 'Lily was becoming such a huge star, of course she would be headlining at the Palladium! This was the new reality for Paul.'

It had been Brendan Murphy who'd promised to make Paul's ambition of starring in a sell-out show at the venue a reality, and he hadn't let him down. The finale saw Lily and friends perform 'There's No Business Like Show Business' on the Palladium's iconic revolving stage. It is no exaggeration to say that it was a dream come true for Paul, and he later described the evening as 'the icing on the cake' of that year, and a 'magical night' that he would never forget. In 10 years or so, Lily had gone from pubs and small clubs to headlining at the most prestigious theatre in the land. As Jo Brand explains, 'It was an incredible achievement, and testament to how the character of Lily Savage had a broad appeal. Up until that point, most drag queens were somewhat niche and Lily wasn't.'

It was in the guise of Lily Savage that Paul would also reinvent the role of the Wicked Queen in *Snow White and the Seven Dwarfs*. Lily would star in the pantomime numerous times, kicking off at the Birmingham Hippodrome in 1999, with Paul tinkering with the show's script with producer Paul Elliott. It was a huge success and Lily returned with the same production in 2001, this time in Southampton. Trade paper *The Stage* reported that, 'at times, it is almost like *The Lily Savage Show*, extending the Wicked Queen part to the biggest baddie you are ever likely to see'. Remarkably, given how much he detested repeating himself, and with how busy he was on television, Paul returned to the role and headlined the production in Bristol in 2003 and again in 2004 at London's Victoria Palace Theatre. By this point, Paul was sharing the writing credits with Tudor Davies, Paul Elliott and Carole Todd. During the pantomime Lily performed 'I Put a Spell on You', 'Trouble', 'No More Mister Nice Guy' and 'Female of the Species' – all songs Paul loved and ones he'd encourage me to play on his radio show. The production also featured an unreliable animatronic raven whose head would sometimes fall off during a scene, leaving Lily stuck with a malfunctioning bird.

'It was an absolute gift for Paul,' remembers Michael Harrison, who had just started out in the business as a junior producer, 'and if I could rewind the clock and go back to three or four theatrical experiences in my life, one would be the Saturday night watching Lily Savage at Bristol Hippodrome because I'd never seen anyone like that before in a pantomime. I can remember the lines, when Lily made her entrance, lying on a bed … [with] her handbag, and she would say, "I've got everything you need in here: a bottle of vodka, last night's kebab and a brick." It was the first time I realised how you can miss someone in a show, because the minute Lily wasn't on stage, the rest of the show fell flat – the audience really missed her, you longed for her to come back.' Russell T Davies also recalls seeing Lily as the Wicked Queen. 'As the man who wrote *Queer as Folk*, I can be a right old prude. And I went along to his panto thinking, "If there are dirty jokes in this for kids, I'm really going to object," because I don't think you should do that. I could not have been more wrong. Paul gave the most perfectly judged performance I have ever seen. It was a great night in the theatre. There was nothing filthy and yet Lily was as funny as ever, and that's when it clicked for me – I could see what would become the great entertainer, Paul O'Grady.'

When he wasn't tempting Snow White with a poisoned apple, in September 2002 Paul was back at the Palladium, this time in the sinister, black-suited role of the Child Catcher in the stage musical version of *Chitty, Chitty, Bang, Bang*. *Chitty* had opened 6 months earlier to good notices from the popular press, though one paper suggested that many in the audience were there just to see the famous flying car, which Guinness World Records recognised as the most expensive stage prop, costing a reported £750,000. The production had experienced unexpected technical issues with the titular vehicle, and some performances were blighted by its unreliability. But when everything worked, seeing the champion race car take to the skies was something to behold. The stage production was directed by Adrian Noble – at the time the artistic director of the Royal Shakespeare Company – with musical staging and choreography by Gillian Lynne, whose many theatrical credits included *Cats*, *The Phantom of the Opera* and *Aspects of Love*. Paul loved being associated with such theatrical nobility. Towards the end of the musical (spoiler alert), when the Potts children have finally defeated and captured the Child Catcher in a net, Paul would be flown on a wire up into the ceiling of the Palladium's auditorium, where he would then have to quickly climb through a door onto the roof, run along the top of the theatre, and scramble back inside so he could take his rightful place on stage at the finale. For those in the Palladium's audience, it was an exhilarating sight to see; while for anyone high enough outside the building, it must have been nothing short of bizarre.

His 3-month stint as the Child Catcher, in which he only had one number to sing, 'Kiddy-Widdy-Winkies', was an important one for Paul because, this time, he wasn't billed as

Lily Savage, he was Paul O'Grady; he was beginning to pack Lily's bags. Even so, when speaking to the press, he explained spending hours in make-up while they applied exaggerated features to his face, then performing and listening to the musical's songs nearly every day of the week, was taking a heavy toll. 'I'm going round the Chitty Chitty bend. I wake up every morning singing songs from the show. They are all stuck in my head and sometimes I think, "Dear God, just save me from this insanity."'

Paul would later flinch when I suggested playing something from the cast recording on his Radio 2 programme: 'I think I've got some sort of PTSD, Malcolm!'

He would often talk to me about the attraction of working in theatre. 'You're in this family', he'd say, 'and if you have the three Gs – a great company, great audiences and a great production – then you're laughing.' And he usually experienced that winning combination when he was starring in pantomime, something that I'll always associate with Paul. Panto kept pulling him back, the genre suited him – most probably as it was a limited run, so he knew when he'd be able to escape. Mind you, he did once ask, 'Which bugger★ invented matinees?'

Panto gave Paul the opportunity to showcase his talents, though his initial delight was usually followed by weeks of regret, often moaning that it was hard work being stuck in a theatre repeating himself. He didn't appear in one every year – far from it – but when he did, it was always accompanied

★ The word he actually used would upset my mother.

by a fanfare of publicity. And while he sometimes had to miss the odd performance due to his health, he always delivered. 'I love the insanity of it all!' he once said to a journalist. 'Although if you asked me that question the third week in, I'd turn on you and say, "I hate it, I want to go home!" But I love it really.'

When Paul signed up to a panto, he took it very seriously. The money was always important, yes, but he also understood the mechanics of the genre and was keen to get it right. And it was a panto in 2010 that persuaded Lily Savage out of her enforced retirement.

When remembering that Mayflower Theatre production of *Aladdin – A Wish Come True*, Paul told Southampton's *Daily Echo* newspaper, 'When I did panto, I realised how much I missed [Lily]. I knew we'd have a good time with it.' Reviewers agreed, calling the show 'a winner,' and they praised Miss Savage for 'a delightful, multi-layered performance'; *WhatsOnStage* even went so far as to write: 'Lily Savage is the ultimate Dame for the modern age.'

Paul loved working at the Mayflower, calling it 'the greatest theatre on the south coast', and had performed at the venue many times before. After one evening's performance of *Aladdin* in Southampton, a group of us, including the actor Matt Rixon and Vera – who was working as Paul's backstage dresser – went for a drink at the nearby Encore pub. Playing Lily's son was S Club 7 singer Jon Lee whom, Paul explained, called him 'his mam'. As Vera got the drinks in, Paul took centre stage again, revealing a show secret: the mechanism used to fly the magic carpet in the Mayflower panto was the same one the Palladium had employed to help *Chitty* take flight. He was delighted by my surprised reaction.

Seeing Paul in that pub, sharing tales and titbits about the show, are still some of the happiest non-radio memories I have of him. That night, I witnessed Paul O'Grady as I hadn't seen him before: he was a social butterfly, holding court, enjoying the company of a close-knit group of actors and backstage crew, and he was loving every minute of it.

In March 2012, following Lily Savage's return 2 years before, it was reported that Paul would revive his much-loved drag creation for another pantomime run, this time in a purpose-built pop-up 1,900-seater theatre at London's O2.

I was a tad surprised, given that Paul had told me he'd never 'do panto ever again', but I had by now discovered he regularly said he wouldn't do something, only then to change his mind.

If his outbursts at Radio 2 were anything to go by, however, his stint at the O2 wasn't the happiest time he'd had in panto, and he disliked performing there. He missed 'a proper theatre, with bricks and a real dressing room'. Even so, that didn't stop him joining the line-up of another panto in 2015 in a similarly unexpected venue, playing to an audience of almost 5 thousand in a sporting arena in Birmingham.

This time it was Paul O'Grady and not Lily Savage starring as the Fairy Godfather who was seen flying across the vast stage, in what was billed as 'the world's biggest pantomime'. Paul's co-stars included Bradley Walsh, and Dick and Dom, plus a company of over 100. Undeniably ambitious, this new production of *Cinderella* was described by *The Stage* as being, 'Brave but fatally lacking', blaming its scale and not its stars for being 'a disappointment.' The following year, the organisers in Brum tried again, this time with *Snow White* starring Melanie Brown and Rylan Clark-Neal (as he was then), but Paul O'Grady was nowhere in sight. He had other plans.

In May 2016, it was announced that, after an absence of 30 years, pantomime was returning to the London Palladium with a brand-new production of *Cinderella* starring Paul O'Grady. For decades, panto had been synonymous with the famous theatre, dating as far back as 1914 and a production of *Dick Whittington and His Cat.* The theatre had soon established itself as the home of some of the most lavish annual pantos ever seen, offering top-tier talent including Julie Andrews, Max Bygraves, Frankie Howerd, Arthur Askey and Charlie Drake.

The news that pantomime would be returning to the London Palladium in 2016, after such a long hiatus, was widely reported, and with the casting of Paul O'Grady as the Wicked Stepmother, aka Baroness Hardup, channelling his inner Cruella de Vil, and Julian Clary as Dandini, *Cinderella* became the season's must-have ticket.

The show's producer and director was Michael Harrison. 'I had asked Julian, and he said to me, "You should really ask Savage." I could tell straight away it was something Paul would want to do. [When] he came into the office for a meeting, there was something so normal about him that it was easy to forget that he was a megastar.' For Julian Clary: 'I knew it would be hilarious. Paul and I had never worked together, and I thought it would be interesting in the convention of panto. For me to do what I do, I need the right people to bounce off, so I was very excited at the thought.' Paul later described the new double-act with his friend as being 'like Bette Davis and Joan Crawford: I'm Bette, he's Joan.'

Before one Sunday radio show, Paul and I discussed his plans for the role and the songs he would be performing. He also showed me some of the designs for his costumes, which he deliberately kept to a minimum, but were stunning creations. In fact, Paul loved them so much a photograph of him dressed as the Wicked Stepmother appeared on the Christmas card he sent to friends and family that year.

Paul and Julian would be headlining an impressive company of star names including Amanda Holden, Nigel Havers and Lee Mead. Lee had found fame on the 2007 BBC talent series *Any Dream Will Do* and was, by now, a headliner himself. Lee recalls attending rehearsals with Paul: 'It was his first scene. It was the first time reading the script as the Wicked Stepmother. He read the first few lines and then proceeded to go completely off book. It must have lasted ten minutes and when Michael Harrison asked him several times to go back to the script, Paul refused. It was hilarious and the whole company, including Michael, were in hysterics. It was a privilege to witness this impromptu performance but I now realise what Paul was really doing that day was trying to find the character within himself, and although he was making us laugh and going off the script, what he was also doing was getting a feel for us – the people he would be spending so much time with in the coming weeks. It was very clever.'

Perhaps unsurprisingly Michael Harrison interpreted Paul's behaviour somewhat differently: 'I would go so far as saying he was undirectable, but I enjoyed that, because the best performers in pantomime are dangerous. You are sitting there; the curtain is about to go up and you don't quite know what they're going to do. You have a rough idea, but they could say anything that night, they could play off a heckler, they could play off another cast member, and there was nobody like Paul, he was a one-off, because pantomime wasn't really his natural home, but it became it.'

For Lee Mead, Paul was 'always professional but he wasn't afraid to say if he was unhappy about something, which I really admired. You could tell that he was a true performer, old school, and if there was any opportunity to make us laugh, he would. For him, it was about making people happy, and he went on to do that for every performance of the run at the Palladium.'

Be it in a rehearsal room, or minutes before he was to go live on radio or TV, Paul often enjoyed an unplanned anarchic rant. And yet, as Michael Harrison observes, 'Paul was a brilliant pro, and nothing was going to go wrong in his hands on stage, but there was nothing safe about him at all. He could not do the same show twice. You would perfect something in rehearsal, and you'd think, "This is brilliant." But he couldn't replicate it. And once we had opened, I'd call in to see the show, a few weeks in, and he'd be doing things I'd never heard before; he simply couldn't deliver the same performance twice, because he got bored.'

Critic Michael Billington described *Cinderella* as, 'a tsunami of smut … it's the filthiest panto I've ever seen. It's less a show for all the family than for highly sophisticated grown-ups.' A grumpy *Daily Telegraph* also reported the production was far too crude, while acknowledging, 'Paul O'Grady oozes the necessary boo-able villainy as the wicked stepmother', while the *Financial Times* noted Paul's role as 'one of his increasingly rare returns to drag.' Looking back at the press coverage for the production, much was made of its innuendo and the hefty price of its tickets, and some reporters did question its suitability for a younger audience. Their criticism only gave the panto more free promotion: 'We were delighted,' confirms Michael Harrison.

The rebooted production of *Cinderella* was a hit and, for Michael, Paul's entrance – in a Rolls-Royce – was highly memorable: 'I've produced thirteen shows at the London Palladium … but the single best reaction I have ever heard in that theatre is when Paul O'Grady came on as the Wicked Stepmother. Audiences were so pleased to see him … and there he was, they were really showing him their love and appreciation.' Paul was genuinely excited to be appearing in such a lavish production with so many of his pals, but without wishing to take anything away from the other members of the impressive cast, for his fans, seeing Paul on stage again was a theatrical treat.

There was one scene which, if you'd been lucky enough to witness, left a lasting memory. It featured simply Julian and Paul in the woods discussing an item of Dandini's attire, namely the state of his over-sized muff. I'll never forget it. Paul stood there, chipping in about how the item had been stretched and kicked about a bit. 'It was like a game of tennis,' recalls Julian. 'He said, "You could get the seven dwarfs in there," and one day I replied with, "I've only ever managed five," and then left the stage. Neither of us cared about who got the last laugh. The thrill was making each other laugh and the subtext of it all.' Michael Harrison again: 'They were magic together … The infamous muff scene was magic, watching two old pros stand there and basically riff off each other in front of a crowd, you could never plan that. Julian got the big laugh at the end, but it took everything that Paul did to get the tag, and he didn't care as long as it was working for the both of them.' The pantomime and the audience had to come first.

Paul's then ten-year old grandson Abel was one of those who saw the show. In 2024, he recalled, 'I was so proud of him, my GanGan, on the stage of the London Palladium. It was surreal. And we went backstage afterwards, and he asked us what we thought. He showed us the costumes and his wigs. And then, after ten minutes or so, he just started moaning about something. And it would be funny because he had a face full of make-up on, with his normal hair, and he was wearing a dressing gown, but it was still just GanGan, having a moan as usual.'

Along with Julian Clary, Paul helped to re-establish the tradition of pantomime at the Palladium. He didn't appear in 2017 and 2018, when Dawn French and Elaine Paige shared top billing with Julian respectively, but in May 2019 it was reported that Paul would return to the famous theatre once again for that year's lavish production of *Goldilocks and the Three Bears*. This time, Paul would be playing a character called Baron von Savage, with a cast which included Matt Baker,

Paul Zerdin, Nigel Havers, Gary Wilmot and Julian. Wisely, perhaps, this time the Palladium warned patrons: 'The production contains adult innuendo and intimation which may not be appropriate for everyone.'

Paul later explained why he was going back for more: 'I moan like hell doing two shows a day and frequently ask myself, as I'm eating yet another Marks and Spencer's sandwich for lunch in my dressing room, "Why do I do it?" The answer is quite simple when I think about it – it's because secretly I really enjoy it. The money's good and to be part of one of the Palladium's extravaganzas is something pretty special.'

The press, once again, moaned about the innuendo, while the *Guardian* suggested, 'As the villain Baron von Savage, Paul O'Grady is pleasantly disdainful, if a little light on one-liners of his own. It's clear that a lot of money has been flung at this show. Next time, a little finesse wouldn't go amiss.'

But for Paul, there wasn't going to be a 'next time'.

Eight months after Paul died in March 2023, Michael Harrison's production of *Peter Pan* moved into the London Palladium for the festive season. As usual, the pantomime's company featured Julian Clary and Gary Wilmot, plus guest star Jennifer Saunders. Julian explained, 'Michael told me he felt we needed to pay a tribute to Paul, and I thought yes, because you can do anything you want in panto. Gary Wilmot quickly adapted the words of the song "As If We Never Said Goodbye" and we did it the next day in technical rehearsals. I liked it because it was the elephant in the room in a way, because everyone there was thinking of Savage. It was quick and it was heartfelt, we were expressing something on the audience's behalf. And when I performed it on stage, the applause was for Savage afterwards. It was hard to do, it got me; there was a fine line between being emotional but being in control as well.'

'*Peter Pan* got the best reviews of any pantomime we had done at the Palladium,' explains Michael, 'and I think we got an extra star because of that number. People choked up when they saw it and it's a credit to Julian that he was able to do that number every night.' Especially as he was dressed in a giant seashell.

The touching tribute highlighted just how much Paul was missed by all those who'd worked with him at the theatre. It also celebrated his panto expertise while acknowledging his involvement was always accompanied by a moan and a groan.

Without a doubt, Paul O'Grady was a highly accomplished stage performer, be it in a prestigious two-thousand-seater or on the small stage of a pub in Vauxhall. He could impress an audience almost anywhere, and he did.

But the job that would propel him to international fame – changing his reputation and image completely – saw Paul working in the unlikeliest of locations, and with an entirely different sort of cast.

14.

A Dog's Life

'You couldn't keep me away from the place'
Paul O'Grady

Many years before Paul stepped onto the 'Welcome' doormat
of Battersea Dogs and Cats Home in London, his affection
and respect for animals – dogs in particular – was already well
documented. Lily too was a fan: when she published her guide
to life called *A Sort of A–Z Thing* she explained, 'I'd sooner
have my Buster in the bed than a husband.'

As far as Paul was concerned, 'all a dog needs is love', and he
was more than generous with his affections. During one of his
radio shows, Hollywood legend Doris Day phoned in to thank
him. 'I bet you didn't expect to hear from me,' she said. 'A little
bird told me about all the wonderful things you do to help our
four-legged friends, so I send a big thank you from me and the
Doris Day Animal Foundation; it is wonderful what you're
doing, really and truly.' He was shocked and thrilled.

Paul and animals went hand-in-paw. In April 2013, he
fronted the first 'animal Oscars' on ITV. The British Animal

Honours, as it was called, recognised brave pets and the people who had dedicated their lives to them. Even though the televised awards were a one-off event, the programme further cemented Paul's association with animal welfare and the nation's pets; it also followed his recent appointment as the host of an ITV series set at one of the most famous charities in the world.

Founded by Mary Tealby in 1860 as 'The Temporary Home for Lost and Starving Dogs', Battersea also started to take in cats in 1883, following a surge of felines found to be roaming the streets of London. One hundred and fifty or so years later, the charity became the focus of a weekly TV series presented by Paul, who took to the new job like a duck to water. Over 13 years, he would go on to present 100 or so episodes of *For The Love of Dogs* (aka *PogDogs*), including special programmes at Christmas.

In 2013, the show was nominated for a television BAFTA in the Best Features Programme category – it lost out to *The Great British Bake Off*. *PogDogs* went on to win many other prizes though, including a special recognition honour at the 2018 National Television Awards. The series was also shown abroad and was popular in Canada and New Zealand. While Paul was happy to be the figurehead, he acknowledged such prestige didn't come from the work of just one person, and was always quick to assert it was borne from the combined efforts of hundreds of people – and dogs – over many years.

The format of *Paul O'Grady's For The Love of Dogs* was a straightforward one: in each programme, he followed a few select animals from their arrival at Battersea through to their adoption. Audiences embraced its good-natured simplicity and heartfelt storytelling, and the series regularly attracted 5 million viewers every week. For some tuning in, it was reminiscent of Johnny Morris's Bristol-based children's series, *Animal Magic*, which had run on the BBC from 1962 until 1983. This was especially true when Paul spoke – and seemed to communicate – with the dogs in question, just like Johnny had done before him.

But the television show for which Paul O'Grady is now perhaps best remembered wasn't the one he'd originally hoped to host. From 1994 until 2004, BBC One broadcast a series called *Animal Hospital*, which focused on animal welfare stories from RSPCA sites in London and Salford. Presented by a now disgraced Australian entertainer, *Animal Hospital* was a success: there was even a children's Christmas annual published to go with the series. Just like the many millions who tuned in each week, Paul enjoyed following the real-life stories of animals who had been injured or needed assistance, especially as most concluded with a happy ending. Even during an episode of *The Lily Savage Show* broadcast in 1997, the star claimed her sister Vera often watched 'that vet's programme'. It was a series Paul was keen to revive, but at that time he wasn't working with Auntie.

The original idea for a show featuring Paul O'Grady and his love of animals came from his former television producer Robert 'Bert' Gray, but by the time Waheed Alli met up with ITV, the concept – which would have seen the presenter getting to know the animals of Port Lympne Safari Park in Kent – had changed and it was the broadcaster, who already had an existing relationship with the charity, that suggested the series could be set at Battersea.

According to Joan, Paul was a perfect fit: 'He could get on with staff, he enjoyed being there, and his love of dogs was unquestionable.' Vanessa White, who worked on the series, agrees. 'He could show a side of himself to animals which he would never show to any of us. Probably due to embarrassment. Invariably the animals in Battersea had endured some sort of trauma, so Paul could see that, and he'd think, "How can I help?" He would walk in, and the dogs would genuinely react to his voice. He had this way about him that was calming for the dogs ... he had a kindred spirit with them.'

I have a very specific memory of Paul arriving at the studio one wet Wednesday afternoon for another recording of his radio show. It stands firm in my mind because he was in a good mood, so much so one might even say he was buzzing.

'Are you alright?' I asked.

'Yes!' he replied with gusto, 'I couldn't be happier. I've just come from Battersea where I've been talking to a wonderful Staffie!'

This would become a regular occurrence. I could always tell when he'd been filming the series: his appearance gave it away. His clothes would also be covered in dog hairs and, if I'm being completely honest, he would be accompanied by a very distinct odour. 'Have you been playing with the dogs again?' On another occasion, he came storming into the studio ranting in explicit detail about what some 'lousy bastard' had done to a bitch and her puppies. It did nothing for his blood pressure.

Paul knew why the series was a success. Modesty aside, he explained, 'It's popular because it's a feel-good programme. You'll get a dog coming in that's in a terrible state and terrified of its own shadow. The staff in Battersea are so good that you'll see it blossom and go off to a really nice home. They always show the dog playing with the kids, catching a ball and sitting on the sofa and the new owner saying they wouldn't be without them. It's a Cinderella story.'

It wasn't all fairy tales, as Vanessa White recalls: 'Paul had it in his contract that he would have make-up, which was great, and invariably it was me. He wasn't fit, he ate appallingly, and he smoked. So, coming into Battersea first thing, he would look, as he would say, like "the wreck of the *Hesperus*" as he got off the motorbike. His hair would be a mess, and he would look pale and very grey, and because he was on blood thinners, his skin would easily mark. So he always had to be made up for television.'

But once he was filming, it was the perfect job for him. Joan, who often accompanied Paul when he was working at Battersea, commented: 'He loved the people there, and the dogs obviously, and even if it was repetitive, we could always find him a dog to play with, to keep him occupied.' Paul later explained that he always felt good about life after a day at Battersea, 'particularly if I'd helped rehome a dog'.

Soon after he completed the first series, Paul was invited to become an ambassador for the charity, a role he readily accepted.

If truth be known, when it came to the canine subjects featured in the series, he preferred dogs which some would describe as 'ugly or damaged', and they sometimes became a new addition to the O'Grady clan. In all, he took five dogs home with him: Eddie was first, then Conchita, Arfur, Nancy and Sausage. I can still picture them all, in various baskets on the floor of his kitchen in Kent. His affection for, and friendship with, those dogs was something to behold, and his conversations with each of them never appeared to be one-sided. If you ever tuned in to the radio shows broadcast from his home, you'll have heard them all participate. Such was his love for his dogs that when Paul died, he left a significant amount of money for their future care, with instructions that the ever reliable Joan and Moira Stewart should arrange their rehoming.

As Graham Norton explains, 'You saw a different Paul on that Battersea show. And that was because it was the purest Paul. Dogs are singularly impervious to anything verbal. Paul couldn't be sharp, witty or sarcastic – all that stuff he depended on, all the stuff he relied on, was useless on that show. And with that stripped away I think you saw a very sweet and sincere Paul. *For The Love of Dogs* was the closest to him an audience ever got.'

After Paul's death in 2023, Battersea set up a fund in his honour, which rapidly raised £480,000. Its chief executive, Peter Laurie, told the press that, 'We've been overwhelmed and deeply touched by the generous donations from thousands of people … It really is testament to how loved Paul was, and we shall always be forever grateful for everything he did for us.' And in October 2023, on what would have been the eleventh anniversary of Paul becoming an ambassador for

Battersea, the charity's veterinary hospital was renamed in Paul's honour. He had been present for the Royal opening of the building by the then HRH The Duchess of Cornwall in September 2016, and during his time filming in London, SW8, the veterinary hospital had become one of Paul's favourite areas on the site.

Some £100,000 of the money raised in Paul's name was later evenly distributed to five animal charities, all of which were reportedly close to his heart, including three near Liverpool. Battersea invested the rest of the funds in helping cats and dogs in need of specialist medical care and treatment. They explained, 'Paul's impact on our charity has been phenomenal, helping drive up donations, legacy pledges, and the rehoming of our animals – but, more importantly, by shining a spotlight on the vital work of rescue centres, he's helped transform the way people view them, encouraging a new generation of pet owners to consider rehoming the many animals that are in desperate need of a new home, rather than going online and fuelling the trade in puppy farming.'

I believe Paul would have been touched by that summary of his legacy.

Paul's pal Dale Winton once said, 'Don't quit the hit,' but it probably won't surprise you to know that Paul told me every year he'd had enough of 'the dog show' because he felt he was on a bit of a treadmill. His filming days were long and some-times the stories he was telling he had shared before. Even with the chance to make a spin-off series like *Paul O'Grady's Animal Orphans*, which saw him travel to South Africa, Zambia and Borneo, meeting some of the animals which had been orphaned in the wild, Paul was wary of repeating himself. But there's no doubt he was proud of *For The Love of Dogs*.

Looking back at the first series, it's easy to see why it made such an impact with viewers. There was the white Boxer, Carmine, whom Paul would try to smuggle out of Battersea each week, and then there was Frank the Staffie who went to Birmingham with Paul to compete at Crufts – spoiler alert: they didn't win. And it would be hard to forget seeing Paul in the final episode arriving at the dogs' home on his limo bike, only to be met with a life-size bronze sculpture of his much-loved Buster. Donated by sculptor Christine Close, Paul was genuinely surprised and delighted. The statue still greets visitors to Battersea, and its staff continue to leave a tennis ball by the Shih Tzu's feet.

And it wasn't only in South London where 'the Paul O'Grady effect' was felt: rescue centres across the UK reported an increase in rehoming applications, and during the early series, the number of Battersea animals rehomed was three times higher than average.

It could be no surprise, therefore, that Battersea and ITV decided to continue with *For The Love of Dogs* and, less than a year after Paul's death, they announced a new host: Alison Hammond. You can see why ITV chose Alison: she is a natural and popular presenter, but fans of *PogDogs* were split by the decision, so ITV began a charm offensive. In a carefully worded press release, Alison was quoted as saying, 'I am very aware that I can never replace the iconic Paul in this wonderful series … But if I can continue to shine a light on the brilliant work done at Battersea and help to tell the stories of these beautiful dogs, then it will be an absolute privilege to give it my all.'

Towards the end of 2023, the animal rights charity Peta posthumously named Paul as its person of the year. '[We recognise and thank] Paul O'Grady for his lifelong determination to make the world a kinder place for animals … He never wavered in his commitment to protecting the most vulnerable among us. We will always treasure his legacy of compassion.' As Alan Carr observes, 'He was a philanthropist, and he made people feel special. And the same was true at Battersea. If a dog had three legs and its tongue hanging out, Paul would treat it like an absolute queen. And he would always gravitate to the underdog, be they a pet or a person. If they'd had a rough start in life, if he could help, he would.'

15.

Visiting Neverland

'I go in and I see a child ... [and] ... I think
where the hell is the justice here?'
Paul O'Grady

Paul 'met' the Boy Who Wouldn't Grow Up, and Tinkerbell, in December 2006. The location wasn't Kensington Gardens but a television studio in London. The occasion was the Paul O'Grady Players' annual pantomime on Channel 4's *New Paul O'Grady Show*. Featuring a cast of special guests which included Dawn French as narrator, Lisa Maxwell as Peter Pan, *Coronation Street*'s Julie Goodyear as the Fairy, Jo Brand as Tinkerbell aka Tinkerball, and Paul as the villainous Captain Hook aka Hooky-Wooky, the programme featured all the traditional panto tropes and followed the central storyline of J.M. Barrie's classic play. Much like the rest of Paul's teatime shows, it was a little rough around the edges, but it was obvious that the cast – and the host in particular – was having great fun hamming it up. For Jo Brand, the only celebrity to appear in all of Paul's TV pantos, being asked was a pleasure:

'It was hilarious, I'm not sure the audience felt that, but we did. And the biggest joy was simply being in a room with Paul. It was just surreal to be with the other guests he'd invited on; I remember once being behind a bar with Joan Collins thinking, "What the fuck am I doing here?" There was a great contrast of the glamour of it – the costumes, the starry cast – and the down-to-earthiness of him.'

I've often wondered why Paul was so fixated on panto-mimes – his name seems to go hand-in-hand with them, both on screen and on stage, even as far back as his early drag days when he and a group of other acts would stage a seasonal panto in bars around London. But the choice of *Peter Pan* for his Channel 4 show was a significant one.

Paul had been a fan of the story ever since he'd seen a re-release of Walt Disney's version in the 1960s. When the animated tale first hit cinemas in 1953, its title sequence included the words: 'Walt Disney Productions is grateful to the Hospital for Sick Children, Great Ormond Street, London to which Sir James M. Barrie gave his copyright of *Peter Pan*.' Some 65 years later, Paul O'Grady's own story would become forever entwined with the same great institution.

Paul had a lot in common with Peter, the boy who never grew up. During the research for this book, one four-letter word kept on rising to the surface (no, not that one, and not that one either) – it's the word 'play'. It's no stretch to say that in almost everything Paul O'Grady ever did, he really just wanted to *play*. You could see it in the toys and mementoes on his dresser behind him on the teatime shows, or in the assembled knick-knacks he accumulated at his homes in London and Kent. And you could find it on screen when he played with the dogs and cats at Battersea, or hear it when he spoke to Elsie the studio mouse on the radio. Paul O'Grady was just a big kid, and I for one believed he had never been in a hurry to grow up.

In August 2018, Great Ormond Street Hospital (GOSH) became the focus of a new ITV series called *Paul O'Grady's Little Heroes*. It was billed as 'A unique insight into the famous hospital and the lives of the brave and resilient children who are treated there every day.' The subject matter wasn't a new one for television, and there had been other behind-the-scenes hospital-based shows before – as is often the case in television, there's no such thing as a new idea. But what set this series apart was its host.

Already an ambassador for the charity Save the Children, Paul was keen to participate in the project, which would follow a child's journey through specialist and pioneering treatment. The content also drew heavily on his own experiences working as a peripatetic care officer for Camden Council in the 1970s. After moving to London from Birkenhead, he had initially helped elderly people and dysfunctional families. He told the *Independent* in 1995: 'If a single mother had to go to hospital, I'd move in and look after her kids, so they didn't have to go into care.' Speaking to the *Mirror* in 2016, Paul recounted a story of the night he had been forced to flee a flat where he was keeping watch on an 18-month-old baby, following a terrifying confrontation with the child's drunken father. He escaped and made a desperate call to The Salvation Army for help, which they provided – no questions asked, an incident that helped to forge his long-standing admiration for the charity.

The experience of working for the North London council never left Paul, and he would often mention his time in Camden and, before it, working as a housefather at a children's convalescent home in West Kirby, where he cared for youngsters with disabilities. Paul had only been 18 years old when he got the job as a live-in carer at 'the Conny Home', looking after children with muscular dystrophy, diabetes or spina bifida. He stayed there for 3 years. 'I was always in and out of hospitals. I trained in a kids' home. I was only a bit older than the kids themselves. I had 11 kids to look after … We did 14 hours a day. Telly is a doddle compared to that.'

Paul's eagerness to present *Little Heroes* was evident. In a promotional press release, he was quoted as saying, 'I can't wait for you all to meet the children, young people and brave families who inspired me so much during my time at this very special hospital.' One afternoon at Radio 2 during a 'Triple', however, he confided to me he was finding making his new series at the children's hospital a somewhat taxing one, not because of the demands of filming, but because of the emotional drain. But he then added quickly, 'It's nothing compared to what the kids have to go through, Malcolm.'

During the course of the two series he filmed at GOSH, Paul followed the stories of a young brother and sister who had been born with the life-long genetic condition cystic fibrosis, a teenager diagnosed with chronic kidney disease, and an 11-year-old who had to undergo a life-changing 8-hour operation to reconstruct the bone around her eye and cheek using bone taken from her leg. He also met a 5-year-old who had spent her whole life being treated at the hospital, two brothers who had unrelated cancers, and a little lad from Leicester who required life-changing brain surgery. Sadly, not all those who were included in the two series had favourable outcomes. Paul explained, 'It's tough. I get emails from parents letting me know how their children are doing … We try to keep it light. But it is harrowing, seeing kids that are seriously ill.'

The episodes were carefully crafted ensuring there was light along with the shade, and heart-warming, uplifting stories featured prominently. One saw Paul playing the patient himself to show a youngster needles do not have to be feared. 'It's amazing I can make that difference … You bond with the kids, and they with me.' Another followed the presenter as he flew around a teenage ward in a blue plastic apron and surgical mob cap worn at a rakish angle, taking lunch orders, and asking one young patient, 'Would you like to see the wine list?'

GOSH welcomed Paul, calling him a 'national treasure' and valued the attention his status brought to its work. The press agreed. The *Express* reviewed the series, saying, 'Paul O'Grady and sick children will make you explode with happiness and celebrate the spirit of human kindness. O'Grady is a selfless presenter, not afraid to work with both children and animals, [who] spreads a good deal of happiness and goodwill in the most heart-wrenching situations and letting the children on the show shine … The bravery of these young people against adversity would bring tears to a glass eye and O'Grady was their perfect foil. He sensitively asked them and their parents questions and gladly played the fool to make them happy.'

Paul was adamant that the series should focus on the children and show how witty they were, in spite of their health problems. The *Daily Mail* proclaimed, 'If laughter is the best medicine, Paul O' Grady should be on prescription … The easiest, most natural subjects for television sometimes seem the hardest to get right. Any shows about poorly children ought to grab the heartstrings and never let go – but too often they end up maudlin and sanctimonious … [GOSH] is a medical miracle factory – but Paul treated it like a panto stage. And everyone loved that.'

As Joan Marshrons told me in 2024: 'He loved everything about the series: being with the doctors and staff of the hospital, meeting the parents, and interacting with the children who often spoke back.' Paul told the press at the launch of the series, 'It has been an absolute honour to film at GOSH, meeting the children, and their families as they go through some of their toughest days. They were truly inspiring. I have so much admiration for the truly dedicated staff who treat and care for them.'

Ironically, it was another health problem – Covid – which dashed hopes of a third series. During 2022, Paul told me he was expecting to return to the hospital as both ITV and the institution were keen. It wasn't to be, but the 12 programmes he did complete showed Paul as an adept and versatile presenter, capable of drawing on his own life experiences to bring empathy and humour to the darkest of human situations.

Paul O'Grady's Little Heroes was universally well received, and this time, more than any other in his TV career, he was delighted the emphasis for once wasn't on him, but the youngsters he had met.

Sick children, stray dogs, injured cats, homeless adults, the lonely and the downtrodden, Paul was often there, giving his support or lending his name to a good cause. And while many of these occasions were seen on screen or reported in the press, he did much more away from the glare of the public eye. I admired him greatly for that. He was savvy and chose his causes with care and consideration; not because they would make for good publicity, but because they were close to his heart. He used his fame with finesse, and it's no wonder many regarded Paul O'Grady as show business royalty.

Speaking of which …

16.

Unlikely Friends

'Now I'm part of the establishment ...
I'll have to start moaning and writing
letters signed "Disgusted of Kent"'
Paul O'Grady

Six months before he died, something quite incredible happened. Paul O'Grady was appointed a deputy lieutenant of Kent, a prestigious position made by the Crown. His Majesty's Lord-Lieutenant of Kent, Lady Colgrain said Paul's 'wide breadth of experience will further enhance an already strong team of deputies who support the lord-lieutenant and act as the eyes and ears for the lieutenancy throughout our wonderfully diverse county'.

Paul's new role made the news, as you would expect, and he spoke to the regional ITV News programme which he still, incorrectly, called *Meridian Tonight* (it became *ITV News Meridian* in 2013). He couldn't hide his excitement or pride as he explained how he might be asked to participate in citizenship ceremonies or be required to offer advice during the organisation of important events. He was, he said, looking forward to helping community groups raise awareness of their work. In another interview, this time on BBC Radio Kent, Paul confirmed he would be taking the appointment 'seriously' and suggested his new role 'could be handy' to others, as he often heard 'horror stories' from Kent's residents, and he wanted to use his position to help. When he called me at home to share this latest bit of news, I asked if I'd have to curtsey the next time I saw him. 'Too bloody right you will,' he replied. The *Independent* declared, 'The ultimate outsider had become a pillar of the establishment.'

Lady Colgrain later explained, 'I knew how much Paul O'Grady loved the county that he had made his home for over 21 years. His love of Kent saw him travelling around the county highlighting many of the coastal areas, with a particular fondness for the Romney Marshes.' That was true, as was his affection for things royal, something that in many ways was a little surprising.

Paul's formative years were populated by queens, but not the one who lived in London SW1A – at that time, the closest he got to Her Majesty was watching her speech on Christmas Day, much like the rest of the country and Commonwealth. And yet Buckingham Palace would feature in his story.

In 1972, Paul decided to pack his bags, leave Birkenhead and head down south. In his first autobiography, he details that journey to the 'Promised Land' where he was looking forward to a new career in hospitality and catering at a 'fabulous hotel in London's swish West End'. To Paul, London was

Avenger-land, where everyone lived in a swanky apartment and drove a Lotus, just like Tara King.

If you've read the account in *At My Mother's Knee*, you'll know things didn't work out quite as he had expected, but that life-changing ride, aboard the X61 Crossville Coach, culminated with a glimpse of Buckingham Palace, at which point 17-year-old Paul tried to imagine the Queen in bed – complete with a heated blanket. He could have had no idea that the monarch and her family would ultimately feature in his own story and while, for the next 20 years or so, he would frequently encounter queens' camp, drag and evil, he could never have known that Paul O'Grady and Queen Elizabeth II would become the unlikeliest of acquaintances.

Thirty-eight years after his first sighting of Buckingham Palace, Paul returned for a closer inspection. It was 14 June 2008, his birthday, and this time, he didn't arrive on a coach from Birkenhead. Accompanied by his sister Sheila, his daughter Sharyn, and André, his partner, Paul was there to receive his MBE from the Prince of Wales. At the time, he told the *Liverpool Echo*: 'It's a very nice present. I'm really pleased, really surprised. It's something I'd never even thought about.' Indeed, he believed initially the offer was a practical joke. 'I've got a weird friend who always sends me letters, looking really official, saying, "Dear Mr O'Grady, we have reason to believe you are running a brothel at weekends" or "Dear Mr O'Grady, this baby-farming has got to cease". So, I thought it was one of those. I thought it was quite a weak attempt. And then they rang up and said, "Why haven't you sent your letter back?" And then the penny dropped … and I rang the family. It was my cousin in Ireland, a lovely old fellow, who said, "It would be very crass and ignorant if you turned it down.""

Paul O'Grady was in good company that year: also honoured for services to entertainment in the Queen's Birthday Honours list were Russell T Davies, *EastEnders* star June Brown, and entertainers Des O'Connor and Victoria Wood. The popular press speculated Paul might go as Lily Savage. As if.

Sharyn told me, 'Dad asked me if I'd go to the palace with him … I was so nonplussed by it, [but] an honour was what I sort of expected for him. He looked so pleased when he received his MBE from Prince Charles. It was a real moment, and I was touched he shared it with his daughter and sister.' Afterwards, Paul celebrated his new honour with a big birthday lunch at the Ritz Hotel in London with his family and friends, but that special day wasn't the only time he would spend in the company of royalty.

Back at Radio 2, during a piece of music, Paul would often entertain me with stories about the British Royal Family, informing me that Princess X or the Duchess of Y listened to his radio show, and I used to wonder how he knew. One afternoon in 2019 explained everything, when Paul arrived at Wogan House to record his weekly programme. He was wearing a long gabardine trench coat and, as ever, he was holding a ubiquitous carrier bag.

'You'll never guess where I've been,' he said.

With Paul, there was no point in trying to answer because, frankly, he could have been anywhere and with anyone. 'Go on,' I replied.

I discovered that that afternoon Paul had paid a visit to the home of Lady Elizabeth Shakerley, first cousin once removed of Queen Elizabeth II and sister of Patrick Anson, 5th Earl of Lichfield (aka Patrick Lichfield, the famous photographer). For many years 'Lady Anson', as Paul knew her, was a party planner who had organised events for the Queen and various other members of the Royal Family. My husband René and I had been introduced to her at Paul's wedding to André Portasio in 2017, which was held at the Goring Hotel in London's Belgravia. Lady Anson had a long-standing association with the prestigious venue and, while a hundred or so guests had enjoyed a lavish lunch at the hotel that afternoon, the actual wedding ceremony was only witnessed by a select few in the Drawing Room, an intimate and beautifully decorated private chamber on the hotel's ground floor. René and I were flattered to have been included in that small group, along with Joan, Waheed, Vera, Moira and Lady Anson. Later, she sat with a delighted Paul and his husband at the top table, her presence low key: she was the epitome of discreet English politeness.

Paul had been a regular visitor to his friend, and he would often pop round to her home to see how she was getting on, especially when Lady Anson's health began to decline. Such visits were typical of Paul: when the chips were down, he was there. Much as he'd done with the hundreds of young men lost to AIDS in the 1980s and 1990s, Paul would be a regular visitor to those suffering in their final days. He often referred to himself as the 'Grim Reaper' and I used to joke with him that if I was sick and in hospital, I didn't want him stopping by wielding his trusty scythe.

On this particular mercy mission, Paul was greeted at the front door by Lady Anson's housekeeper who advised Paul that 'we have informal company'. He was ushered into the kitchen where, much to his surprise, he discovered Her Majesty the Queen sitting, having a cup of tea. Now, for anyone else, this might have flummoxed them, but not Paul, though he later admitted that he was a bit embarrassed to be chatting to the Queen carrying a WH Smith's bag. Paul told me Her Majesty thanked him for being such a loyal friend to her cousin, and for being a regular visitor to her during her illness. Paul replied he had been friends with her for many years and his concern was the same he would show to anyone. The conversation between monarch and subject continued, covering family, mutual friends and the events of the day – all of which shall remain private.

It was, I have since learnt, one of many such encounters Paul enjoyed with the Queen. He kept his association relatively quiet, and rarely mentioned it on air or in public. If he did mention the royals, his viewers and listeners wouldn't know if he was joking; after all, would *you* have believed him if he told you he'd had tea with the Queen?

According to Michael Cashman: 'Paul wasn't impressed by wealth or privilege. He loved truth and he loved honesty, and I think that is why the Queen found him so interesting and why she engaged with him so often as she did.'

While there were more private assignations than public ones, perhaps the most widely reported encounter between the star and monarch was at the Royal Variety Show in 2001. This time, she would have seen him blowing a trumpet with his head between his legs performing the burlesque classic 'You Gotta Have a Gimmick' with his pals Cilla Black and Barbara Windsor. It was a routine he had given a decade before with Betty Legs Diamond – aka Simon Green – and Gayle Tuesday. Speaking about the royal performance, Paul recalled, 'I remember her [the Queen] asking me where I practised playing my bugle, and if my neighbours objected. I told her I went down the field and, whilst the neighbours didn't seem to mind, a couple of sheep had died of fright.'

The entertainer and monarch also bonded over their mutual affection for dogs. In 2015, during a visit to Battersea Dogs and Cats Home, for the opening of the Mary Tealby dog kennels, Paul encouraged the Queen to adopt her own rescue corgi. To the best of my knowledge, HM didn't take one home.

Paul's regal connections weren't limited to Queen Elizabeth II: he also forged a relationship with the Queen Consort, Camilla. In late 2022, he told reporters, 'I don't know what her title is, I'll have to ask her when I next see her. I've always called her Camilla; I get on really well with her … She's great with people and we both love dogs. I think she's what the royals need.' As a patron of Battersea Dogs and Cats Home, Camilla appeared in an episode of Paul's television series, *For The Love of Dogs*, to mark the charity's one hundred and sixtieth anniversary. In a visit to their Brands Hatch site in Kent, Paul praised the then Duchess of Cornwall's commitment to Battersea, saying: 'I just love her, she's great.' He was a frequent guest at royal lunches, sometimes hosted by Camilla in Fortnum and Mason's private dining rooms on Piccadilly, where he would make the assembled diners laugh, though he never did his fire-eating act.

When Paul died in March 2023, Camilla was one of the first to pay tribute. The Royal Family's Twitter/X account posted a statement which said, 'Deeply saddened to hear of the death of Paul O'Grady, who worked closely with Her Majesty in support of Battersea, providing lots of laughter and many waggy-tailed memories'. And, at his memorial later that year, Celia Imrie read a further, more personal, message on Camilla's behalf. In it, she shared that she missed Paul 'very much' and explained how she had been 'touched by the kindness of his heart'. She went on to highlight their mutual interests – namely of the four-legged variety – and described her 'dear friend' as both a 'legend' and 'luminary'.

The warmth of the royal tribute was at odds with the decidedly frosty atmosphere Paul had experienced a few short months before at the BBC.

17.

Saving Sundays

'Let's face it, it wouldn't have been
the same without you'
Paul O'Grady

Paul left Wogan House in central London for the very last time on Wednesday 11 March 2020. He had just recorded his show for broadcast the following Sunday. He didn't know he wouldn't be back – none of us at the BBC did. The following week, with the threat of Covid, the nation entered lockdown and, as he was in a group deemed as 'vulnerable', he wasn't allowed to return to work.

For the next few weeks, while the alarming drama of the pandemic played out across the country, Paddy O'Connell held the fort, playing requests and reading emails. I was then asked to repeat a selection of my documentaries in Paul's Sunday slot, which saw the re-run of various programmes about Kylie Minogue, Simon Fuller and Walt Disney among others. The repeats went on for almost 2 months, during which time the BBC continued to pay

Paul and the other 'older' presenters it had also told to stay at home.

While Sundays were temporarily taken care of, I was told I had to continue to go into London every Saturday morning to produce Graham Norton's weekly live show, which was an important programme for the station, one the *Daily Telegraph* had called 'the best chat show on radio'. By this time, Graham and I had been working together for 10 years. Saturdays with him were always a bit of a whirlwind and, unlike Paul and me, we didn't have much of a relationship away from Wogan House.

Although Paul and Graham were both gay comedians-come-presenter-writers, they couldn't have been more different. Naturally, there was a cultural and age difference, but I always felt Graham was the more ambitious of the two. Paul seldom told me he tuned in to the Saturday radio programme, but he always showed an interest in how I was getting on with Graham. Paul knew I loved producing the starry show. Not only was it broadcast live, but I also got to choose all the music and had free rein to book whomever I thought would make an interesting guest.

Wogan House during the pandemic could be unnerving and, as Graham broadcast at the weekend, there was even fewer people about, with no one in the main production office at all. Along with this, there were social distancing signs everywhere, and copious tubs of sanitary wipes placed all around the building. The infamously cramped lifts to the studios on the sixth floor were now designated only for one person at a time, and for many weeks the BBC insisted my assistant producer Flo had to work remotely at home.

Up on the sixth floor, Graham and I were also kept apart, with him in the studio and me around the corner in the green room, with our simple means of communication being a talk-back unit. With guests only available via glorified Zoom sessions, it was no way to make a radio show. But somehow we did. When I spoke to Paul about this arrangement he said, 'Don't expect to get any thanks from management.'

I've often been asked what it was like to produce the two huge stars in parallel. Graham, of course, was a major BBC name, his Friday night chat show being an important asset to BBC One. I always took great pleasure, though, in telling the big guests we had on the radio programme that *our* audience of some 4 million listeners was larger than that of his TV show. Paul, by comparison, had 1.7 million listeners every Sunday. Graham was also the presenter of Eurovision, having inherited the mantle from Sir Terry Wogan, and he was still associated with the successful talent shows that had discovered Jodie Prenger, Lee Mead, Jessie Buckley, Samantha Barks et al. As a result, while I was working with him, Graham Norton was one of the BBC's highest paid stars. When, in 2018, the Conservative government forced the Corporation to disclose the top salaries of 'talent' and executives, Graham was singled out, and the publication of his BBC earnings annoyed him. He told me he found the whole debate embarrassing. His agent had secured a lucrative deal for him at the Corporation, and Graham's need for privacy became one of the factors which would contribute to a major decision about the future of his radio show. While I believe his earnings should have remained private, I also thought he was worth every penny.

And I wasn't alone: guests would often tell me as they left the Radio 2 studio after their interview with him that there really wasn't anyone else in his league, and that was true.

Paul O'Grady, on the other hand, was a commercial television name. Admittedly, Lily had hosted *Blankety Blank*, and Paul had presented a handful of documentaries for the Corporation, but his biggest small-screen triumphs were over on ITV with the 'dog show'. It had also been ITV which had taken a gamble on employing him, and not Lily Savage, as the lynchpin of its new-look afternoon schedule. Paul always told me he felt more liberated at ITV and Channel 4, and I would suggest the programmes he made for both networks showed him at his best. That's not to say he didn't respect the values of the Corporation, but by 2020 he wasn't its biggest fan either. He had suffered some dreadful experiences on BBC TV shows and was quite happy to tell you about them if you had the time to listen. He loathed the seemingly endless layers of management and, in the case of Radio 2, the interfering 'content editors' who, he felt, knew nothing about his radio show. As Julian Clary told me, 'Paul was anti-authority, anti-management. He saw them as something to push against. He knew they could be ruthless people.'

To be fair, Paul's animosity towards senior managers wasn't just limited to those of the BBC. He would seldom have a good word to say about anyone in a management position, be it at the Corporation, Channels 4 or 5, or ITV. It's also important to note that he didn't dislike the people he was working *with*, just the ones he was working *for*. And he had a particular dislike for anyone who carried a clipboard and pen.

As summer 2020 approached, Radio 2 said goodbye to its latest boss, Lewis Carnie. Most of the staff were gutted to see him go, and so were many of the presenters, including Graham and Paul. Unlike some in BBC management, Lewis had a flair for spotting creative opportunities and then actually giving the production teams the space and freedom to deliver programmes. Personally, Lewis had always encouraged my endeavours, and he supported the shows I produced: it was because of him I got to launch new weekly programmes for Graham, Alan Carr and, of course, Paul.

I wasn't alone in thinking that Radio 2 was about to undergo more sweeping changes, especially as the focus now seemed to be on trying to find the elusive and, as far as the top management was concerned, all-important 'Mood Mums', those defined by the BBC as 'working-class, tight-for-money women, aged 35 to 44, who [are] time-poor, family orientated, and who put their children first'.

You can understand why Paul and I were worried.

We knew his audience on a Sunday was an important one. Throughout my time at the station, the Radio 2 weekend schedule was skewed a little differently from the rest of the week, with Sundays featuring what were known as 'specialist shows'. These included ones devoted to classical music, jazz, easy listening and musical theatre, and most were intended, in part, for older listeners. Paul and I began to realise those shows, along with ours, might be under threat.

As Graham Norton began his long summer break, Helen Thomas was appointed as the person who would run the UK's most listened-to station. I'd known Helen for years and we had often spent time discussing radio, and what we thought made it work. She had produced Chris Evans and, once he left the network, Helen later took up a role in management, eventually working alongside Lewis Carnie; I used to joke that Lewis was the 'show' in their partnership, while Helen was the 'business.' By the time she got the top job in June 2020, her appointment came as no surprise. But I was wary – Helen had thoroughly bought in to the BBC's mission to seek a younger audience for Radio 2, a plan I was somewhat dubious about. However, she assured me she valued Paul's programme.

With the end of Covid nowhere in sight, one of Helen's first Paul O'Grady-related decisions was to ask me to dig out some of his old 'specials' and repeat them. I had no objection, but I did think the umbrella title she chose – *Paul O'Grady Again* – was an uninspired one. Paul, though, was keen to have a presence on Sundays, even if it was in the form of a repeated programme. And so, in June of that year, from his home in Kent, he introduced his well-informed interview with legendary singer Barry Manilow from 2014, and another sensitive and considered conversation with *Britain's Got Talent* star Susan Boyle from 2011.

Using what felt like a piece of string and two tin cans, we managed to record a new introduction for each, Paul sounding like he was on a very poor telephone line – which, of course, he was. No money had been spent on this new way of working, but he was pleased to be back and so was his audience. For the next 5 weeks, we managed to cobble together more repeats: the Cilla Black documentary we'd made in

2003 received yet another airing, as did a *Lost TV* special featuring 2 hours of old theme tunes. There was also Paul's first – and last – *It's A Small World Special* featuring connected songs from around the world, the fiftieth anniversary *Crossroads* reunion, the tribute to the TV executive Sir Bill Cotton, and an in-depth interview with Dame Shirley Bassey.

By August, the BBC had finally found and despatched an old microphone and some headphones to Paul's home in Kent. With me in Surrey, we started to make new programmes for the first time in over 6 months, Paul explaining to his loyal listener he was broadcasting from his back bedroom with a tea towel over his head to make it sound more professional. It didn't, and interruptions from his barking dogs became a regular occurrence.

As the weeks went by, we got into a rhythm, and Paul encouraged me to contribute – and chuckle – more and more. We carried on with no feedback from anyone in BBC management; we had no idea if the show we were making was what they wanted, and just assumed they were simply pleased to have us back on air.

In September, Graham returned to his Radio 2 show after his summer break. We were still working in a socially distanced way and we hankered for the atmosphere we'd forged in the early days when travel reporter Bobbie Pryor was present in the studio, alongside agony aunt Maria McErlane. As we started that eleventh series, I was told Helen had agreed with Radio 2's head of music that his team would now pick all the music for the show. I was very unhappy about the decision; even my immediate line manager thought the change was a disappointing one. 'They'd better not try that with my show,' said Paul, and suggested to me that it was a 'daft idea' – he was right.

Listeners might be unaware that the likes of Zoë Ball, Jeremy Vine and Ken Bruce had very little input to their daytime playlists on Radio 2. Graham's programme, just like Paul's, had from day one featured a hand-built playlist and, for me, it was an integral part of my job. While Graham acknowledged my exasperation, he basically advised me to let it go. This confused me because, up to this point, he had always been on my side. And I soon discovered why his stance had changed.

The following Saturday, Graham called me into the studio to tell me he had decided to accept an offer from Virgin Radio. I was gutted but understood that after 10 years, he might want a change.

When I returned to my desk, a socially distanced colleague noted my paled expression and jokingly asked if someone had just died. It felt like someone had. Later that afternoon, I phoned Paul and shared the news. He consoled me and explained he wasn't surprised by Graham's decision.

And suggested we should jump ship as well.

Graham left Radio 2 in December 2020. A few weeks after his elegant and well-orchestrated exit, I received an impersonal text from Helen Thomas advising me to tune into that day's breakfast show to learn who his replacement was going to be. It was Claudia Winkleman, and she was going to be produced by an independent production company – not the BBC department I worked for.

In March 2021, the *Spectator* reviewed Claudia's first show, explaining that Radio 2 had booked the new presenter 'to focus on its target audience of "Mood Mums", but from the evidence of this show, the station doesn't regard them as very clever.'

Both Graham Norton and Paul O'Grady had contracts for a specific number of programmes per year. But unlike Graham, who saved up his 'holiday' to take it in one long block, Paul would intermittently be required to film overseas for his TV documentaries. As such, his breaks from Radio 2 were less structured and, in some years, he presented more shows than he was contracted to. Lewis Carnie had simply been happy to have him on air – if Paul wanted to do extra shows, that was fine.

Lewis's replacement had other ideas, however: Helen was sticking to what had been agreed upon and insisted Paul should take time off. And so, throughout 2021, listeners were faced with a confusing Sunday mishmash: Paul would be on air for a month, then Patrick Kielty sat in for a run of shows, then it was Paul again, then back to Patrick, until Paul returned once more.

Patrick was respectful of the format and wanted to do Paul justice, and I enjoyed working with him. Even so, listeners grumbled about Paul's erratic and prolonged absences, and many asked, 'Why can't he just pre-record his programme?' Radio 2 didn't seem to mind the complaints. It was almost as if they wanted to alienate Paul's audience. When I discreetly shared my thoughts with Patrick on how the BBC was treating Paul, he suggested something might be on the cards.

Sadly, he was right.

When Paul was on air during 2021, he was still broadcasting from his home. The physical distance between us actually brought us closer and we really did have a laugh together. And that camaraderie was evident on air. A typical example was when he mistakenly introduced that week's 'Classy Classical Choice' by Edvard Grieg as 'Morning Wood' instead of 'Morning Mood'. My hysterical laughter was genuine. During another show, he left me high and dry while he went to the gate at the end of his drive to let a courier in. And his location in Kent meant there were regular interruptions from low-flying aircraft that had taken off from the local airport in Lydd. 'I'm just turning on the landing lights in the garden, Malcolm.' When he queried one week if I'd ever been on a murder-mystery weekend, I asked him if working with him every Sunday counted. Our on-air partnership flourished and, during this period, we produced some of our favourite programmes. Not once during this run of socially distanced shows did we receive any feedback from anyone at the BBC; once again, we thought their silence meant management was happy.

In the summer of 2021, Radio 2 contacted Joan Marshrons to discuss a new contract for Paul. What was proposed came as a huge shock. Instead of a new 2-year deal to continue the show, Paul was offered a 1-year contract for just 26 programmes in two blocks of 13 each. He would normally present over 40 editions of TeamPOG a year.

Joan phoned me. We were both flabbergasted. And when Joan broke the news to Paul, he too was shocked. He phoned me. 'Fuck 'em, Malcolm. We'll just do the first thirteen and then we'll bugger off.' I'd never known him be so angry – which was saying something. Joan and I kept Paul's reaction between ourselves.

Radio 2 insisted Paul couldn't mention the new arrangement to the outside world. He complied. That changed when the BBC's press office prepared a draft release which announced the comedian Rob Beckett would be joining Radio 2 to 'save Sundays'. When Paul was told, he hit the roof: '"Save" Sundays?!? How dare they say that!' he bellowed down the phone to me. I was equally insulted by the proposed wording, and I couldn't believe how disrespectful the messaging and optics were. Our listening figures were robust and, while other parts of the new Radio 2 schedule needed help, Sunday afternoons between 5 and 7 did not.

This time Joan did inform the BBC that Paul wasn't happy, and he received an email apologising for the insensitive use of words. Radio 2's boss even volunteered to visit Paul at his home in Kent. It was an offer he declined. A rewritten press release was published. When the news of Paul and Rob's new job share finally went public it went down, to use Paul's words, like 'a bucket of cold sick'.

As 2021 drew to an end, Paul and I motored on with the first block of 13 shows, with me believing they would be our last. Three months later, on 13 February 2022, Paul posted a message on his Instagram account explaining, 'It's my last Radio 2 Sunday show for quite some time, our listening figures have shot up, so a great big thank you to everyone who listens. While I'm on the subject I would also like to thank my producer (sounds very grand) Malcolm Prince who is one of the best in the business and hasn't cracked once in the 14 years we've been on air. There's a new regime now, I do 13 weeks on and then 13 off, which is nothing to do with me as it's a management decision. So, all being well, and providing I'm not in India or Borneo, travel restrictions permitting, I should be back sometime in May.'

Although the BBC hadn't registered it, the clues were there that he had little intention of coming back at all.

Paul and I didn't know Rob Beckett. Gaby Roslin, Paul's longtime friend, reassured him that Rob was a fine man, something we never doubted, and Paul even encouraged his listeners to welcome their new Sunday afternoon host. The *Daily Express* wrote, 'What on earth possessed [Radio 2's] bosses to shift Paul O'Grady off ... in favour of Rob Beckett? ... Regular listeners are now talking about boycotting him. O'Grady and his producer Malcolm Prince are radio's greatest current double act. While the former's health sometimes means the show requires stand-ins, this bears all the hallmarks of another pointless tinkering. It succeeds only in alienating an existing audience, while doing Beckett no favours either.' The journalist wasn't wrong.

The BBC issued a statement explaining that, despite Paul's valued presence on the show, plans 'do evolve over time ... Paul is much-loved by many of our listeners, and whilst we're making this change to Sunday afternoons, he very much remains a firm favourite here in Wogan House ... Rather than have a range of deputies host the show throughout the year, we'll now have Rob Beckett on Sunday afternoons with his own series, alternating with Paul's.'

What that BBC announcement didn't mention was that Paul was only contracted for 2022, and there was nothing on the cards for 2023.

As Rob Beckett settled into his new slot in February 2022, Paul went on holiday and I took a break. Away from the routine of making weekly radio, I decided it was time to leave the BBC altogether. Radio 2 was becoming less ambitious, and as the station began to focus more on plundering Auntie's audio archives, the money for the carefully crafted programmes I used to make apparently no longer existed. I was also missing Graham's show. Now in my fifties, I noted many of my colleagues were all much younger – and cheaper. During a staff Zoom meeting, yet another editor told the assembled producers – all of whom were in their 40s and 50s: 'Let's be honest, none of you here will be asked to produce a daily strand like *Breakfast*, Ken Bruce or *Drivetime*.' It felt as if ageism at Radio 2 was rife.

Remembering something which Graham had once said to me about taking voluntary redundancy at the BBC – 'It's a chance in a lifetime to receive money for doing nothing' – I wrote to my head of department saying I was interested. As the Corporation was regularly trying to make redundancies and save money, my show of hand was accepted immediately – my boss never questioned it, nor did she raise the issue of who could work with Paul after I'd left.

When I told Joan I would be leaving the BBC in September 2022 she replied, 'You know he won't stick around without you, don't you?'

Paul said the same thing to me. But a few weeks after we had discussed my exit, he called to ask if I would consider doing the final block of 13 shows after all. He had changed his mind about not coming back after his break, as he felt we owed it to the fans. It also meant he could honour his contract, something he was extremely concerned about. 'Don't worry, Malcolm, I'm still going to leave when you do, but let's do the last thirteen.' As I was still employed by the BBC for a few more months, I began to prepare the programmes.

The final TeamPOG programme rapidly approached and, days before it was broadcast, Paul formally handed in his notice. He was true to his word; he wasn't going to stay at Radio 2 without me. Looking back now, Paul and I had probably given BBC management exactly what they wanted, but it did feel like a mixture of constructive dismissal and ageism.

Two days later, Radio 2 posted on social media that it was, 'sad to say that after 14 years on Sunday afternoons, Paul O'Grady has decided to leave Radio 2. We wish Paul the very best of luck and hope to work with him again in the future.' His listeners weren't impressed and the response to that post on Twitter (as was) was scathing. One wrote, 'You pushed him out,' while another suggested, 'Radio 2 has lost [its] focus, and you are fast losing your audience,' and another summed up the news with, '[It's] madness by the management.' Unlike Graham Norton, Paul O'Grady's exit from the BBC was turning out to be anything but graceful. The press noted that Paul was part of a group of presenters who had recently left the station – either by force or by choice – including Simon Mayo, Don Black, Clare Teal, Jools Holland, Bill Kenwright and Craig Charles, causing the *Daily Telegraph* to write that 'Radio 2 has a death wish'.

In a post on his own Instagram account, Paul clarified his decision, saying, 'The reason I'm leaving is because I wasn't really happy with the 13 weeks on, 13 weeks off business.' He added: 'Thanks very much and good luck to everyone on Radio 2 and long may it continue.' He would later tell the press, 'I'm a great believer in continuity. If you go off for 13 weeks and somebody else comes on, the listeners don't know when you're back … [They're] trying to aim for a much younger audience, which doesn't make sense because you've got Radio 1. Radio 2 was always for an older audience.' In March 2023, the *Guardian* wrote: 'The fact that O'Grady resigned after being asked to share his slot with comedian Rob Beckett – in his 30s, more given to playing Blur and Dua Lipa, less inclined to discuss dead pets or thank a grand-daughter – tells you rather more about Radio 2's ageism-with-impunity, its desire to skew its audience younger, than the departure of Ken Bruce [who announced his own departure in January]. Frankly, it was their loss.'

'I could not believe it when I heard Paul was leaving Radio 2', remembers his friend Jayne Tunnicliffe. 'Asking him to share the Sunday spot with Rob Beckett must have been such a slap in the face for Paul. Imagine someone saying, "We love you and we love what you do, but we'd like to hear less from you." The move by Radio 2 was unforgivable and definitely ageist. And it turned into such a disastrous decision because had Paul been allowed to continue the show with Malcolm, he might have still been with us today.'

Jo Brand believes, 'You could say the BBC's decision to reduce Paul's contract was under the umbrella of ageism, but they were aware that his audience was aging too, and people who work in radio who have any power always think they need to offer something new that might attract another raft of young listeners. I think that humiliation happens to most older performers in the end, there isn't much you can do about it. I wouldn't have let him go, but he was in good company. But just sitting another comedian who is very popular on social media in the chair of a show doesn't necessarily mean that it's going to work.' Speaking in 2025, Graham Norton told me, 'It was interesting, at the time people were trying to say it was ageism – because there's still loads of old people in that building! No, I wasn't surprised he left Radio 2. Paul threatened to leave every week, so finally somebody called his bluff.'

Graham Norton is right. I can't tell you the exact number of times Paul said he was going to quit the show, usually citing a lack of interest from the BBC. But, as I have since learnt, Paul only ranted about things he cared for. I remember when the station's then controller, Bob Shennan, received a particularly dramatic resignation email, in which Paul explained he wouldn't be returning to the airwaves after his summer holiday. I was summoned up to Bob's office. A sincere reply was prepared, urging him to reconsider, and when Paul received it he was extremely flattered to read that Bob regarded Paul O'Grady's programme as a 'jewel in the crown of Radio 2'. Paul promptly withdrew his resignation.

For me, 10 years later, it was bizarre to think that under new management, the network's valued gem had become nothing more than a disposable bauble.

Sangeeta Bhabra suggests: 'The decision to let him go showed that they had forgotten that Paul had a genuine relationship with his audience. And because of his emotional maturity and empathy, he realised that a lot of them were on their own, they were isolated, they needed his show.' This was especially true during the pandemic.

For fellow listener Jonathan Harvey, it wasn't just about his older listeners: 'Paul was an expert at gabbing away to his heart's content, so his show was a pleasure to listen to. But for the audience I think it was an intimate thing … we felt he was our best mate talking to just us.' Alan Carr agrees: 'I was saddened when Paul O'Grady lost his Radio 2 show, it was such a unique programme full of idiosyncrasies and "Paulisms", and a real mixed bag in a good way – you didn't know what was going to happen next! Paul made radio look and sound effortless, he made you feel that he was there with you in the room, a confidante, a companion, and that is a rare quality these days. It wasn't cookie-cutter radio; it was unique, and it felt special.'

We pre-recorded our final Radio 2 show. As always, the programme had the regular features which had proved so popular, including one last 'Muck in A Bucket' recipe for a Hawaiian-style cocktail, and Paul paid tribute to one final batch of listeners' pets that had recently died. After playing 'Friends' by Bette Midler, he signed off, thanked me, then asked his listeners to, 'Look after yourselves, stay safe and well. Ter-ra everyone.'

And that was that.

A few days after the broadcast, fellow presenter Vanessa Feltz quit Radio 2. The two events were unrelated but in her memoir, *Vanessa Feltz Bares All*, she explained Paul's exit was a bit of a wake-up call for her, stating that he was a 'beloved and irreplaceable … radio genius. The decision was ludicrous.' Russell T Davies agrees: 'The surprising thing is, if you wanted a diversity hire – which we do – he ticked all the boxes: he was outwardly gay … he appealed to the working class, pet owners, older listeners, everyone … it was the longest list in the world. That's what mystified me. He ticked more boxes than anyone else. It was dreadful how they treated him. I do work for the BBC and it's staggering, I just don't know how it happens.'

The final TeamPOG programme was broadcast on 14 August 2022. Afterwards, my husband and I threw a small party at our home in Kent to mark the end of an era. As we raised a glass, my phone rang. It was my dear pal, Steve Wright.

'Wrighty' and I had known each other for years. We had worked together on some big-name documentaries, and for a time I had been his executive producer. We would also sometimes travel to and from work together. I treasure memories of those journeys, during which we discussed radio, what was happening in the world of show business, and the latest moves and errors made by the Corporation we both loved.

Steve also greatly admired Paul, who had regularly appeared as a guest on what most people knew as *The Big Show*. And when we had to record an edition of Paul's Sunday programme during the week, Paul would stay around afterwards to chat to Steve about the latest goings on at Radio 2 – a subject that never failed to fascinate them both. They respected each other – one hugely successful on stage and screen, the other radio royalty. Their conversations would sometimes go on so long, I'd just leave them to it.

But on this evening, Steve's call was an unexpected one. He congratulated me on the final TeamPOG programme and acknowledged the work which had gone into making Paul's show the success it was. For the next hour or so, we discussed his thoughts on the sweeping changes at Radio 2, which included the end of his own afternoon programme: a few weeks before, it had been announced that his long-running and hugely popular show would be finishing at the end of September. Publicly, Steve thanked the BBC, explaining, when the end of his 'big show' was announced, that the head of Radio 2 had told him she wanted to do 'something different' in his slot, a decision he graciously accepted. But, privately, the diktat to end the high-profile programme after some 23 years broke Steve, and during our call he kept on saying, 'I just don't get it, Malcolm, we haven't done anything wrong, have we?'

To hear Wrighty sound so despondent saddened me. He was a radio hero of mine. I reminded him that his own programmes, and the way he approached and created them, had inspired me in the way I produced those of Graham and Paul. He asked me to send his love to Paul and we bade farewell.

In the 2024 New Year's Honours, Steve Wright was made an MBE. He died just 7 weeks later.

Terry Wogan once shared some pearls of wisdom about what made a great radio programme: 'You have to create this little club. We're not talking to an audience. You're talking to one person and they're only half listening.' And those wise words applied to the shows presented by Steve Wright and that of TeamPOG. Paul's programme wasn't the biggest show on radio, but for his listener it was an important one and it had a loyal audience, in the main because Paul was so relatable. As radio executive David Lloyd observed, 'When Paul reached for stories, he did so from a normal listener's world – a world of aunties and uncles and bay-fronted semis, not headphones, mixing desks and VIP red carpets … His show was targeted perfectly at the audience he sought to attract.'

As soon as Paul had decided he was going to leave the BBC, in the summer of 2022, we contacted Lewis Carnie to see what he thought our next steps should be. He had contacts with Global – a huge group of media companies that included some of the most popular radio stations in the UK, including Heart FM, Capital UK, LBC, Classic FM and Smooth Radio. He kindly set up a meeting with Global's chief broadcasting and content officer, James Rea, which Paul, Joan and Lewis attended. I couldn't go as I was still working out my notice from the BBC. The meeting, I was told, went very well and Paul left the Global headquarters in Leicester Square telling the receptionist, 'You'll be seeing a lot more of me!'

Once I was free of the BBC, Joan and I went in for another meeting, this time with two other executives of Smooth Radio. To say it went badly was an understatement. I've never witnessed such apathy; they didn't even try to make us feel welcome. We were told we would have to deliver a pilot to hear what Paul sounded like on air – a strange request, given he'd been broadcasting successfully on Radio 2 for 14 years. I pointed out that their equivalent Sunday programme featured a presenter who spoke for approximately 4 minutes in each *hour*, and that Paul's first opening link could often last that long. It was quite clear that the Smooth execs weren't interested in having Paul on their network. Adding insult to injury, when Joan and I were finally escorted out of the building it was via the back door.

Paul O'Grady wouldn't be joining Global.

In November 2022, three months after his last BBC show, Paul was interviewed by the local press in Bristol. One reporter asked if he missed doing the radio programme. Paul admitted it was now strange not having his Sunday show: 'I still get approached by former radio listeners who miss it being a part of their weekends … and I do miss it, to tell you the truth. It was really good fun to do together, me and Malcolm.'

A few days after that disastrous meeting with Smooth, Joan and I had tea with Paul at his house in Kent where we discussed our options. Paul wanted another home for his radio show. We agreed it was time to find some new digs.

18.

A Country Life

'I'm a city rat turned country mouse'
Paul O'Grady

For Paul, home was everything. And Kent, where he lived for almost 25 years, encouraged him to retune his life. He said it 'soothed the soul' and brought a sense of peace that he couldn't find anywhere else. 'It's in the quiet moments, surrounded by the tranquillity of the countryside, that I find my greatest inspiration.'

As is sometimes said, necessity is the mother of invention, and when foreign travel became almost impossible during the Covid pandemic in 2020, Paul's adopted county became the subject of a beguiling television series called *Paul O'Grady's Great British Escape*. And it proved to be a ratings winner. Promoting the ITV series, he explained, 'I was getting a bit sick of Kent's reputation for lorry parks, the M20 and Operation Stack … it's such a beautiful county and I think it's getting overlooked. [It's still] the Garden of England … and I've lived here over 20 years now and I absolutely love it.' As Sangeeta

Bhabra notes, 'That was the kind of publicity the Kent Tourist Board could never have afforded. He was so proud of his adopted county, and he realised the lovely spot he ended up in was a privileged place to be. It was where he could be himself, but it wasn't a retreat; he was part of a community.'

Like Paul before me, the county I now call home isn't where I grew up: I moved to Kent from Surrey in 2022. I now live in Sandgate, a little village on the coast overlooking the English Channel. On a clear day, you can see the white cliffs of Calais – yes, they have some too. It's a beautiful part of the world and minutes from Paul's home in Aldington, near Ashford. I should put on record it wasn't planned; it just happened my friend was living down the road. He was delighted when I told him we were relocating: 'Oh, I'll pop round and bring the dogs with me.'

Paul treasured Kent; and why and how he ended up living in the county involves Enid Blyton, Pippi Longstocking and Bilbo Baggins – typical O'Grady! What connects those three names are *stories*, all of which depicted the countryside, admittedly idealised and fictionalised; but it was the promise of a quieter, slower and idyllic existence, combined with the possibility of countless adventures, that attracted a young Paul O'Grady to a life in the country. For years, he had fantasised about living in a crumbling old farmhouse, inhabited by a few animals and a pack of dogs, surrounded by woods and wildlife. And, eventually, his dream came true.

Growing up, Paul enjoyed the annual visits to his father's family in Ireland who, back then, lived in County Roscommon. He embraced the rural life on his Uncle James and Aunty Bridget's farm, and those early memories – encountering cows and cowpats – stayed with him for the rest of his life. Reading his account of those times in his books genuinely does sound like an Enid Blyton story – all that's missing were the lashings of ginger beer.

Thirty or so years later, with the success and wealth that had come with Lily Savage, Paul was able to recreate those idyllic and exciting times once again. A chance visit to Kent with Brendan Murphy encouraged Paul to find a property, away from close neighbours, where he could 'play his music as loud as he liked'. He later wrote that he had, 'this fancy to wake up to green fields, fresh air and birdsong and not the racket that comes with living in central London'.

The five-bedroomed house he eventually bought in Kent in 1999 was almost everything he'd ever hoped for. It was Brendan who discovered the idyll while Paul was in Manchester playing Miss Hannigan in the musical *Annie*. Encouraged by his friend Janet Street-Porter, Paul put in an offer sight-unseen. The house had been on the market for some time and its then current owner, the comedian Vic Reeves, happily accepted Paul's offer. But despite being a successful entertainer, Paul struggled to find a mortgage. His bank advised him to put up a guarantor, which he did, asking Elton John and Ian McKellen. 'There you go, a multimillionaire global pop star and a knight of the realm – stick that up your arse!' he later said.

Paul O'Grady never did anything by halves.

He fell in love with Knoll Hill House a few months later when he saw it in person. The property had a commanding position: Aldington Knoll was one of a chain of viewpoints used for the Anglo-French Survey, which linked the Royal Greenwich Observatory with the French equivalent in Paris.

According to its new owner, Paul's house itself wasn't what you'd call 'grand' or 'elegant', instead it was unassumingly comfortable. 'The first time I visited,' recalls Jayne Tunnicliffe, 'Paul was in the garden wearing shorts, fag in hand, twigs in his hair too, telling me to "Mind that dog poo" and showing me "his woods"! He seemed so at peace and happy and proud of how far he'd come.'

Spread over 52 acres, the press later described his home as a 'farm', but Paul would usually refer to it more accurately as a 'smallholding'. He would go on to spend two decades turning the property into a flourishing natural environment, planting a wildflower meadow, coppicing the woods and buying a patch of land nearby for his sheep – the latter was a clever move because it also prevented the area from being turned into a possible and unwelcome site for motorbike scrambling and outdoor paintballing.

Prior to his move to Kent, Paul had lived in a succession of 'dumps', as he called them, including 'Vicky Mansions' which was a period block of flats on South Lambeth Road in London. After his career began to take off, he had bought 'a little house near Tower Bridge out of Lily Savage's immoral earnings' which had taken a year to renovate, and which soon became just as cluttered with 'junk' as his previous rented homes. By comparison, his Kent residence was no hovel – it included a swimming pool, a small orchard and unrivalled views of Romney Marsh, down towards Dymchurch and the

English Channel. But even with all that space, as Brenda Gilhooly observed, 'Paul simply brought Vicky Mansions to Kent, along with all the funny knick-knacks, Disney memorabilia, all his quirky clutter; it was all over the place.'

'I took Abel there, who was just 2 weeks old,' explains Sharyn Mousley. 'Knoll Hill House was such an important place for us and the family. We have so many happy memories of summers there, parties with him, it was a happy place. At first, we used to stay in the Blue Room, and you'd wake up and see the bunny rabbits outside. He filled the house with everything for my children, he ordered highchairs and bought a *Thomas the Tank Engine* bed for Abel. Dad was over the moon with the kids. He would do so many things for us but never made a big deal out of it, he was dead blasé about it, but inside I knew he was just made up. And when Abel and Halo were older, he built us [a] cottage and Dad was so excited with how it was progressing, he kept sending me pictures and, when we got there, he had decorated it with fairy lights.'

Sharyn's husband, Phil, remembers that his father-in-law had always wanted such a place: 'He said that if we as a family were going to visit him more often, he'd build one for us, which he did. It had a wood burner in it, a small kitchen, underfloor heating, a nice bathroom; he really splashed out on it. And upstairs, the galleried bedroom was just magical. He would come over from the main house and he'd just be sitting there, talking to his grandchildren, reading them a book, and he was happy for me to see him doing that. I think that was when he was happiest.'

Paul filled the cottage with ornate wooden carvings. He painted small front doors to the homes of fairies who he explained also lived there. Halo – whom Paul often called 'Hailstones' or 'Minnie', after Mickey Mouse's girlfriend – recalls her grandfather 'decorated the walls next to my bed with all sorts of stuff Abel and I would like. There were pictures of the orangutans he'd fostered for us whom he'd met when filming abroad. There were also paintings of little mice which he knew I loved when I was small, a clock, and there was hand-painted lavender all the way up the wall by the stairs.' Paul would continue to add further decorations each time his family came to stay in the whimsical building. Jayne Tunnicliffe encouraged him to make a cabinet of curiosities, which was on a wall downstairs. This delightful piece, which Paul made during the pandemic, was 'filled with all manner of junk found in drawers knocking about the gaff,' including a small ornament of Disney's Snow White, a petite pair of porcelain Dutch clogs, a tiny poster advertising the delights of Folkestone, and a miniature Punch and Judy theatre.

The cottage was pure Paul: the property had his DNA running through it, a physical embodiment of the affection he held for his family.

According to his friend Moira Stewart, the cottage also had another function: 'It was to give Paul space because Knoll Hill House itself wasn't really a great place for having guests as it was hard to get away from them. So, the cottage solved that problem too.' This wasn't missed by Sharyn, either. 'Dad liked to get away to his bedroom and shut the door. We got used to that after a while. When I first took Phil to meet my dad, Paul stayed in his room upstairs, and then he'd come down and take us to an antique shop in Hythe. But a lot of the time, Dad would sit with us; it just depended on who was in the house, really. We understood his behaviour, though, because if you're constantly performing it was exhausting, and he just wanted peace and quiet.' Sharyn continues, 'When the house was full, though, like when Julian Clary had a birthday party there, the house had so much life in it. Dad just thrived on it. They were really special times.'

Paul once told me he had invited a soap actor and his partner to spend a weekend with him in Kent. But when his guests arrived, he thought the better of it and stayed upstairs hidden away for two days until they left.

Escape rooms aside, Knoll Hill House was a welcoming residence and it suited Paul down to the ground. And when he was in the mood 'he was a great host', remembers Brenda Gilhooly. 'Just like when he was on stage he had a natural, effervescent personality, and as host he wanted people to have a good time. He would always have a story to share, and he'd make sure you always had a drink – he was brilliant like that.'

When guests visited his home, if they had to use the loo, they would be shown to a bright room on the ground floor with an old wooden-seated toilet at the far end. On the walls of said room were posters from Paul's stage career. There was one of him as the Child Catcher in *Chitty, Chitty, Bang, Bang*, an image it must be said that traumatised many children, including Halo. There was also another as Lily, the star of *Prisoner Cell Block H: The Musical*. In other rooms, there were select mementoes and awards from his career on display, but it wasn't a museum to his achievements.

Paul's home would go on to feature in his television and radio shows, with film crews, photographers and journalists often visiting the property over the following years. As Sangeeta Bhabra remembers from one of her times there, 'The house itself felt very homely, it wasn't show-offy.' Sangeeta's first visit was accompanied by a crew from *ITV News Meridian*. 'It was such a big deal, I mean, who lets you go to their home for a TV interview? Knoll Hill House was really about the animals and making sure they were in a lovely place. When he opened the fridge, he had so many different types of milk for all his animals – he even had milk for the alpacas!' For a man who enjoyed his privacy, he wasn't shy of sharing his home.

Paul delighted in regaling his guests with stories about the property's history. He explained to René and me that Noel Coward used to visit Knoll Hill House, as Goldenhurst Farm, Coward's own home, was just down the road – it was later acquired by Julian Clary. Speaking to me in 2024, Julian recalled, 'I told [Paul] I was thinking of buying somewhere to escape to. He told me about Goldenhurst and as soon as he mentioned Noel Coward I was gripped because I loved him; I grew up in Teddington where Coward was born. So, I went down to Kent to look at the property with Savage. The owner lit the fire and left us to it, and we just sat by the fire and Paul said, "Ooh, can't you just imagine sitting here and having a nice think?" And I thought, "Yes, I can." I sort of knew, as you do, straightaway that I was going to buy it, and it did amuse me that Paul was up the hill.'

'Paul felt so blessed to have his house,' says Moira. 'It had all these little bits of fun. In one of the bedrooms, there was a bookcase that opened revealing a wardrobe behind it – very *Harry Potter*. It was pure him.'

Paul's home was where he could play, and he wasn't the only one, as his good friend Amanda Mealing recalls. 'He was just a giant child in the eyes of my boys. He had access to ice creams and sweets, the remote control, the animals; having that freedom to do whatever was really important.' When Amanda asked Paul to be godparent to one of her sons in 1999, 'it was one of the first times I had ever known Savage to shed a tear,' she remembers. 'Not cry, but he choked up and said, "No one's ever asked me before." And once he agreed, some people around me queried if it was right for a drag queen to have that role. But for me, there was no question about who would imbue my son with the best perspective, attitude, and ethics … Like me, he was old-fashioned, working class, and he knew what it was like to graft. Savage was always present in the lives of my sons. My two boys look like opposing sides of the same coin: Milo has a blonde afro and very white skin like my mother, while Otis is more my colouring and [has] a tighter afro curl. So, they grew up not looking like anyone else. As a child you just want to fit in. And having Savage in their lives, they understood it was OK to be different.'

His grandchildren also have happy memories of time spent playing with their grandfather. 'GanGan would bring us down to the lavender field at his home in Kent to play,' explains Halo. 'There was loads of stuff down there and Abel and I would search for all the little gargoyles that were everywhere.' Halo would also write stories, which Paul would read and tell her what he thought and then, 'I'd go back and rewrite it. GanGan loved to play with us.' Abel recalls the fun that was had in his grandfather's pool. 'We'd go swimming with him. He often got in the pool with me and Halo, and he'd chase her pretending to be an alligator, or he'd help me when I couldn't go into the deep end. And if he didn't want to go in at all, he'd be there with the hose spraying us with cold water. But he always made an effort.'

Paul also liked to draw – he was an accomplished illustrator. One of the first posts he made on his Instagram account was his drawing of Kaa the snake from *The Jungle Book*, and both Abel and Halo treasure the pictures he drew for them of favourite Disney characters including Snow White, Dumbo, Thumper and Cruella de Vil. Abel and Halo's dad Phil explains that when Paul spent time with his grandchildren, 'he didn't have a care in the world'.

For Vanessa White, who worked with Paul on the ITV series *Paul O'Grady's Great British Escape*, Kent was his sanctuary. 'And it probably saved his life because if he'd stayed living in London, partying every night, he might not have survived for as long as he did.' Moira remembers: 'He would walk through the door, say "Hi" to the dogs, sit on the sofa [and] then usually make himself a slice of toast and marmalade with a cup of tea, and then watch *The Avengers* on TV. The house had the clutter of creativity, but he knew where everything was. He could just potter there, and pottering is fundamental to creativity.' Joan Marshrons agrees: 'He loved being able to walk around in his pyjamas or sitting out in the summer house painting a watercolour.' Moira continues, 'He always had something different on the go that would tweak his imagination. He would then have a burst of activity doing things, making cakes, being a country boy; and then he would get bored and would need to go back out into the world.'

'And that was the problem,' confides Joan. 'Looking after him was a bloody nightmare. It was endless, worrying about him. Partly because of his heart and partly because I knew he got lonely, especially after Brendan died. And it was always trying to pre-empt that, and make sure he was OK. There was a small group of [his friends] who would always make sure one of us was with him at weekends and I would check with everybody, especially if I knew Savage was going to be on his own. I'd say to Moira, Vera, Chad [Rogers, who had worked on many of Paul's television shows and whom Paul had taken under his wing], "What are you doing this weekend, do you fancy going down to Kent?" And we would rotate and make sure Savage was never there on his own because, although he loved it, he needed people to bounce off and he needed an audience.'

As with everything about Paul, it wasn't all black and white. While he appreciated the peace and tranquillity of Kent, he also regularly complained about Aldington being the back of beyond, with 'weather that was like something you'd witness in an Ingmar Bergman film' – grey skies and non-stop rain – muddy fields and equally muddy dogs, and a kitchen that sometimes had a whiff of 'eau de pooch' about it.

It goes without saying that Paul O'Grady loved animals, but he couldn't stand rodents; he once said he would rather be in a room with a couple of tigers than a mouse or a rat. 'They're wily buggers, Malcolm, just like BBC management.' He claimed that his greatest fear was to find a rat swimming in his loo. Thankfully, to my knowledge, that never happened, but during lockdown he did tell his radio listeners that he had discovered a cheeky rabbit in the toilet bowl one morning.

I often thought if he left show business, Paul would have made an excellent tour guide. When I moved to Kent, he phoned me with recommendations of places to visit, what shops to try on Hythe's high street, and where to buy the best fish and chips and fresh fish. 'There's a marvellous place where I get my kippers. Rick Stein devotes a whole chapter to Hythe in his cookery book, I'll send you a copy.' He was keen to point out that Folkestone's art scene was burgeoning: 'Go and have a look at some of the triennial installations around the town,' and that H.G. Wells had lived in and written about the village of Sandgate where I now called home. It wasn't all Judith Chalmers, though: he warned me of the challenges of finding a decent dentist, the ever-increasing number of 'craters' (potholes), and the ongoing problems with his nemesis – the M20. He also explained I'd have trouble using a mobile phone as finding a signal was always difficult, and while he loved the local wildlife, especially the bees and butterflies, he wasn't a fan of the increasing numbers of wasps and mosquitos: 'They're the most irritating bugs ever created,' he'd say. He was also wary of the fungi he discovered in the woods and fields near his house – 'I don't have the knowledge or skill to identify the edible from the deadly' – but he did seem to be an expert in another countryside topic: how to deal with moths. My husband has a phobia about them, and Paul eagerly discussed and shared the best methods of deterrent with him.

Seeing Paul at home in Kent was fascinating for me; it might sound a bit hackneyed, but when he was mooching around Knoll Hill House, he was a very different person to the one I worked with. At Radio 2, the man I usually encountered there could be volatile, restless and attention-seeking. He'd walk into the messy, noisy, open-plan office, often moaning about his journey into work, or complaining about someone who'd asked for a selfie outside but who didn't know how to use the camera on their phone. He would declare 'I'm like a coiled spring, Malcolm!' as he settled into the chair next to my desk. And while his bluster was never directed at me, I would tread carefully. I was always keen to get him up to the studio as soon as I could, as his outbursts, though funny, were a distraction for the other production teams working there. I'd be quick to get him a cup of tea – white, two sugars – and settle him into the presenter's chair in the studio and I was often anxious to get started, in case he wound himself up so much that he decided to walk out.

Looking back now, I do regret not taking more notice of what might have been irritating him so much, but I was there to work. My job, as far as the BBC was concerned, was to do anything and everything to make Mr O'Grady happy, but, ultimately, we had a show to produce for his listener at home – even if he was in a bad mood.

But that sometimes frenzied and erratic Paul O'Grady wasn't the man I saw in Kent. 'When I am not working, I'm quite lazy,' he'd say. Gone were the three-piece suits he wore on the telly; instead, he would simply don a pair of chinos and a comfy sweater. 'After a few days down here, Malcolm, I end up looking like Catweazle.'

Speaking with his friends after his death in 2023, I was comforted by the knowledge that Paul's house was – for the first few years he lived there, at least – a very happy place, and the get-togethers and revelries were a thing of legend. For Julian Clary: 'His parties were not for the faint-hearted. A sort of high-end carnage.' I can't tell you the number of his pals who told me their version of how Vera tumbled on the fire in the garden, leaving Paul in hysterics. Poor old Vera – she was fine, by the way. And dancing around the large kitchen table also seems to have been a regular activity, often to tunes from *Gypsy*. Julian remembers it with affection. 'His kitchen was where he held court. We would have dinner parties and Paul would stand near his Aga and perform. I recall that one night he got these cassette tapes of his early drag act The Playgirls, and he did the whole show. It was like an hour-long cabaret.' Sharyn agrees, 'The kitchen was a very special part of the house for Paul. I can still see him, coming in with his dressing gown on, his hair a mess, and making his Weetabix. He was happiest when we were all in our pyjamas, just sitting there, Sean [Paul's loyal and long-serving handyman] would bring in the newspapers, my dad would turn the radio on, and he'd just look through the papers in his kitchen.'

Phil Mousley also has fond memories of spending other times at Knoll Hill House: 'Christmases were fabulous.' I know, I was surprised to hear this as well, considering how often Paul moaned about the dreaded 'C' word. But if he wasn't working in pantomime, Paul would surround himself with family and friends at that time of year. He would put up a tree, hang some fairy lights and distribute gifts.

Having said that, one of my favourite seasonal O'Grady quotes is the jolly: 'I'd rather do community service than sit and write a load of Christmas cards,' so if, like me, you were lucky enough to receive one from him, it felt as though you were privileged.

Paul objected to the commercialisation of Christmas and how it started far too early. For as long as I knew him, it continued to be a thorn in his side. I would often include an email from a listener on Paul's Sunday radio show which mentioned the fast-approaching season of good will, and Paul would feign disgust. I'd then play a snippet of 'It's Beginning To Look a Lot Like Christmas', which would push him over the edge, especially as this would all be happening in the middle of August.

Phil continues: 'Christmas, though, could be a bit fraught down there in Kent – because you didn't know which Paul you were going to get on the day: he could be good tempered or in a bad mood – the more visits we had, the more relaxed he got with us. They were great times.' Easter was celebrated too, and Paul would hide chocolate eggs in the garden and then scare his grandchildren dressed up as a giant bunny.

As well as entertaining, Paul also had an interest in local fairies (stop sniggering, please). In the 1901 story by H.G. Wells, 'Mr Skelmersdale in Fairyland', the reader discovers that Knoll Hill is endowed with magical qualities, something which fascinated Paul. On my first visit to his home, he directed my attention to the knoll and explained it was believed to be the burial site of a giant and his sword, both of which were, he said, protected by murderous ghouls who would kill anyone attempting to flatten the area. His property was, according to him, a place where 'the little people' could be found if you looked hard enough, especially by the gnarled hawthorn tree in the nearby field. Such stories all stemmed from Paul's fascination with pagan rituals, old traditions and superstitions, and he took it all very seriously. He explained in his book *Paul O'Grady's Country Life* published in 2017: 'I grew up with it, having a mother and two aunts who could've given a very realistic performance as the three ladies in the Scottish play.' He was an expert on everything, from white rabbits and broken mirrors to horseshoes and whistling in a dressing room.

As Moira observes, 'He had a kind of magical view of the world and nature, and as far as he was concerned, the Borrowers *were* under the floorboards; he still maintained all that childhood sense of wonder.'

Paul found trees and the nearby woods therapeutic and calming, and taking a walk in the seemingly endless grounds of Knoll Hill with his dogs would allow him to relax and clear his mind. Sadly, as his health declined, the property essentially shrank in size for him, and the long walks became fewer. But he continued to appreciate two ancient majestic oak trees at the bottom of his field and often spoke of the magnolia he had planted when he moved in in 1999. It had become what he called, 'a ridiculously beautiful sight'.

During the first Covid lockdown, Paul would often phone for a much-needed natter. For me it was a highlight because we were still off air at that time, just repeating old editions of his radio show, and I missed talking to him.

'What's René up to?' he'd ask.

'Oh, he's in the garden, pruning the trees,' I'd reply.

'You should get out there and help him,' Paul would suggest. 'You're never too old to climb a tree.'

He obviously had no idea how much banana bread I was consuming.

Paul's own relationship with food was a complicated one. I've been on a diet since 1983 and, while I am no expert, I think I can see the signs and would suggest that Paul possibly had some sort of eating disorder. I recall as far back as 2010 sending him an emergency food hamper. He was doing panto in Southampton, and I was worried he might forget to eat, so I included a month's supply of Fray Bentos corned beef, various jams and plenty of Turkish Delight: he was a self-confessed 'picky eater'. David Ames observed that, 'Eating was more about socialising than the meal itself for Paul,' while Amanda Mealing explains, 'Food was a necessity, he didn't particularly like [having to eat] it.' Moira would often do the weekly shopping when she looked after the dogs in Kent: 'There was something about food that was tough for him,' she agrees. 'He told me that his aunty, Chrissie, who was a major influence in his early life, was probably anorexic. And Paul either binged or didn't eat for days.' Vanessa White agrees: 'He was a very tricky eater, and on filming trips abroad with him, I would always take a box of Weetabix, just in case, because often he just wouldn't be able to eat anything. And sometimes, in a hotel, he would order British food instead of eating the local dishes, or ask for oysters in Africa – it was the worst thing you could do, really. I think it all stemmed from his days with Lily, when he was wearing corsets, and he had to be slim.' Vera explains: 'Lily always looked great, but it was hard to maintain that. Getting her ready could take an hour or more, and it was tiring for Paul. That was one of the reasons he eventually retired her.'

Whether or not his issues regarding food began during his days trying to maintain Miss Savage's figure – Lily's legs were insured for a significant sum when she used to advertise Pretty Polly tights – one thing I can confirm was just how hard it was to get Paul to eat. Personally, I don't think it was about his vanity. During the radio show, he would sometimes nibble on a sandwich from M&S, or a sausage roll from Greggs, but he seldom finished anything you gave him. And even though he would often bring cakes in with him, sharing them around, I don't recall him enjoying them himself. 'He was a feeder,' Moira told me. 'We would be watching something on telly, and he would say, "Do you want some ice cream?" and he would bring me a bowl full of it and I would say, "Can't you just do two scoops!?" I also remember now, he didn't sit at the table to eat. He would cook a roast dinner, and he'd have the end bit of the meat because it was well cooked with a couple of potatoes, and then I'd see him scraping it all into the bin saying, "Oh, that was lovely," but he hadn't really touched it.' Moira continues, 'It didn't help that one day he would eat meat, the next he was vegetarian. The things he liked last week, he wouldn't this. He didn't like eating at other peoples' places, and he didn't particularly enjoy going to restaurants. But he would graze during the day. And he could stuff his face, usually with Turkish Delight, or simply just not eat at all. Eating was absolutely a problem for him.'

Even so, Paul installed an Aga, which became the making of him. He admitted it was an expensive buy, but one that was, along with his bed, one of 'the best investments I ever made'. Taking up prime position in his country kitchen under an impressive mantle that held all sorts of paraphernalia, including an obligatory clock, candle lamps and Disney figurines, Paul held his Aga in high regard: it was his pride and joy, along with his KitchenAid (other kitchen appliances are available, obviously). He gave his old 1920s Rayburn oven to his neighbour, Julian Clary. 'It was beautiful and such a wonderful house-warming present, literally, because it was a cold day when I moved in, and I couldn't get the central heating to work, and I was thinking, "Oh, what have I done?" Savage's gift was perfect for my house, and it warmed everything up. He was very thoughtful, he wouldn't make a big show of doing acts of kindness, but that was a very well-thought-out, helpful thing to do.'

I can still see Paul's cream-coloured Aga, with assorted steaming casserole dishes, his brown teapot with matching egg timer, and a copy of a Gary Rhodes' cookbook. He described himself as a 'pretty boring' cook, in that he was only interested in preparing good, plain food that didn't involve a lengthy and tiresome search for obscure ingredients. His soups were legendary – oh, to enjoy his tomato with dill soup again! Or the Thai one he made with prawns …

Paul was also a master baker, and desserts were never in short supply when I paid a visit. Even though he thought there were far too many cooking shows on the box, I believe he could have shown Mary Berry or Prue Leith a thing or too. Paul put his skills down to the fact his uncle, Hal, who had worked for the Cunard Shipping Line, was a baker. 'It's in the genes. I'd make a cake a day if I could.' Paul's strawberry trifle was something to be believed, and I suggested he sell his Victoria sponges and lemon drizzle cakes in supermarkets, next to Mr Kipling's.

Let's not forget, he already had a successful and popular range of dog food.

His allotment and small orchard ensured his larder was well stocked, and he was highly proficient at making bread, jams and preserves. I was particularly enamoured with his chutneys. And it wasn't just food he was adept at making. Alan Carr recalls, 'I was having a bit of trouble with a boyfriend and Paul suggested he could make a concoction that could get rid of him! You know what, I believed him!' The promise of a magical potion was often mentioned during my own conversations with Paul, and he had an answer for any ailment going. His book about life in the country featured quite a few of his favourite recipes. There was one by his Aunty Chrissie for an apple pie, and another for his Aunty Sadie's rhubarb tart. And he was quick to explain that he enjoyed collecting them because they reminded him of his friends and family.

His life in Kent was also an expensive one. Cilla Black had warned him that a big place in the country wouldn't be a cheap existence, and she was right. 'If you're going to buy an old house as I have,' Paul later wrote, 'be prepared for the expense of its upkeep'. For every uplifting anecdote about his beloved animals, there would be a fistful of fictions about broken gas boilers, the perils of feeding time in wintery conditions, and unexpected and unwelcome power cuts. But he was undeterred. 'Paul worked his arse off,' explains Amanda Mealing. 'He slogged his guts out for every thread of carpet in that house, everything. He never boasted about it, but he was so proud of Knoll Hill House.'

Trials and tribulations aside, Kent was a productive place for Paul. While we never got around to building a permanent recording studio for a much-discussed possible podcast – or 'POGcast' – it was at Knoll Hill, once the animals had been fed and the visitors had left, that he became Paul O'Grady the author. 'I can only write when the house is quiet, and the dogs are asleep.' It was usually at the kitchen table, listening to his favourite radio broadcasters – David Jacobs or Janice Long, both now sadly gone – where he would sit with his little laptop, writing his best-selling autobiographies and children's books.

Kent, in part, had inspired Paul to enter the celebrity-fuelled world of children's fiction. In 2021, he launched what he intended to be a trilogy of stories featuring 10-year-old Eddie who can speak to animals, including his dog Butch. Paul had sent me a copy of the first in the series – *Eddie Albert and the Amazing Animal Gang* – with a note that said, 'Here it is, fifty years in the making,' and it really was a labour of love for him. With stunning illustrations by Sue Hellard, Paul had originally written the story for his own amusement – and his grandchildren's. Abel recalls, 'My sister Halo and I enjoyed being a part of it. GanGan told us the stories before they were published ... Eddie went to school, but GanGan hadn't been in a school for years, and he had to make Eddie's [school] relatable to kids who go now. He'd ask what happens to naughty kids, what games we played in school; he was basically doing research. I recall he asked me what a SENCO was and I explained it was the teacher who was the school's special educational needs co-ordinator. He wanted to get things right.'

On Radio 2, we would also regularly dedicate an edition of his show to Halloween, Paul's favourite time of year, and writing late into the night only added to his conviction his home was haunted. I shall always remember when he told René and me about the perfumed ghost of Knoll Hill House. We were sitting once again at the table in the kitchen and he explained, 'When I first moved in here, guests would say they could smell perfume, but I couldn't. Then, a few years later, I popped downstairs for a drink, and I got a whiff of a perfume on the stairs, but I didn't know how it could be there.' The scent in question, he later discovered, was called Joy by the French fashion designer Jean Patou. René and I never encountered the ghost, nor smelt Joy, but the story did seem to suit Knoll Hill.

Paul's fascination with ghosts was well known, and he was a huge fan of the Yvette Fielding paranormal reality television series *Most Haunted*. In 2008, he participated in a special edition called *Ghost Hunting with Paul O'Grady and Friends* which was filmed in Palermo, Sicily's cultural, economic and tourism capital. He had enjoyed the spooky expedition but returned home disappointed as he hadn't encountered any ghoulies.

And Paul always promised to come back and haunt me – assuming he went first – a threat I usually just shrugged off until, that is, his death …

When Paul used to visit my home, as well as bringing a dog with him, he'd always have a smoke on the balcony. René would provide him with an Hermès ash tray which, after he left, would be emptied in the bin under the kitchen sink. The last time he paid us a visit was 2 weeks before he died, in March that year, so it was genuinely spooky when, almost 12 months later, as René and I were talking about Paul, I opened the lid of the bin to put some rubbish in it only to smell cigarette smoke. Neither of us smokes and no one had had a fag since Paul had last set foot in the apartment. The smell of his ash was so potent it genuinely unsettled us both, and I reminded René that Paul had always promised to come back and bother me.

This visitation has happened a couple of times since, normally when we are talking about Lily, Paul or both.

I can hear him chuckling away as I type this.

In pre-Covid times, Paul was often invited to attend Aldington Primary School's Nativity play, and he also took great pleasure in opening the local fete, where, according to co-headteacher Ben Dawson, 'Paul wouldn't rush off, he would stay and chat to everyone, children and parents alike.' Occasionally, he could be found at the Walnut Tree pub where he would enjoy a drink, some oysters and a corned-beef sandwich made by local resident Jean. For a time, he was probably the village's most famous resident, but even though he was often seen out and about, he didn't mix too much with his neighbours and kept pretty much to himself.

During the pandemic, like most of the UK, he isolated at home. There were worse places to be than a smallholding in Kent, but he still had to keep busy, looking after his animals and supporting the local community. He discreetly gave money to the landlady of his local pub which, like so many businesses during the initial lockdown, was struggling to keep afloat. As Michael Cashman puts it, 'If there was an Achilles' heel, it was that Paul could not stop giving: himself, his talent, his encouragement and enthusiasm, his life. Kent was Paul's refuge; at home he could shut himself away.'

But he wasn't alone there: 20 or so years after he had moved to the county, Paul O'Grady wrote, 'I bought an old house with more land than rooms as my main objective was to keep animals.' He was true to his word. He was joined by Solly, his favourite bantam chicken; there was Tom Tom, one of six extremely vocal New Zealand Kunekune pigs, and in the early days, another called Blanche, with whom he would go for walks. 'She's such a sweetheart, Malcolm. I know she understands everything I say to her.' He'd then moan that, 'Pig nuts cost a fortune.' Paul was also fascinated by cows and, on one Sunday afternoon radio show, instead of picking on me, he decided to tell the nation he wanted one. I didn't take his wish too seriously; after all, a few weeks before, he'd requested a Lotus Europa Mark II. A listener, however, happened to have one – a cow, not the car – and so Dot, a black and white Jersey/Dexter cross became part of the O'Grady household. So much at home was she in fact, that she once popped into the kitchen for a spot of smoked haddock. The affection Paul held for Dot was matched only by that he gave to Waupie, a Romney Marsh lamb Paul had hand-reared. Paul's smallholding was also home to Christine the psychotic sheep, Minerva the rescued barn owl, a colony of pipistrelle bats, and some sadistic geese. Then there was Winston, the Weetabix-loving lamb originally from Manchester; and, in later years, La Verne, Patty and Maxine, the pregnant alpacas.

While Paul also appreciated his trips overseas, be they for pleasure or work, as Joan observes, 'It was the return to his home in Kent he anticipated and appreciated the most.'

19.

Final Adventures

'My maxim is "be adventurous in life,
but not in restaurants"'
Paul O'Grady

Apparently it was the American comedian W.C. Fields who suggested, 'Never work with animals or children.' Well, whoever said it, Paul O'Grady was happy to ignore the advice because the peaks of his career involved them both. And, in 2022, he unknowingly made the decision to spend his final months with elephants *and* orphans.

For some time, he had wanted to highlight the plight of the largest living land animal – 'Whisper it quietly, but my love of elephants runs dogs a very close second,' he once said. The TV project *Paul O'Grady's Great Elephant Adventure* had been postponed due to Covid travel restrictions, but finally in December it was all systems go.

Unfortunately, things didn't start off well. There was a mix up: Paul had been expecting a late afternoon flight to take him from London to Thailand, and not one first thing in the morning, and he wasn't even packed when his car had arrived to collect him. Paul was no fan of long day-time flights because he preferred to use the opportunity to get as much sleep as he could. As Joan explains, 'He loved an [overseas] adventure, though he never enjoyed travelling.'

Vanessa White remembers that trip. 'We finally got off that plane in Bangkok, after a fifteen-hour flight. Paul was grey, literally grey, and he could barely walk from the aircraft to the lounge, where we had to sit for another six hours, waiting for the connecting flight to Laos. He looked so ill, so ill, and he was so thin.' Paul persevered, the chance to film with elephants seemingly being a big enough carrot to entice him through the project.

Mostly recovered and back on his feet, Paul explored the hills surrounding the ancient city of Chiang Mai, 400 miles north of Bangkok, known as the elephant capital of Thailand. He also visited the Elephant Nature Park, the largest rescue and refuge centre in Thailand. 'I'm so privileged to get this close to an elephant, you don't do this every day of your life,' he explained as he played football with a couple of young calves. 'They are so cute, baby elephants. They are like puppies, aren't they? A big puppy … not a care in the world … What I love is, they are safe, that's the thing.' He later shared: 'It took quite a lot of persuasion to get me away from the elephants and get me on to the plane home.'

Despite its rocky start, and being a challenging shoot, Paul's final overseas expedition resulted in a moving and sincere piece of television for him. When the two programmes were finally broadcast in March 2024, a year after his death, the

Daily Telegraph described the accessible and accomplished production as a 'joyful, jolly jaunt … a heartfelt film and a fitting farewell'. According to the show's producer, despite being covered in mud for much of the time, Paul had declared that he was 'in heaven' working on the project.

It was in stark contrast to one of his first filming expeditions, as Vanessa remembers. 'Going abroad with him was often difficult because he was out of his comfort zone. Paul was initially at a bit of a loss. I remember, we were on a bus in Zambia or somewhere, and the bus caught fire. Joan was with us, and Paul had brought a brand-new and very expensive Louis Vuitton case with him. Suddenly there are all these flames and smoke, and the bus pulled over and we had to jump off. And all I could hear him shouting was, "Leave Joan, save the Louis! Save the Louis!" It was hysterical. Luckily, both survived but he never took that case with him again because he realised how stupid it was for travelling around Africa.'

Following his adventure with elephants in Thailand and Laos, Paul returned home to Kent for Christmas 2022, where he spent a relatively quiet festive season with André, Joan and Moira. René and I popped over on Boxing Day to see him and enjoy one of his famous 'cold spreads'. Paul was relaxed, though he was tired and did look gaunt. But, as always, he was full of plans and there was talk of him filming a possible companion programme to *Paul O'Grady's Animal Orphans* (2014–2016), which would have seen him reunited with African elephants. He also mentioned he was about to make a new series about wild dogs and wolves in Canada, and another series which would see him return to Ireland.

All these projects, though, would have to wait until he had completed his commitments to a musical he had agreed to star in.

This wasn't the first time Paul had appeared in the hit Broadway show *Annie*. Lily Savage had first played the tyrannous, gin-swilling harridan Miss Hannigan at London's Victoria Palace Theatre for 2 months in late 1998. The musical has more grit than you might expect, and as Paul would happily tell you, 'There is a bit more to it than just a sweet little red-haired girl naively singing, "The Sun Will Come Out Tomorrow".'

Paul and the company were also chosen to take part in 1998's Royal Variety Show, where they performed a 10-minute piece which highlighted the key production numbers from the musical. It can still be viewed online and to see Lily as Hannigan in close-up is a treat, especially when she performs the song that 'nearly killed him' (Paul's words): 'Easy Street', with Peter Gennaro's demanding and larger-than-life choreography – Peter won the Tony Award for Best Choreography for the original Broadway production, and Paul was adamant he would replicate it. The routine is a delight to see and the steps he learnt stayed with him for the rest of his life. In fact, he would often throw a theatrical pose in the radio studio, declaring, 'I've still got it, Malcolm.'

Lily's first night was on 15 December 1998. The *Financial Times* observed that Lily Savage 'stamps her character on the part of Miss Hannigan, but does not literally stop the show in order to do so … the line between the orphanage tyrant and the Scouse caution is expertly blurred.' The journalist also observed, 'It is still a surprise to realise how tightly the nation has clasped her to its bosom – and as a person, not a character.' The journalist noted that Paul's own name wasn't even included or referenced in the programme – this was Lily Savage's show.

Looking back now, the idea of a drag artist playing Miss Hannigan probably shouldn't have been considered such a novelty. 'Lily and Hannigan were both from the wrong side of the tracks,' assesses Brenda Gilhooly, 'and in a way, like many drag acts, the characters pay tribute to what is *not* a "nice girl". Sexism in society says that girls need to be pretty, quiet and unselfish. But if you look at Lily Savage or Miss Hannigan, they are none of those things – they celebrate what the rest of society might consider to be awful women, and what a girl is not meant to be – and that's funny.'

Lily's interpretation was a hit, and that success would stay with her, and Paul, for the rest of their lives. The sharp-tongued orphanage owner with a disdain for her young charges wasn't by any means Lilian Maeve Veronica Savage, but she was an indication of just how far Paul O'Grady had turned the dial throughout his career.

I recall discussing the idea of Paul's return to the role of Miss Hannigan in 2022 when having tea with him and Joan at Knoll Hill House. Joan and I were apprehensive because Paul had recently been advised to have an implantable cardioverter defibrillator (ICD) put in his chest, to monitor his heart rate. Paul's cardiologist was concerned that his heart might just stop, and the small device placed under the skin, usually in the space just below the collar bone, would in theory help to restore it to a normal rhythm. But Paul wasn't keen, telling us: 'I don't want one of those, I won't be able to work again.'

I remember looking at Joan – her expression said it all. She had explained the procedure to Paul at length, shared the rationale for doing it, and listened to his concerns. But there was no point in challenging his decision. Paul told us he was worried about getting insurance – something all big names in show business have to have – and an ICD might raise issues. Plus, if he failed a medical, it could prohibit him from taking on work, especially jobs which included foreign travel. He wasn't frightened about the procedure – Paul O'Grady was made of strong stuff – but he was unenamoured with the prospect of an operation and a long recuperation.

A few months before, Paul had endured an unexpected and painful week-long visit to William Harvey Hospital in Ashford and couldn't face the idea of being out of action so soon again. In a text message to his daughter Sharyn, he wrote, 'The cardiologist just wants me to have a defib. But no way am I having one of them. He's being over cautious and besides, I'm nowhere near as bad as I was.' His daughter continued to encourage him to look after his health, as did we all, but Paul was the sort of person who sometimes just wouldn't listen.

As Joan and I drank another cup of tea, Paul promised he'd think about having the procedure, joking that having an ICD would mean he wouldn't be able to walk past an electronic garage door without it opening automatically.

Quips aside, however, it seems his mind was made up. His friend Moira had collected him from the William Harvey Hospital. 'As we were driving along the lanes back home, he said to me, "I'm not going to be here for much longer." I asked him what he meant and pushed him to tell me what the doctors had said to him. He was contemplative, I put my arm around him, and he just replied, "That's it. I think I won't be here for much longer."' He told me much the same, during a phone conversation a month or so later. It's one I will never forget because he calmly ended our chat with, 'I won't make old bones, Malcolm.'

In October 2022, the announcement was made that Paul O'Grady would star as the mean-spirited Miss Hannigan in the revival of the musical *Annie*. Jo Brand was surprised to hear Paul was taking to the stage again: 'He was the same age as me and there's no fucking way I'd be going on tour in a musical, because it's exhausting. You can do the show with your eyes closed to some extent, but it's the travelling that gets to you.' Brenda Gilhooly saw the decision differently: 'When I spoke to Paul about returning to *Annie*,' she explains, 'he seemed very enthused. He liked to work, he would have made a very miserable unemployed person.' Alan Carr recalls, 'I had seen him recently for dinner and he looked frail and, for once, he looked his age. I mean, his wit was still intact, and he was funny, joking and quick as a whip as always, but I did think he looked a bit fragile … his spark had gone, so I was shocked to hear he was doing *Annie*. But it was a calling for him, and I know how much he enjoyed getting out there and entertaining; getting that response from a live audience was his lifeblood.'

Despite my initial reservations, I suppose I did understand why Paul had agreed to do it: the piece was familiar to him, it was also as sure-fire a theatrical hit as a show could be, plus his return to the stage would be a news story – which it was. Promoting his return to *Annie*, Paul spoke to the local press in Bristol, where he was due to visit for a week at the Hippodrome (tragically, his performances never happened). Paul joked about being plied with whisky by the producer before accepting the job offer: 'He was saying how he'd seen me as Miss Hannigan years ago in 1998 … I'm easily led, me, that's the problem.' Michael Harrison told me he remembers that drinking session well: 'We were in the Union Jack pub in Southwark, and I'd taken the company out at the start of rehearsals for *Cinderella* [the Palladium pantomime of 2016]. Paul joined us and said, "Get me a whisky," so I brought him a glass over and he said, "No, a bottle." And we sat with [that] bottle of whisky and one by one everybody left, and it was me and him. The subject of the little orphan raised its head, and he said, "*Annie* is unfinished business, I'd love another crack at it." And after the pandemic, I was planning the UK tour and I said to him, "Pick some dates," – I thought he'd do just three weeks. But he selected the biggest theatres: Edinburgh, Southampton, Liverpool, Dublin and Bristol. And then he said, "Plus I'll also do Newcastle for your mother." Now, that wasn't where he was going to make a load of money, it wasn't one of the biggest theatres, but he knew, because he was smart, if I took Paul O'Grady to my hometown, then that was a big deal.'

Paul told reporters, 'In my version [Hannigan] is a bit raggy. I'm going to do her a lot older, where she's got no tolerance at all for kids – all she wants to do is listen to her radio and get drunk.' In an interview with the *Scotsman*, Paul confided,

'Hannigan's a different kettle of fish from Lily, but great fun to play. I've always played villains … I don't get the glamorous stuff. But you can't have good without evil, and the villain is really good fun to play.' As Michael Harrison observes, 'He had done a lot by then, he'd been around, and his craft had changed by the time he returned to the part second time around.'

Just before he left to begin rehearsals, Moira saw Paul from the kitchen at Knoll Hill House: he was struggling for breath as he was climbing the stairs. 'I said to him, "Why are you even thinking of doing this? How are you going to do it?" And he replied, "I don't know." And I thought, "Just *why* is this still happening?"' A few days later, however, *Annie*'s dance captain Tommy Wade Smith shared a typical O'Grady moment on his social media during rehearsals. The short video showed Paul declaring, much to the amusement of the assembled cast: 'I've been forced into this! They said you can either do *Annie* or six months [in jail]. And I should have done the six months! It would have been a lot fucking easier!'

After a triumphant first night in early March 2023, at the Theatre Royal, Newcastle upon Tyne, followed by a 2-week break, Paul O'Grady returned to the musical in Edinburgh, the place where he had always found a warm reception. Promoting the engagement on BBC Radio Scotland, he joked: 'Don't take the elderly for granted. I'm no chicken. I'm 67, I'm 68 this year, and I'm rocking around with Miss Hannigan doing "Easy Street" gasping for air … The last time I was in *Annie* was 28 years ago. It's strange coming back after so long. But Hannigan is such fun.' In another interview with a local paper, given a few days before the start of the week-long run, Paul encouraged his fans to see his performance, 'before it's too late'.

The dates at the Edinburgh Playhouse sold out and Paul received a rapturous welcome. When he made his stage entrance on 21 March, the venue erupted – and he hadn't even said his first line. Two and a half hours later, as he returned for the curtain call, theatre-goers gave him a standing ovation; at his final bow, the whooping and clapping was so deafening Paul's face lit up – he was overwhelmed and delighted in equal measure.

Much like his earlier visits to Auld Reekie, Paul took the opportunity to see old pals, popping into one of the city's longest-running gay establishments, Planet Bar. Manager Darren Patterson told the *Daily Record* that Paul came in for a drink and a catch-up, and he was soon singing on the karaoke. Paul was seemingly on top form, but he apparently declared to the assembled patrons that he was the 'last one standing' out of his iconic group of friends, which included Cilla Black and Barbara Windsor.

The week-long engagement in the hit musical concluded on Saturday 25 March. It would be the last time he appeared in Edinburgh, and his final stage performance. Perhaps it was fitting that both were in the city which, in many ways, had made him, and in the musical he had loved for 25 years.

Packing up Hannigan's wig and dress, Paul returned to his home in Kent one final time.

20.

Ter-ra

'We don't know how much time
we have, Malcolm'
Paul O'Grady

Following the dreadful meeting with the team at Smooth
Radio in 2022, Paul and I had found a new home at a rival
station targeted at baby boomers. Without the might of Global
or the BBC behind them, Boom had launched during the
pandemic and was one of the fastest-growing radio stations in
the country. And, most importantly, they wanted Paul
O'Grady.

Our first show for them was broadcast on Christmas Day
that year. It was a huge success, and his arrival on the station
had generated considerable coverage in the press. The
programme itself attracted the station's largest audience too.
Their faith in TeamPOG had been justified.

Boom's co-founder David Lloyd explains, 'As we launched
Boom Radio – our station for listeners who dared to be aged
over 55 – we knew the voices our listeners really wanted to

hear. Not the supposed "personalities" of today, famous for goodness knows what, but those authentic human beings who simply make use of radio to communicate – and have mastered the art … Paul had a mastery of the language and a way of connecting with ordinary people. His Christmas Day show was legendary … When he left the BBC, listeners campaigned – pleading with us to secure his services. Response to the announcement of his Christmas show was phenomenal … missing Paul would have been a Christmas ruined, and we stood poised lest the internet network could not handle the surge of listeners joining via their Alexa.'

Unlike their competitors, this new station had no studios; instead, presenters broadcast from their homes. So, for Paul's first programme on the fledgling station, they had provided us with a new microphone, a set of headphones and a few cables for his iPad. It was a very simple affair and a far cry from the studios of the BBC, but Paul and I were well versed in creating radio magic from home.

Boom now asked us to make another show, this time for Easter Sunday in April 2023, and there was talk of a regular series, and so, on 28 March, I popped round to Knoll Hill House to test the broadcast kit.

Whenever I paid a visit to Paul's home, I was greeted by a cacophony of dogs barking and yapping, interspersed with Paul shouting commands which they would all ignore. Paul's kitchen was, like most, the centre of the home, but it was no show kitchen. There were dog baskets all over the floor, and a large dresser against one wall which was filled with an impressive selection of the usual miscellaneous knick-knacks: a ceramic pumpkin, a small Santa, an old wireless, a Thermos flask, small Disney figurines, a trumpet, photos, assorted cups and mugs, a nodding Buster, and pumpkin fairy lights – even in March. There was also a large kitchen table with numerous chairs positioned around it, each having a different cushion, none of which seemed to match. The table, Paul had told me, came from Julian Clary. Much to Paul's disappointment, his neighbour down the road had sold up, leaving Paul in Kent while Julian had returned to London. Paul explained, 'That table was filthy! I spent the afternoon cleaning it before we could use it.'

The kitchen was always welcoming and genuine: it felt lived in, and the room was filled with light and warmth; it was a very easy place in which to settle down for a natter. As Moira explained, 'He didn't like it being super organised – he aspired to it, but he knew it wasn't him. I've never known such a messy person in the kitchen, it was a disaster zone!' Often, when I paid him a visit, Joan would be there, with Moira, Vera and handyman Sean. They were, as the author Armistead Maupin would say, a 'logical family': a memorable clan of misfit friends and the people who made his life work.

But today it was just me, Paul, and his husband, André, who was soon despatched to the local supermarket.

It had just gone 4 p.m. 'Fancy a cuppa?' Paul asked. 'How's René, how's he doing now?' A few weeks before, my husband had lost his dear sister Marie-Thé in tragic circumstances. I explained that things weren't easy as there were so many questions unanswered about Marie-Thé's death. Paul looked concerned. 'Look after him, Malcolm,' he told me. I have since wondered if he'd had a premonition because we continued to talk about death, and 'not knowing what was round the corner'. He reminded me of a quote by the creator of Snoopy, Charles M. Schulz: 'Just remember, once you're over the hill, you begin to pick up speed,' and Paul joked about his own age and how he wouldn't be surprised if his own exit would be 'sooner rather than later'.

'Don't say that,' I replied.

As he made the tea, I set up the radio equipment and microphone for him. It was very straightforward, and once the test was successfully concluded, Paul put the kettle on for another cuppa.

I took the opportunity to play him his new Boom Radio jingle. The one we had used for 14 years or so – inspired by *The Avengers*, and featuring a sung refrain of 'Paul-O-Gray-dee-on-the-wire-less' – was owned by the BBC, so we couldn't use it for the show on Boom. The new jingle, though less ambitious, charmed Paul: 'At least they bothered to do something!' he said.

We chatted about the show we were going to record the next day, and I explained that the singer Rumer had recorded a special message for us. He was always surprised people had bothered to do such things, especially for his Christmas shows, which in previous years had included messages from Mariah Carey, Julie Walters, Sue Johnston, James Blunt, Kelsey Grammar, Donny Osmond, Kylie Minogue, Bette Midler, Cliff Richard and most of Radio 2's 'family'. Hearing Sir Ian McKellen talk on the show about my mother's infamous mince pies remains a career highlight for me.

I reminded Paul how well his Boom Christmas Day programme had been received. He was pleased and happy to hear that the team at the station were equally delighted.

'Are you really up for doing another weekly show?' I asked him.

'Yes, I think so,' he replied. 'It'll be good to do a new one for them, as long as I can do it from my kitchen.'

I reassured him that was the plan and, while we had yet to sign the contract, once we'd re-established the programme, Boom would be looking for a sponsor which would result in an increased budget – and our fees.

'What time will we be on?' he queried.

'From 2 p.m. until 4 p.m.,' I replied.

'That'll dent Elaine [Paige] and Johnnie [Walker].' He smiled wickedly. 'Yes, I think we should do it, and show them [the BBC] what they've lost. The listeners want us back, don't they?'

Judging by the many messages on social media I was still receiving 8 months after our last Radio 2 show, I confidently replied, 'Yes, they do.'

'OK then, Malcolm, deal!'

Because of what happened a couple of hours later, I have detailed notes on the remainder of our conversation in his kitchen that afternoon. When I received the shocking news about Paul's death, I knew if I didn't write down everything we chatted about that final time, I might forget it. I recognised that what Paul had said would be important to his family, his friends and his many fans.

For the next hour and a half or so that afternoon, we did what we often did: we nattered. It's the one thing all his pals miss; his phone calls were legendary too. Talking to Paul was effortless, enjoyable and always resulted in laughter, especially when he kicked off.

This day was different. As with any conversation between two friends, there were many topics we discussed that final time including self-assembly furniture (don't ask); his animals and how grateful he was that Moira was looking after them; Vera (obviously); Hinge and Brackett (why not?); and his two grandchildren, of whom he was so proud. Yes, he was on form. And yes, we laughed. But he didn't have a rant – there seemed no time or need for one. Looking back, everything about that chat instead felt measured.

Paul began by telling me all about his recent stint as Hannigan in Edinburgh. He showed me some photos of the set and the cast and explained how happy he was with this new production. He was pleased the musical would keep him busy in the coming months. It was a delight to hear his excitement and pride, especially given that only a year before we had sat at the same table with Joan contemplating whether he should accept the role, fearing it would be too much of a physical stretch for him.

He was next scheduled to don Miss Hannigan's costume in Southampton at the Mayflower Theatre. He was looking forward to it, even though he was, 'knackered, absolutely knackered … I'm 67, remember. And I have just received this' – he waved an official-looking letter from the Department for Work and Pensions – 'to say I'll be getting my pension!'

'That'll make Joan laugh,' I said, 'working for a pensioner.'

He laughed in turn: 'That bloody woman, she'll have me working when I'm six feet under!' He went on to say he would be lost without Joan, adding, 'But don't tell her I said that!'

Continuing with the topic of pensions and money, Paul explained he was planning to review his will. These words seemed to just hang in the air and, feeling awkward, I changed the subject.

I mentioned the state of the BBC's local radio network. Paul was incensed how Auntie had recently announced plans to reduce its service considerably, axing local shows and replacing them with generic regional programming, or worse.

'It's a disgrace!' he said. 'Mind you, look what they've done to Radio 2!'

Yes, one of our favourite topics had risen to the surface again.

'Speaking of the BBC, I'm putting them in purgatory.'

Not for the first time, I had no idea what Paul was talking about.

He clarified his comment: 'Paul Merton has asked me to appear on his new series of *Room 101*.' The comedy series invited guests to discuss pet hates and then persuade the host to consign their choices to oblivion. 'I've agreed. I told him, I'm not just putting the bloody BBC in it, I'm placing them in purgatory!' He explained he would be recording the episode for Radio 4 in the coming weeks.

The subject turned to theatre and Michael Harrison. It transpired that the two had recently discussed the idea of Paul appearing in the UK tour of *The Wizard of Oz*. Now, I know he was a great performer, but even I thought a 68-year-old Paul in a gingham dress and a pair of ruby slippers was a bit of a stretch. No, I was mistaken, he wasn't talking about playing Dorothy, he was contemplating the role of the Wicked Witch. Just like he had with *Annie*, Michael Harrison had encouraged Paul to select some key dates on the forthcoming tour. While Paul considered the idea, he was more interested in taking *Annie* into the capital for the festive period, something Paul revealed Michael was planning to do.

Paul's love of live theatre extended not just to the shows he'd appeared in, but also those of his friends, and our conversation turned to former *Coronation Street* star Tracie Bennett. We reminisced about her performance as Judy Garland in *End of the Rainbow* at the Trafalgar Studios in 2010. 'She was bloody marvellous,' he said. 'She was channelling Judy on that stage, night after night. God knows how she did it.'

We stayed with *Coronation Street*: Jodie Prenger had recently become a Weatherfield resident. Jodie had stood in for Paul on his Sunday radio show a few times and later became a regular voice on TeamPOG, telling listeners how they could get in touch. Paul would then describe what she was wearing, making up a different outfit every week, 'Oh, today she's in lovely Alpine lederhosen,' that sort of thing.

For many years, Paul had suggested on air that Jodie would make an ideal barmaid for the Rovers Return, and he was thrilled when, in 2022, she joined the cast of the nation's favourite soap as Glenda. And, as luck would have it, she was the sister of the *Street*'s resident undertaker, George Shuttleworth, played by Paul's pal from *Eyes Down*, Tony

Maudsley. 'I hope they give Jodie something good to do, more than just pulling pints, because she's such a talented woman.'

The soap talk continued, chatting about Noele Gordon. As far as Paul was concerned, Nolly was a real star, and he remembered seeing her in London: 'I'll never forget her at the stage door of the Victoria Palace Theatre when she was doing *Call Me Madam* in 1983. She seemed like the Queen Mother as she came out to this throng of fans who were all fainting, swooning and screaming. There she was, all in mink, looking fabulous, doing the whole thing and then she got into her Rolls and swished off, and I thought, "That's a star, a real star." She had a very commanding presence.'

Paul's own fans probably would have been surprised to hear he could be as starstruck as the next person.

The dogs started barking: something in the garden had set them off. 'Stop it!' Paul shouted but, as usual, Arfur, Nancy, Sausage and Eddie ignored him and simply continued yapping. The only one who wasn't bothered was Conchita who sat quietly, ignoring the commotion. Seeing Paul with his family of dogs is a comforting memory and one which I hold dearly. They clearly loved him as much as he loved them. Once the dogs had finally settled down, Paul quietly told me that he'd had to say goodbye to another of his beloved pigs. His family was getting smaller. Even after knowing him for 20 years, I still couldn't cope when Paul O'Grady looked sad.

Again, I changed the subject and congratulated him on an award he had recently won, this time for the second Eddie Albert adventure *The Curse of the Smugglers' Treasure*. He had dedicated the book to his two grandchildren, and it had become a hit with its intended audience. Paul had just heard it had been recognised in the St Helens Schools Library Service book awards, in Merseyside, and he recorded a short video message on his phone thanking them just after I left. Paul went on to tell me about his idea for the third adventure for Eddie. It would, he explained, involve a Russian oligarch who, accompanied by a sidekick called Olga, was kidnapping animals to populate a private zoo on the Isle of Skye. Eddie and his gang would save the day. Once again, Paul's imagination knew no limits. He told me there were also discussions to turn the books into an animated television series; he had seen some of the early artwork and he was impressed. The same was true of the full cast audio book adaptation of the first Eddie Albert story which, unlike Paul's many autobiographies, he had contributed to.

For me, seeing Paul being so positive about his work was really pleasing. We recalled how the original press release for Eddie Albert's debut described it as 'a Technicolor cinematic adventure packed full of friendship, animals, action … and … a wicked sense of humour.' I had joked, 'Sounds just like your own life!' It had come as no surprise the first outing for Eddie Albert had included a visit to Amsterdam. Paul had bought a property in the city, and he enjoyed spending time in the Dutch capital. He was heading there, he told me, for Easter, taking Joan and Moira for a much-deserved break.

Making yet another cup of tea, he said he'd just had a call with his beloved Tara King, aka Linda Thorson, which led us to the subject of favourite women. We would often share stories and opinions on the famous stars we'd both encountered, from Julie Andrews to Liza (with a 'z'). Today was no different. When it came to big-name interviews, we enjoyed a friendly rivalry. In my work as a producer of feature documentaries for Radio 2, I'd had the good fortune of meeting and interviewing Nina Simone, Whoopi Goldberg and Carly Simon, among many others. He'd remind me: 'I shared strawberries with Barbra Streisand,' and I'd retaliate with, 'I went to George Michael's home for a coffee,' to which he'd reply: 'Well, I had tea with the Queen.' He would usually win.

I encouraged Paul to tell me about the times he had run into the great Thora Hird, Dora Bryan, Beryl Reid and Marianne Faithfull. Sharing such tales put him in his happy place. Paul had a story about everyone – don't forget, he'd interviewed hundreds of people on his chat shows – and his memory was surprisingly good; even though he often happily repeated a good yarn.

The subject then changed to Melanie Sykes, who was just about to publish her memoir, and I told Paul that she had been in touch to tell me she had written about him. 'I hope she slags off Radio 2.' We were back on that subject again. Paul asked if I'd heard from the BBC. 'No', I replied. Publicly, he hadn't said anything negative about the station since we had left the previous August, but he still found the BBC's decision bewildering, believing they didn't understand who the real Radio 2 audience was. It was clear Paul hadn't forgiven the Corporation for the way he had been treated.

'In any other business it would have been constructive dismissal!' he continued. And he was probably right. 'I wonder how long Rob Beckett will last?' he mused. (In February

2025, Radio 2 announced Paul's permanent replacement was stepping down from hosting his Sunday afternoon show. He had lasted just 2 years. His departure was another notable example of some of the changes to its schedule the station had made that hadn't really worked, including Claudia Winkleman's brief stint on Saturday mornings, and Dr Rangan Chatterjee's fleeting Sunday 'wellbeing' show.)

We parked Radio 2, and the conversation changed to something less irritating. As I've previously mentioned, one of the striking things about the position of Knoll Hill House is that it often affords a very clear view of the surrounding area. The night before my visit, the locals had witnessed a remarkable evening sky as Mercury, Jupiter, Venus, Uranus, Mars and the moon aligned in an arc in what is known as a 'planetary parade'. Paul explained that it had been visible after sunset and said that he'd been out in his garden, planet spotting. For him, though, it was also a 'sign' – and an omen. He said that we should 'check the babies who were born last night', and went on to clarify, 'such events usually signify new beginnings … and potential danger'. I smiled at his explanation.

Some of his outstanding fan mail from the Radio 2 show had been forwarded to me by a pal at the station, and there were a few photos of Lily that loyal listeners wanted signing. She was still haunting him. 'Look at those legs!' he said. 'Eh! You'll never guess what happened while I was in Edinburgh … the things people were asking me to autograph at the stage door! *Doctor Who* DVDs, a TeamPOG tea towel, and a book all about [the TV sitcom] *Hi-De-Hi*. Someone even asked me to add my signature to a copy of *The Bill* annual!'

I had no idea there *was* an annual celebrating the police series and made a mental note to buy one on eBay as part of Paul's birthday present that June. I never knew what to buy him, but a quirky gift often went down well. I recall his delight when I gave him the sheet music for one of his favourite songs, 'I See the Moon', which we played on the Christmas Day show, every year.

It was time to go, and Paul had to feed the animals and take the dogs for a walk. André had returned from the shops, and I suspected I wouldn't be popular if I stayed any longer. 'Now, please don't stand at the door and watch me attempt to reverse the car,' I said.

Paul chuckled. I'd always struggled with the layout and constraints of his driveway. There was a low-standing wall just in front of the house which I was fearful of hitting with my car. 'Talk to you tomorrow, then.'

I replied: 'Yes, looking forward to it.' I gave him a hug and unusually he kissed me on the cheek. 'Ter-ra.' He closed the front door, once again the dogs were making a din, and this time I successfully manoeuvred the car and drove down the long drive, waited for the gates to open, and headed off towards Hythe. I had the radio on and was beaming. Knowing that Paul wanted to do a new weekly radio show meant we would be able to do what we did best together.

I know now that there were three elements to him arriving at this decision: firstly, he enjoyed the work. Yes, it annoyed him from time to time, and he was forever threatening to give it up, but he genuinely loved reading the emails and messages from his many listeners. He also found great pleasure in sending me up, hoping that things would go wrong, and crit-icising my musical choices. The second reason he was happy to return to presenting weekly radio was because it would 'put two fingers up' to the BBC – his words, not mine. He was still wounded and slightly embarrassed by what had happened, and he wanted to show them that his audience was still there and mattered. But the third reason was that making a weekly show would give me some financial security. Paul didn't need the money, but he knew I would.

And that was typical of him.

At 9.28 p.m., my mobile rang. It was Joan. A late call was unexpected, but not unusual. My immediate thought was something had happened, and Paul wouldn't be able to record the radio show the next day.

'Hello, Joan, you OK?' I offered.

'He's gone,' was the succinct reply.

I didn't understand quite what she was saying. 'What?' I asked.

'He's gone, Malcolm … Paul's gone … He's gone.'

★

It later transpired that Paul had died about an hour or so after I'd left him. Moira phoned Vera with the news around 7.30 p.m. 'She just said, "Savage is dead. Savage is dead."' Vera had replied: '"What? What do you mean?" I just couldn't take it in.'

The news of Paul's death broke in the middle of the night, so I had a few hours with René to reflect on a world without our friend. I was concerned for Joan and Moira who I knew

– despite their shock – would have to sort everything out, with the help of Waheed. I was also worried about Vera, and Paul's family: his sister Sheila, Sharyn and his grandchildren. It was such a dreadful shock for us all.

René and I agreed there was no point in trying to sleep, so we stayed up monitoring the news channels and social media. Around midnight, out of the blue, a showbiz editor from a tabloid paper started to follow me on Twitter, and another sent me a personal message asking how I was. I suspected the news had leaked.

Moira and Joan had arrived at Knoll Hill House around 9 p.m. only to find numerous ambulances at the property, plus the local police. The commotion of blue flashing lights must have alerted Paul's neighbours, and Moira recalled seeing a reporter trying to peer over the garden fence. The medical team had attempted to save him, but Paul had died in his beloved kitchen. The radio microphone and his headphones were still on the table where I'd left them that afternoon.

A few hours later, I received numerous invitations to appear on TV shows and radio programmes. No doubt they were hounding Paul's other friends and family, but I declined everything. Honestly, I just couldn't speak coherently about my friend. I decided to post a few words on Twitter which were reported on the main news shows throughout the day, along with a photo of Paul and me smiling in my kitchen. It had only been taken days before. And while I was happy to answer a few phone calls from my friends and former colleagues, I was surprised how many just wanted a juicy bit of gossip.

I suppose I was simply being naive.

As soon as the news of his death was announced, countless celebrities appeared in the press, online and on TV, declaring they were his nearest and dearest. I recall phoning Joan Marshrons a few days later to say that I didn't realise that XX, who had just posted a heartfelt tribute on social media, was such a close pal, or that YY, who had spoken about him on breakfast television, had even known Paul. When the production team which had worked with him on the TV series *For The Love of Dogs* made a tribute programme for ITV, I was invited to take part. One of the things I said that didn't make the final edit was that I had been surprised by how many people thought they were Paul's 'closest friend'.

Hours after his death had been announced, BBC Radio 2 got in touch saying they 'wanted me to make a programme about Paul'. There wasn't even a hint of condolence. It was such a blunt request and I declined: I knew Paul wouldn't have wished me to produce something for them. The buzzer to my apartment rang, it was two journalists from national newspapers, both asking for me to comment. René told them where to go.

If it was unpleasant for me, the media attention was considerably more intrusive for Paul's immediate family in Liverpool. 'We spent probably a week in the house, with all the blinds down,' explains Sharyn. 'There was press in the street for the whole time. The doorbell just kept on going, it was relentless.' She was doorstepped by the *Daily Mail* who eagerly reported her few words. 'All I said was, "What can I say? We are all devastated, I am, my mum is, everyone is. We loved him and we will miss him. We are all distraught." The headlines made it look like I had given them an exclusive. I hadn't. It was really upsetting because my friends thought I'd given them an interview.'

Understandably for a public figure like Paul, the media's thirst for information didn't let up. Linda Thorson appeared on the ITV breakfast show, *Good Morning Britain*. Sharing the information she had been given, Linda explained that Paul had died peacefully in his bed. It was a version of events the public would have wanted to hear at that time, but it wasn't true. 'It breaks my heart, the fairy tale account of his last minutes,' Amanda Mealing told me in 2024. 'I'd love that to be true because the reality hurts my heart. That my soulmate, my fiercest protector, my friend beyond words … the man who would give you the shirt off his back, the man who helped so many, who cared for and uplifted so many, would die alone is something that haunts me. If only I had been there. If only … if only.'

Since the first report of his death, two other accounts of how Paul died have appeared in the media: all three differ, and sadly the only thing they share is the ultimate outcome.

The press later reported the cause of his death was sudden cardiac arrhythmia, in other words, a cardiac arrest. Paul's heart had just stopped working, just as his cardiologist had predicted a year before.

Another phone call I received soon after Paul's death was announced was from David Lloyd at Boom Radio. He asked if I would produce a tribute show to replace the scheduled Easter Day programme. Again, I declined. I wasn't being awkward; it just didn't feel the right thing to do. Instead, I suggested he could repeat the one we had broadcast on Christmas Day; it was a lovely show, upbeat, funny and full of glittering guests. More importantly, having Christmas at Easter would also amuse Paul. David agreed.

A couple of days later, I recorded a short introduction to explain why Boom was repeating Paul's Christmas show on Easter Day. I began by explaining that I was usually referred to as '… Paul O'Grady's "long-suffering radio producer". Right now, you should be hearing the song, 'Stop Me If You've Heard It All Before' by Billy Ocean. It would have been the opening track of the TeamPOG Easter Day show. But sadly, that's not to be. Paul's sudden death on March 28th shocked us all – his family, friends and fans – we all feel robbed. But I think we should count ourselves lucky because Paul O'Grady will never really leave us. We have his award-winning books, we can still watch his hilarious chat shows and sitcoms, learn from his travelogues and documentaries, and remember thousands of his live performances on stage.

'And then there's Miss Savage. It's an enormous and unique legacy.

'And part of that was his radio show. Paul loved it, pure and simple. That's why he did it for so many years. And there was one programme in particular that Paul knew was just as important for his other listener. Yes, he joked he couldn't stand the run up to the Big Day, but he knew it was a privilege to be there on Christmas Day with you. So, by popular demand, here is his first show for Boom Radio.

'It was supposed to have been the start of a brand-new adventure for him, me and you. It's Christmas Day 2022 all over again and regular TeamPOG listeners will know, it won't be the first time we've played festive music in April. Oh, and that description of me being his "long-suffering producer"? Well, don't believe a word of it. I loved every minute.'

A few weeks later, on 20 April 2023, hundreds of mourners, along with their pets, turned out in the village of Aldington to view Paul's cortege and say farewell to their friend. Shortly after 2.30 p.m., a horse-drawn carriage carried his wooden coffin, along with husband André and their dog Conchita, through the village and on to St Rumwold's in nearby Bonnington.

A dog called Ernie, from Battersea Dogs and Cats Home, greeted attendees at the small church, including Rolling Stones' guitarist Ronnie Wood, as well as Dame Sheila Hancock, Alan Carr and Jo Brand. It was so moving, especially when Michael Cashman read Shakespeare's sonnet number 18: 'Shall I compare thee to a summer's day?' Joan read Pam Ayres' 'Woodland Burial', which set most of us off, while Julian Clary gave a perfect eulogy.

He told me later: 'Straight away I thought it had to be funny, that was what Savage would have wanted. You needed the release of having a laugh. And it wasn't difficult to come to that conclusion because if you're talking about him, you know there would be funny anecdotes. But the doing of it was something else, but I knew I had to. And maybe he knew the organ in the church didn't work, maybe he'd planned it all along, because it was funny. I think I did skip the last paragraph because I suddenly couldn't speak.'

Obviously, while no one wanted to be there on that day,

Julian's heartfelt speech was a blessing and it perfectly summed up the person we all loved. Afterwards, the mourners walked out of the small church to Elvis Presley's version of 'Trouble', Paul's favourite song.

As his coffin was placed into the grave shared with his former partner Brendan Murphy, the weather turned: right on cue, the heavens opened, the wind picked up, and we all scrambled to deploy umbrellas. 'We had to force him into that grave,' remembers Michael Cashman. 'It wasn't wide enough: we tried the legs first and then headfirst, and in the end, they had to shove him in, and I looked to Julian Clary and said, 'That's Savage saying I'm going fuckin' nowhere!'''

Paul O'Grady had such a huge personality, and his work reached far and wide, so I wasn't surprised by the number of people who wrote to me after his death saying how greatly they missed him, and the programmes he had made. Many asked me if he knew just how much he was loved and admired, and the truth is, although he'd joke that all he had done was impersonate a middle-aged prostitute and done a bit of telly, he did. The recognition he received from royalty played a part in it, as did the volume of fan mail he received at his home in Kent. But the real measure was the countless people who came up to him in Waitrose and Greggs, asking for yet another 'bloody selfie'. While the love of his family and his animals had been never-ending, Paul recognised he had been fortunate to have so many loyal friends who had been with him on his astonishing journey. And he knew he had surrounded himself with the 'right people', too – those who had helped and supported him to make informed professional choices, organise his life and make the most of his singular talents. Yes, he had known he was loved.

As Moira put it, 'He was a one-off. He was a good friend to a lot of people, he was loyal, he took people with him on the way. He gave good advice; he was someone who always supported me. And he could be this massive bundle of fun. Everyone thought they knew him, and in some ways that's true. But Paul O'Grady was very different from the person you thought you knew, and part of him just couldn't believe he was secure and that he'd made it.'

For Michael Harrison, 'So many people in the industry are boring off-stage, but he wasn't. He was as entertaining off as he was on. The void he left is huge. The working-class persona is fading, with that journey coming up through the clubs, learning your craft, playing to hard crowds and rowdy audiences and all that he went through, you can't teach that and I'm not sure we will see it again like we did with Paul … more than anything, the business is made of characters, and he was one.'

Russell T Davies adds, 'We certainly lost that working-class voice which could be radical when it needed to be. He was on the side of the audience, and they loved him. I miss that laugh on the radio, and his sentimentality – he was unashamedly sentimental – there is literally no one like him. I've never met anybody who didn't like Paul O'Grady.'

For Jo Brand, 'We weren't ready to let him go, it happened far too soon. What have we lost? Someone very special, with a huge amount of warmth and talent. His death was an appalling loss, but at least he avoided a poor end where he had no control. His stardom is preserved in our memories, and we are fortunate for that.'

As someone who had benefitted from Paul's support throughout their career, Jodie Prenger believes, 'He was such a star, a real star, and I looked up to him, I admired him, his northern humour and his love of animals. I can never repay him, but I just hope I can do him proud. I miss hearing him on the radio now.'

Julian Clary agrees: 'People come up to me and tell me how much they miss him. A woman flung her arms around me and started crying in Marks and Spencer's. Paul had that connection with so many people and that doesn't happen very often. He was very no-nonsense about negativity in life. He was very centred with his own, and he knew what he wanted and what would make him happy. He would find a solution for you if you shared a problem with him. And what drove all of it was his innate intelligence. Yes, he complained, but there was never any self-pity. He laughed a lot. For me, I lost a friend and that particular kind of laughter he brought out in me. And apart from watching clips of Lily Savage, I don't know how he did that to me. The thing with laughter is that you are out of control, you are very helpless, and I miss that and the way it would leave you feeling alive and that all was well with the world. And now it's gone.'

For Vera, 'I lost the best friend I ever had, he was always there for me, and he never changed in all the years I knew him. That's incredible, really. I miss his phone calls, sometimes one after another – and another! And we all lost a great entertainer and storyteller who appealed to so many different types of people; you know, he achieved things you could never have dreamt of – even though he was never really satisfied.'

'The joy of a friendship with him was seeing the different colours of emotion and seeing how much he was moved by the simplest of things,' explains Michael Cashman. 'A child battling with cancer, a soldier trying to walk after becoming a paraplegic, an animal being rescued, a friend being uplifted out of tragedy. To see him witnessing that and supporting people in those situations was not only to enjoy a privilege, but to be wrapped in it.'

Jonathan Harvey remembers, 'Years back my friend Annie Kirkbride passed away. She played Deirdre in *Corrie*. I was of course very upset, but seeing the national outpouring of grief, seeing people on the news being upset about it ... grief is such a personal thing, so to see it as a group thing really helped me. I really hope that the national outpouring of love when Paul died helped, in some small way, and comforted his loved ones. I think we lost a wit and a talent who was up there with the likes of Noel Coward.'

Alan Carr suggests, 'We lost another twenty years of entertainment to be honest, you know, more pantos, more Miss Hannigan, more radio, more telly. He was just too good not to be used. He was like a Brucie. He'd moan about working so hard and yet he would sign up to new things. I think he would have kept on going and going and going. We lost a gorgeous man, the kindest, loveliest, wittiest person. We lost twenty more years of people laughing, and him giving dogs a beautiful home. You know, the longer you work in this business, the more stories you hear about what people are really like, behind the scenes, and how their true character comes to the fore. But I can say, hand on heart, when you mention Paul O'Grady's name now, a smile comes across their face: I haven't heard a single negative thing about him. He was the warmest person; of all the bloody people to go early, it had to be him. It's just not fair.'

Joan Marshrons, who knew Paul O'Grady so well, explains, 'We lost somebody who was a very funny, clever, entertaining, a caring man; he had so many strings to his bow. He was the last of a very talented group of entertainers. Paul had a particular skillset which he had honed in pubs and clubs. He was always watching other people, learning from them, and he learnt so much from those who had gone before him. You might say he had borrowed all these things from previous performers and then put them all together and made them his own; he could turn his hand to anything.'

Sangeeta Bhabra believes, 'Paul shone bright because he transcended everything and everyone: black, white, rich, poor, gay, straight, humans and animals – he was the best, and a unique breed of person.'

As Mic Wright wrote in his blog, 'Telling jokes, being kind to dogs, and ensuring job opportunities are open to the widest possible range of people, (especially working-class people) are all good ways of honouring O'Grady, but the best one of all is to speak up and resist.'

For Graham Norton, 'Paul was more important than he would have understood in the cultural landscape, he kind of punched above his weight in a way because there was something so uniquely British about Lily Savage and Paul O'Grady.

He was the sort of personality I don't think you would find in other countries' entertainment scenes. He took enormous pride in his success, and he never got over it. He loved being part of the entertainment world and I think he felt loved because there were a lot of people in his life who adored him, supported him and put up with him.'

As Christmas 2023 approached, David Lloyd invited me to produce a new musical celebration of Paul's life. He explained Boom Radio would like to broadcast the show in TeamPOG's customary seasonal slot: Christmas Day at noon. 'Paul would have been a huge asset for us,' admits David, 'and, putting personal feelings aside, the loss of his services dealt us a blow. For a single human being to have that effect is a tribute to his gifts.' We both agreed that a programme for that special day just felt right. I had kept a long list of songs and recordings Paul enjoyed, so there were ones from Elkie Brooks and Barbara Dickson, a performance from The Salvation Army Band, one of his favourite seventies' hits 'Uptown Top Ranking' from Althea and Donna, a festive carol and a dose of Northern Soul.

'What do we do, Malcolm?'

'We keep the faith, Paul!'

'Hallelujah, brothers and sisters!'

We also played the obligatory 'Sugar Town' by Nancy Sinatra, which fans will know was the first single he bought, a track from Jools Holland and, naturally, 'Trouble' by Elvis.

The resulting 2-hour show also featured messages from many of his friends, all introduced by Julian Clary. I managed to track down the jazz artist Madeline Bell, whom Paul adored, and she recorded a tribute, as did Dawn French and singers Hazell Dean and Sonia. It wasn't the usual TeamPOG show – how could it have been? – and I won't deny it was a tricky project to make because it still felt too soon to be saying a final farewell to Paul, but everyone who took part was keen to do so. Vera shared a story about a Spike Jones song which Paul played religiously in the 1970s as they prepared for a night out in Liverpool. Amanda Mealing recalled her infamous ride with Paul during a visit to Disney's French theme park on 'it's a small world'. The attraction, with its permanently jolly singing dolls, broke down, leaving the friends stranded and listening to the ride's well-intentioned but notorious signature song on a constant loop – so yes, I played *that* music, of course I did, just as I had done for over 500 shows because I knew it still irritated Paul. I also persuaded Joan to take part and she spoke about Paul's theatrical endeavours. And I was especially thrilled when his daughter Sharyn agreed to record a personal contribution. Her words added greatly to the final programme, and we were all delighted the show was selected as one of the year's ten festive highlights in the *Radio Times*.

Even though he would have been embarrassed about all the fuss, I hope Paul would have been impressed, especially as Michael Bublé sent a heartfelt message from his home in Canada: 'There are so many words I could use to describe Paul O'Grady: generous, humble, funny, kind, empathetic, romantic … I mean, I thought I was well versed in the art of romance until I got stopped in my tracks by the master himself, Paul, who chose to shamelessly flirt with me with abandon while I was on stage for my first *Audience With Michael Bublé*. I think I was blushing for the full hour on national TV. And I have got to be honest with you guys, I loved every single second. I miss you so much Paul, thank you for making the world a better place. I love you.'

Three months later, to mark the first anniversary of Paul's death, a few of his friends decided to have lunch and raise a glass. What started out as a group of six or so people ended up being nearly 80. Joan organised a gathering at Port Lympne Safari Park, where Paul's wake had been held the previous year. It's just a few minutes down the road from Knoll Hill House. Acquired by John Aspinall in 1973, the estate is now an animal park, set in 600 acres of a Kentish 'savannah.' It was the perfect location.

René and I decided against joining the animal safari before lunch, but quite a few of the other attendees braved the inclement weather. It was a very cold day, and I was pleased to be inside with Jo Brand, Amanda Mealing, Sharyn and her family, plus Paul's sister, Sheila. However, word reached us that one of the open-sided trucks used on the safari had broken down and the guests were stuck. Unable to leave the vehicles because of safety concerns – lions, leopards and tigers roam free on the safari – it took over an hour for everybody to be rescued. Finally, Vera and company returned to the relative warmth of the main house, frozen and in need of a cuppa.

'Did you see any of the potential life-threatening inhabitants?' we asked.

'No,' came the reply. 'They were sensible and stayed indoors in the warm!'

We all joked that Savage had had a hand in the drama that day which, hypothermia aside, turned out to be a joyous and uplifting reunion of Paul's nearest and dearest. Joan gave a terrific speech and while there were tears, we also laughed and remembered our dear friend with great affection.

The following evening, ITV broadcast a new documentary called *The Life and Death of Lily Savage*. It featured archive footage and new interviews with Vera, Moira, Joan and Sharyn. It also included contributions from Graham Norton, Ian McKellen and Jo Brand. I invited Sharyn, her husband Phil and their children, Abel and Halo, to watch it at home. We were also joined by Moira and Joan. It was a very special evening and one I shall always treasure. As Paul and Lily's story unfolded on the screen, somehow we all managed to hold back the tears.

It was a poignant programme, one that showed that Sharyn's relationship with her father had been an unusual and complicated one. Paul's grandchildren are a credit to Sharyn and Phil, and when I interviewed them for this book, I reminded the siblings of something Paul had once said: 'My grandkids are the greatest reward of fatherhood. I became a dad at the age of 17 and didn't really get to see a lot of my daughter when she was little. But I did with the grandkids, [and] watching them grow up is just wonderful. I think, "My God, I've kept the chain going."' And he did.

Paul O'Grady touched so many through his programmes, books and performances. And he truly made a difference, probably more than anyone else I have ever worked with. He made friends everywhere he went, and made millions of people, me included, happy. But was Paul O'Grady a happy individual? These answers are as fascinating and contrary as the man himself:

'He had the capacity to be relentlessly negative,' shares Moira Stewart. 'He was depressive … But when he went out, he could be someone else; it was a different voice, he was performing.'

For Vanessa White, 'Over the 23 years I knew him, he was happiest in his favourite places, with his friends, hosting them, doing things for them and helping them out. I loved him and being with him. But on his own, I think he was frightened to be happy in case it tempted fate. And he never woke up with a big smile on his face.'

Phil Mousley believes, 'Paul was always searching for something, and perhaps he thought happiness was somewhere else, maybe in another country, because he was always on to the next thing. I did see another side to him when our kids were young – that was one of the happiest times I had ever seen him. Yes, his grandchildren made him happy, and it was a wonderful thing to witness. It was almost like a second chance at being a father to Sharyn.'

Diane Jansen, Sharyn's mother, remembers Paul as, 'a happy man when I knew him. And he liked to reminisce about the good times … If we had married each other, it wouldn't have lasted. That was a lucky escape for both of us! But I think Paul was always looking for something, he was looking for adoration from everyone, he had a very low boredom threshold, and he had to be entertained the whole time. He was a whirlwind.'

'I don't think he was a happy person, no,' says Joan. 'But he did have a lot of happy times. He found a way of making the most ridiculous situations funny. And there were things he really enjoyed: meeting people who he would have revered, like Dame Maggie Smith and Queen Camilla; he was thrilled with all that. And he loved being in Thailand with the elephants – if you watched that series, you won't have ever seen him happier than when he was wrapped around the trunk of an elephant. I suppose I was lucky, because people thought they knew him. In a way that was nice. And that was what my job was really, to hide the anger that so often came with him; I tried to make sure people didn't see that side of him.'

It's true that angst surrounded Paul, and his public persona was at times at odds with the person the inner circle knew. The *Guardian* once wrote, 'There is a sort of matter-of-fact sadness to O'Grady.' Joan adds, 'But there were reasons why he was like that, I just think he was sad and angry, really angry. We used to joke about getting him to talk to a psychiatrist, but God help the shrink!'

Paul O'Grady had so many reasons to be angry. I am no therapist, but I would suggest it's easy to see where his fury and frustration stemmed from: Paul had lost his father when he was a teenager, and, soon after, his Aunty Chrissie and his mother died. Paul never came out to his parents, and that unfinished business wouldn't have helped either. He had also witnessed so many of his friends and contemporaries lose their lives prematurely because of AIDS. And, in more recent years, cancer had broken his circle of pals. Then there was the loss of Brendan. 'Brendan was utterly enchanting,' explains Jo Brand. 'I thought he was one of the best-looking people I had ever met, and he looked like a French intellectual. He was excellent company.' For Vera, 'Brendan was key. He was the one who got Lily out of the gay bars, and all the way to Edinburgh; he was the one who got Lily to headline at the Palladium. Brendan could see the potential in Lily, and Paul trusted him. He was never the same after he lost him.' Brenda Gilhooly agrees: 'They just came as a pair. Brendan was so important. Paul completely believed in him. He was very bright, he was savvy, an intelligent man. And he was one of a very few people who knew exactly how to handle Paul. He didn't have the same personality as Paul, but he would give as good as he got. I don't remember when they stopped being in a relationship, they just carried on as partners, the manager and the star. But they were always the closest people to each other, and that lasted until Brendan died.' As Joan told me, 'Even though he was the love of his life, Brendan couldn't be the person Paul wanted him to be. And even if he had been, perhaps their relationship would have eventually blown apart, because Savage really was a bit of a loner.'

The solitude of Paul's life had been compounded in his final years by the deaths of friends including *Daily Mirror* columnist Sue Carroll; Peter Searle, aka the drag artiste Adrella; Cilla Black; Lady Anson; and Barbara Windsor. Sadly, there were many others. As Paul wrote in *Still Standing*, 'I've sat through too many round-the-clock bedside vigils … Now, for the sake of sanity and self-preservation, I prefer to slip away and remember my loved ones as I always knew them.'

Death and his own declining health had been a constant subject in our conversations for as long as I could remember. 'And in the last few years, he worried about his own body letting him down,' says Joan, 'and that was all very depressing for him. He was scared of losing control and I think that's why he wouldn't have the pacemaker because he didn't want to be on camera or in front of an audience when the thing kicked in … he would have been embarrassed about it all.'

'There is now a big Paul O'Grady-shaped void where he was,' explains Graham Norton. 'There'll never be someone like Paul again, because the people who remind you of him do so because they are being influenced by him. When I do *Drag Race* on the BBC, there are some very funny queens on that show, but if they are very funny there's normally a whiff of Lily or Paul about them because they grew up watching *him*. So, it's not like someone has replaced him. When Paul died, we lost a really distinct comedic voice; and I don't think he will be replaced in any meaningful way.'

I believe we also lost someone who often said the things we all wanted to say.

Over 20 years ago, when I first began working with Paul O'Grady, I never imagined what an impact he would have on my own life. He was great company, I respected his opinion, and he was the first person I would turn to for advice and a few wise words, my favourites being, 'Don't go to sleep after a row with someone – stay up and fight!' and, 'I don't live *with* people, Malcolm, that's why my relationships last. I'm not romantic. Separate bathrooms are a must. Actually, separate bedrooms and ideally separate houses, or it's doomed.' He also reminded me why it was important not to allow life to pass you by, and he taught me the value of time – he was so generous with his own.

Paul's life was unlike mine, but he was kind enough to share part of his with me, and I'm grateful the programmes we made together were enjoyed by many, even if much of the radio magic he created has vanished into the airwaves. Obviously, I am indebted to him; I'm the first to admit I have benefitted from knowing the man. Paul was truly a unique friend, and I miss the laughs, rants and excitement we shared both on and off air. And I know I am not alone.

I hope with this book his friends and I have paid tribute to him, and I also hope you now know the man we called a pal a little better. Yes, he was complicated, and yet, in a funny way, so much about him was quite straightforward. He liked a yarn, and he liked to play. He enjoyed the company of good friends, and yet sometimes he preferred his own. He was generous and interested in others, while wishing to keep his private life just that. And when it came to his work, he was a magpie, and just like the diminutive protagonists of his favourite story, he literally *borrowed* from all those around him. And he repaid them – and us – handsomely. Weren't we lucky? As Jodie Prenger reflected when I spoke to her in 2024, 'When Paul died, the nation lost its best friend.'

Now, Paul wouldn't want us to be glum. So, just for good measure, as it's almost six o'clock (somewhere), shall we have a cocktail? Yes! Here's one of his favourite 'Muck in a Bucket' concoctions. Remember, as Paul would say, this recipe comes with a health warning.

Today, we're having a Little Worm. Here's how you make it.

Add the following ingredients into a shaker:

41ml of pear brandy
15ml of lemon juice
10ml of honey
54ml of apple cider
And the white of one egg

Give them a shake, chuck in some ice, and shake again
Strain into a cocktail glass
Garnish with a fan of thin apple slices, and half-a-
Twiglet … (other savoury snacks are available but
won't work)

As always, please drink responsibly.

And if you're daft/brave enough to attempt to make a Little Worm, why not play one of Paul's favourite songs as you swig it back? We included The Stargazers' classic every Christmas Day on his radio show, and he adored it. Fans might remember he gave a festive interpretation on an edition of *Paul O'Grady Live* in 2010, introduced by Bette Midler, no less.

Cue the sound of a harp glissando …

We are in Liverpool, it's 1963, and outside Yates's Wine Lodge stands Paul O'Grady, accompanied by his best friend Vera, members of The Salvation Army Band, and Cilla Black, with whom our journey began.

Put the needle on the record and get your pan lids ready for, 'I See The Moon' …

Afterword

My dad loved working with Malcolm, and I know he was proud of the programmes they created together. When Malcolm called to say he was writing a book about his friend and colleague I was delighted: I couldn't think of anyone better to capture the essence of the man we all loved. There was so much ground to cover, and understandably Malcolm was daunted by the project, but I had no doubt he could do it, and he has.

GanGan (as we called him) made his radio show sound easy, so it's been fascinating to discover the work which went into making it such a success, and the longest job he ever had. He would usually send up Malcolm something rotten on air, but his trusty producer gave as good as he got, and my dad loved that. GanGan lived a busy life and although we stayed in touch by phone and text, and visited him in Kent as often as we could, it was always a comfort for his family to hear him every Sunday on the wireless. Malcolm and Dad cared about their radio show because they both knew it was treasured by so many – their weekly on-air banter is now greatly missed by listeners everywhere.

I hope you feel you know my dad a bit better now; I know I've learnt a lot about him too. He was a fascinating and complex man and, while he left us so suddenly, through this book some of his many friends have now been able to say farewell to someone who was adored by millions and loved by me and my family. So, thank you, Malcolm, for remembering GanGan and for being a true friend to him. I know it's not the same without my dad, but I think this book has brought us all a little closer to him.

Sharyn Mousley, April 2025

Acknowledgements

I am indebted, first and foremost, to Sharyn Mousley for granting me permission to write her father's biography. A mother with her own family and career, she embraced this project unreservedly and was understanding and generous of heart throughout it all. I could not have been given a greater gift.

It should go without saying that I couldn't have undertaken this project without the support of Paul's friends and family. To all I am grateful for sharing their memories.

I must single out Joan Marshrons. Her encouragement, enthusiasm and interest were ever present. It's no wonder Paul trusted you so much.

Katya Shipster, my editor at HarperCollins, contributed enormously to the shape of the book and I am indebted to her. She's living proof you can teach this old dog new tricks. (Gold stars all round.) I must also acknowledge the expertise of her team who helped bring this endeavour to life, namely Daisy Ward, Georgina Atsiaris, Isabel Prodger and Kate Neilan. Thanks also to Belinda Jones for making sure my words and thoughts appeared in the right order!

My agent Gordon Wise. Never has a surname been more apt. My deepest thanks go to him for always being there with guidance, encouragement and excellent company.

Jo Malley, my long-time friend and former colleague, helped so much and put up with my emails headed 'just one more thing' at all hours of the day and night.

I should also take this opportunity to thank all the BBC studio engineers and production staff who worked on TeamPOG over the years.

I am most grateful to Jane Anderson, Carolyn Dennis, Matthew Gormley, Anita Land, Peter Lorraine, Kevin McCabe, Amanda Malpass and Brian Sibley, all of whom I turned to while undertaking this project.

I am indebted to Rowena Webb who was there at the beginning of this endeavour and 'without whom …'.

I also need to acknowledge the many fans of Paul and his radio show. Please know, we never took you for granted while we were on-air, and years later I am grateful so many have shown support for this book.

To my husband René: bless you for understanding so completely the obligations and needs of a work that consumed so much of my time. Thank you for always being there and for holding the fort.

Most of all, my thanks to Paul.

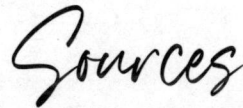

9 Dead Pets, 'Triples' and Keeping the Faith

10 Cuddly Toys and Weatherfield

11 On the Box

12 A Blind Date With Cilla

13 Puppets, Plays and Pantoland

Picture Credits

All photographs from the author's personal collection, with the exception of:

p.1 (top left) Paul Massey, Camera Press, London
p.1 (top right) Rick Colls/Shutterstock
p.1 (middle) © Alpha Press
p.1 (bottom right) © BBC Photo Archive
p.2 (top) Ken McKay/ITV/Shutterstock
p.2 (bottom) ED/CS/Camera Press
p.3 (top) BenStansall/PA Images/Alamy Stock Photo
p.3 (bottom) Simon Harris/PeterTatchell Foundation
p.4 (top) Coltas/Williams
p.4 (bottom) © Paul Coltas
p.5 (bottom left) Courtsey of Stephen Pover
p.8 Courtesy of Sharyn Mousley